THE
HARRIMAN
ALASKA
EXPEDITION
RETRACED

RUTGERS UNIVERSITY PRESS

NEW BRUNSWICK, NEW JERSEY • LONDON

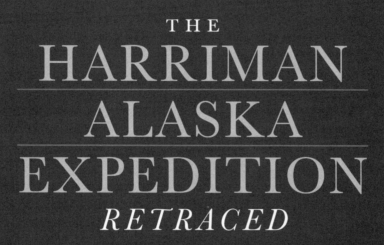

THE
HARRIMAN
ALASKA
EXPEDITION
RETRACED

A Century of Change, 1899–2001

EDITED BY THOMAS S. LITWIN

FOREWORD BY DAVID ROCKEFELLER JR.

LIBRARY OF CONGRESS CATALOGING-IN-PUBLICATION DATA

The Harriman Alaska Expedition retraced : a century of change, 1899–2001 / edited by

Thomas S. Litwin ; foreword by David Rockfeller Jr.

p. cm.

Includes bibliographical references (p.   ).

ISBN 0-8135-3505-0 (hardcover : alk. paper)

1. Harriman Alaska Expedition (1899) 2. Harriman expedition retraced (2001)

3. Natural history—Alaska. 4. Alaska—Description and travel. I. Litwin, Thomas S., 1951–

QH105.A4H27 2005

508.798—dc22   2004003829

A British Cataloging-in-Publication record for this book is available from the British Library.

Manufactured in the United States of America

To Maureen, on our anniversary, for twenty-five years of love and support;
to Megan and Elizabeth, the reason I cherish the future;
and to Richard B. Fisher, Charles R. Smith, and Thomas C. Richards,
mentors all who were willing to take a chance.

Contents

Illustrations

Color plates appear between pages 134 and 135.

Foreword

I N 1899 Edward H. Harriman sponsored an expedition to Alaska. When the first two volumes of the expedition report were published in 1901, he wrote in the preface, "It is pleasant to recall the spirit of harmony and good fellowship which prevailed throughout the voyage." He was clearly pleased with his journey to Alaska, but when he was writing these words, he probably was not thinking that in a little over one hundred years his efforts would be re-created. The contributions of the 1899 expedition did, in fact, survive a century, and they became the foundation for a second expedition to Alaska at the start of the twenty-first century. In 2001, the Harriman Expedition Retraced included artists and scientists, as well as conservationists, who came to pay tribute to the vision of the original expedition and to create another benchmark on the condition of Alaska. My family and I were honored to be among the passengers.

For the better part of two decades I have continually been drawn back to Alaska. A sailing expedition I organized to the Gulf of Alaska in 1991 first introduced me to the wildness of Alaska's marine environment. Soon after, enticed by both the beauty and the challenges facing Alaska, I joined the board of the Alaska Conservation Foundation, an Anchorage-based organization whose mission is to protect the Alaskan environment while also promoting cultural and economic stability. Later, as an appointee of Interior Secretary Bruce Babbitt to the board of the National Park Foundation, I visited Denali National Park in early September 1998, as the snows were first falling. This trip consolidated my belief that Americans have taken Alaska and its wilderness heritage seriously. After all, Alaska's ten national parks—more than 50 percent of all federal parks by area—are the magnificent results of the boldness and vision of many conservation-minded citizens.

What is it that makes Alaska important to us? Because it is a land rich in oil and timber with seas and rivers full of fish? Because it serves as a listening post for early signs of threat from foreign lands? Because its native families live principally in villages, not on reservations, and struggle to balance a subsistence culture with shareholder imperatives? Because of the evidence of global warming that we see in retreating glaciers? Because environmentalists call us to end road building in the Tongass rainforest or to block oil exploration in the Arctic National Wildlife Refuge? Because young people still flock to the adventure and danger of Bering Sea crabbing or train to become bush pilots? Or because Alaska is wilder and bigger than any other place in North America—our last wilderness?

In 1991, as I was just coming to know Alaska, I also first learned about the 1899 Harriman Alaska Expedition, and I have been fascinated by its history and contributions ever since. Several aspects of the voyage struck me. It was a partnering of art and science for the purpose of painting a picture in time. The boatload of large egos financed and led by the larger-than-life Harriman himself moved swiftly through the landscape producing a portfolio of elegant sketches and hastily gathered samples but few finished works. The opportunity to continue the work of the 1899 expedition, driven by the questions above, drew me once again to Alaska and the Harriman Alaska Expedition Retraced.

During Retraced, we were amazed by what had changed since 1899. Glacier Bay had enlarged in equal proportion to the retreat of its glaciers. Canneries and fox farms had shut down. Large sections of rainforest had been clear-cut. And, yes, the residue of the *Exxon Valdez* oil spill still persisted from Prince William Sound to Kodiak Island. But we were equally impressed with what had not changed, as well as the successes of the last century. Salmon stocks are high, and whales are more plentiful since widespread hunting has stopped. Thousands of miles of undeveloped coastline still adjoin open and wild ocean. Massive natural beauty and abundant seabirds and marine mammal populations characterize large areas of the coast. And among Alaska's people, an independence and frontier spirit persist, along with a concern for the future of their societies, cultures, and shared environment.

While sailing the waters of Alaska, I was able to confirm my own answers to the questions raised by the Harriman Alaska Expedition Retraced. I believe Alaska is important because it is beyond human scale. It humbles us. It is wild. It is awe-inspiring. It is abundant in resources, both natural and cultural. But as stories in this book reveal, Alaska's scale and abundance should not blind us to the fact that we ingenious humans can still do considerable harm ("tame it," we used to say). Unless we take care, centuries-old mistakes will be repeated. Equally important is the finding that many human activities are having impacts beyond the vastness of Alaska. Paralleling my participation in Retraced, I served as a member of the Pew Oceans Commission, formed to study living systems in U.S. waters. The commission's principal conclusion is that we humans can no longer afford to take the view that the oceans are so vast that they are impervious to human actions—not even in Alaska. Fish populations worldwide are in serious decline, and many rich, productive coastal zones are faltering in the face of widespread and damaging pollution from cities, farms, industry, and ships.

Alaska represents a conservation opportunity: if we are not vigilant and fail to take care of Alaska's precious resources—its intact ecosystems and indigenous communities—the magnificence of the Alaskan wilderness and the ability to sustain its many resources will be lost. Because this outcome is unacceptable, we must find the will and resources to lead conservation efforts; we are obligated to our grandchildren to be good stewards of their inheritance. I hope that the inspiration of Harriman's 1899 expedition and the 2001 retracing so beautifully organized by Tom Litwin and his colleagues will remind all Americans that a wilderness even as great as Alaska's can be brought to its ursine knees if we choose to do so. In a nation as creative and prosperous as ours, we have the opportunity to do otherwise.

DAVID ROCKEFELLER JR.
CAMBRIDGE, MASSACHUSETTS
FEBRUARY 2004

Preface

OVER A CENTURY AGO, in 1899, New York financier and railroad builder Edward H. Harriman, considered one of the most powerful men in the United States, planned a summer cruise for family and friends to the remote and exotic coast of Alaska. With the enthusiasm and drive that characterized most of his undertakings, the vacation became a scholarly, albeit somewhat zany, scientific expedition. The thirteen volumes of findings produced by expedition members over a decade contained narratives, artwork, photographs, and highly detailed scientific data that provided a snapshot of Alaska in the closing months of the nineteenth century. As the twentieth century drew to a close and a new millennium was ushered in in 2001, the 1899 expedition's wealth of information was a time capsule waiting to be opened. The 2001 Harriman Expedition Retraced opened it.

Unlike the 1899 expedition's creation, which was accomplished in a short two months, the Harriman Alaska Expedition Retraced evolved over decades. As a graduate student at the Cornell Laboratory of Ornithology in the late 1970s, I was surrounded by collections of Louis Agassiz Fuertes's artwork. Fuertes, the naturalist artist, had a long history with Cornell University: his father was dean of the engineering college, and he was a class of 1897 graduate. After graduation Fuertes often naturalized and led walks in what he and Laboratory of Ornithology founder Arthur A. Allen called "the Sapsucker Woods." These woods, now preserved as a wildlife sanctuary, surround the Laboratory. As my own research focused on the birds of Sapsucker Woods, Fuertes's vision provided me with a beautiful window on the golden age of natural history and its transition to the nascent field of ecology. Upon my graduation, another Cornell ecologist-romantic, Dr. Charles R. Smith, gave me a gift of Dover Publications' *Alaska, the Harriman Expedition, 1899*. I discovered that Fuertes, just two years after graduating from Cornell, was invited to join Harriman's Alaska expedition. As Robert Peck writes in *A Celebration of Birds: The Life and Art of Louis Agassiz Fuertes*, this was Fuertes's "first major expedition and in many ways his most important." It was all there, whether in 1899 or 1979, a young naturalist's dream: the coast of Alaska, a ship, and a who's who of late-nineteenth-century scientists, writers, and artists onboard. The ship had a name, the *George W. Elder*, and the expedition had a voice, John Burroughs.

A decade went by, and the only attention my copy of *Alaska* received was wistful looks toward my office bookshelf at the end of long days—the coast of Alaska, a ship called the *Elder*, John Burroughs. In 1990 and 1992 the book came off the shelf when I was asked by the Alumnae Association of Smith College to lead trips to Alaska, where for the first time I used Burroughs's words to help narrate our journeys through the Inside Passage. An idea began to form, inspired by more serendipity. C. Hart Merriam, the person Harriman asked to organize his expedition, had a sister, Florence Augusta Merriam, Smith College class of 1896. Florence Merriam was a noted ornithologist and nature writer in her own right. When asked by her brother to recommend a bird artist for the 1899 expedition, she was ready with a name. He was a young, unknown artist who as a junior at Cornell had illustrated a book she had written. His name was Louis Agassiz Fuertes. As I dug deeper into *Alaska* I realized there was in fact a Smith College Glacier in Prince William Sound's College Fjord. The 1899 Harriman Expedition had named both the glacier and the fjord. Bernhard Fernow, the 1899 expedition's forester, was the founding dean of Cornell's College of Forestry, now the Department of Natural Resources. As a graduate student, I spent countless hours in the building named after him. These wonderful convergences made the story that much richer and more personal.

With another wistful glance at the bookshelf in the winter of 1998 and a quick calculation, the idea of a retracing found a purpose: in another year the 1899 expedition would celebrate its centennial. There it was, a once-in-a-lifetime opportunity to explore one hundred years of change, bracketed on both ends by the poignancy of old century ending and a new one beginning. I took the idea to my colleagues in the Alumnae Association who had extensive experience with chartering ships and to a neighbor whom I did not know—documentarian Larry Hott of Florentine Films/Hott Productions. As in 1899, a serious, but somewhat zany, very human enterprise began. Our ship, the *Clipper Odyssey*, left the dock on July 22, 2001, with the sole purpose of retracing the Harriman Expedition of 1899.

Both as a practical matter and in recognition of the communications technology available to us at the start of the twenty-first century, the Harriman Retraced project did not need to produce thirteen volumes of reports. The documentary film made during the voyage, *The Harriman Alaska Expedition Retraced*, directed by Lawrence Hott, presents Alaska in all its magnificence, while illuminating the issues that challenge its future. Both this book and the film are further described on the Harriman Retraced web site (www.pbs.org/harriman). And an advantage we have that did not exist in 1899 is a flourishing University of Alaska system and a host of agencies that are studying in fine detail Alaska's natural environments and social systems. An Internet search quickly reveals that the primary literature and data regarding Alaska are bountiful and readily available.

The goal of this book is to capture the perspectives of contemporary scholars who opened the 1899 expedition time capsule while sailing the same route as their colleagues did one hundred years before. The challenge for us was to bring our own years of experience and knowledge to bear in 2001, while weighing and evaluating the experiences of those who came to Alaska in 1899. A listing of the 2001 and 1899 expedition participants is provided at the end of this book, in the Appendix and the Notes on Contributors. Although each of our authors examines a specific topic relevant to his or her expertise, all these conversations take place in the context of a maritime voyage that followed the Alaska coastline. To share the sights we saw and the experiences we had along our route, I have written log entries that follow the daily movements of the ship and that connect the stories told in each chapter. The map on pages xxiv–xxv depicts the route of the 1899 expedition and the 2001 retracing. The Suggested Readings and References, at the end of this book, provides bibliographic material for both the logs and the chapters.

The 1899 expedition was extraordinary in its interdisciplinary approach to examining a large, complex subject, and we have worked to retain that spirit in word and illustration. The poems of Sheila Nickerson help set the tone as our voyage passes from one geographic region to the next, or they foreshadow observations and emotions we encountered along the way. Similarly, Patricia Savage's etchings define the start of each chapter by evoking an image from the story that follows. Through the generosity of the Harriman family, we are able to share a magnificent collection of photographs from the 1899 expedition; these pictures are presented throughout the text to illustrate and reinforce our theme, one hundred years of change. As a counterpoint, the color photograph and art gallery, with contributions by expedition photographer Kim Heacox, artist Kesler Woodward, and Young Explorers Team member Megan Litwin, provides the visual images that help define the 2001 voyage.

The Harriman Expedition Retraced was an extraordinary opportunity to look back and forward in time in one of the most beautiful, raw, and wild places on earth. On behalf of all the 2001 expedition members, it is our pleasure to share the story and grandeur with you, our readers.

THOMAS S. LITWIN
NORTHAMPTON, MASSACHUSETTS
MAY 2004

Acknowledgments

T HE HARRIMAN ALASKA EXPEDITION RETRACED would not have been possible without the critical partnership of the Alumnae Association of Smith College, the Smith College administration, the Harriman family, and my friends in adventure, Lawrence Hott and Diane Garey of Florentine Films/Hott Productions. I am deeply indebted to Phoebe A. Wood, who provided invaluable insights, logistical and financial support, and a base of operation in Anchorage. The talented members of Zegrahm Expeditions meticulously translated the 1899 Harriman Expedition itinerary into the contemporary expedition route and provided invaluable logistical and maritime expertise. The support and ongoing cooperation of Clipper Cruise Lines, including Captain Michael Taylor and the crew of the M/V *Clipper Odyssey*, were a critical ingredient of Harriman Retraced's success.

I extend special thanks to Terry Andreas, Paula Bensen, Brenda Bolduc, Carrie Cadwell, Janine Harris, Walter Hays, William F. Hibberd, Laura Kale, Phoebe Lewis, Thomas C. Richards, and Werner Zender for their extraordinary personal involvement with the project. The deep commitment of Irene Dundas, Joe Williams, Diane Palmer, and the clan leaders and elders of Saanya Kwaan to the repatriation of clan objects was inspirational. The Alaska Geographic Alliance, with the support of the Alaska Science and Technology Foundation, played a significant role in shaping the project's educational mission. The highest Internet educational standards were achieved through the talent and efforts of Thomas LaPointe, Alison Hammer, Lawrence Charters, and Robert Aguirre of the National Oceanic and Atmospheric Administration, and Eric Brewer and Tony Caldanaro of Smith College.

The 2001 expedition became the "floating university" we dreamed of as a result of the knowledge, experience, and wonderful sense of humor that the Harriman Scholars brought aboard. It was a privilege sharing the voyage of a lifetime with this extraordinary group of individuals. And to all the visiting scholars, policy experts, and deeply dedicated citizens who came aboard to join the debate, we thank you for your knowledge and for caring. The preplanning organization and scheduling of our community events were meticulous because of Beth Bishop, whose patience was endless.

To Rutgers University Press, senior editor Audra Wolfe, editorial assistant Adi Hovav, copyeditor Pamela Fischer, and Marilyn Campbell, director of the Prepress Department, I extend deep personal appreciation for their help in shaping the manuscript, patience (which was tested often), and endless encouragement. In Northampton,

Massachusetts, the talent and friendship of Brenda Bolduc and Faye Wolfe helped turn a book proposal into a book. Brenda saw it through to the last period, and for that I will be forever grateful.

Gaining insight into the life of contemporary coastal Alaska was a monumental task that could not have been accomplished without the goodwill of the many wonderful communities we visited. The Harriman Retraced project team is deeply appreciative of the support provided by the people of Anchorage, Metlakatla, Ketchikan, Saxman, Wrangell, Juneau, Skagway, Sitka, Yakutat, Orca, Cordova, Valdez, Homer, Chignik, Unalaska, St. George, St. Paul, Gambell, Teller, Little Diomede, Lorino, and Yanrakino.

Many organizations and agencies provided expertise and assistance to Harriman Retraced through all phases of the project. The quality of our experience was immeasurably enhanced by assistance from KTOO–Juneau, the Anchorage Museum of History and Art, Alaska Federation of Natives, Cape Fox Corporation, Father Duncan Cottage Museum, Wrangell Museum, Wrangell Chamber of Commerce, Alaska Department of Community and Economic Development, Alaska Department of Natural Resources, U.S. Coast Guard, Alaska State Museums, the offices of Governor Tony Knowles and Lieutenant Governor Fran Ulmer, Alaska Department of Health and Social Services, Skagway Chamber of Commerce, Sitka Tribe of Alaska, Sitka Conservation Society, Yakutat Tlingit Tribe, Yakutat Cross Cultural Consultants, Alaska Native Science Commission, Prince William Sound Science Center, Cordova Historical Museum, Orca Lodge, Alyeska Pipeline Administration, Pratt Museum (Homer), Kodiak Convention and Visitors Bureau, Baranov Museum (Kodiak), Alutiiq Museum (Kodiak), Unalaska/Port of Dutch Harbor Convention and Visitors Bureau, Museum of the Aleutians, Traditional Council of St. George, Tanaq Corporation of St. George, Aleut Tribal Government of St. Paul, Pribilof Island Stewardship Program, Traditional Council of St. Lawrence, Traditional Council of Teller, Inalik Native Corporation of Little Diomede, and the office of Governor Roman Abramovich in Chukotka. In addition, an expedition along a coast as vast as Alaska's would not have been possible without the assistance and cooperation of the National Oceanic and Atmospheric Administration, the National Marine Fisheries Service, the U.S. Fish and Wildlife Service, the U.S. Forest Service, and the National Park Service.

Many of the 1899 Harriman Expedition photographs in this book are the originals used by E. H. Harriman to produce the souvenir albums provided as gifts to the expedition members or assembled in a series of personal photographic albums for the Harriman family. Many have never before been published. We are grateful to the Harriman family for making them available.

The Harriman Retraced project team extends special thanks to the Harriman Foundation Group, the Gladys and Roland Harriman Foundation, the Mary H. Rumsey Foundation, and the Mary W. Harriman Foundation for their generous support of the expedition and its education programs. Major support for Harriman Retraced was provided by the Natalie P. and Charles D. Webster Trusts, the Paul Allen Foundation for the Arts, the Arthur Vining Davis Foundations, the Andreas Foundation, the M. J. Murdock Charitable Trust, the Town Creek Foundation, and David Rockefeller Jr. Foundation support was generously provided by the Alaska Science and Technology Foundation, the Alces Foundation, the Alumnae Association of Smith College, the William West Grant Trust, Smith College, the University of Alaska Foundation, and the Alaska Geographic Society.

Many corporations contributed to the success of Harriman Retraced, including the Aleut Corporation, Alyeska Pipeline Corporation, ARCO Foundation, Goldbelt Corporation Inc., Holland America Line Westours, Inc., Koniag Incorporated, NANA Development Corporation, National Bank of Alaska, Northrim Bank, Phillips Alaska, Inc., Rockefeller and Co., Inc., Royal Caribbean Cruises, Ltd., VECO Corporation, Motorola Foundation, and Brown-Forman Corporation.

The dedicated support of individual contributors was essential, and we extend deep appreciation to Terry Andreas, Susan Faith, Katherine Fanning, Lile R. Gibbons, Alice and Peter Hausmann, Dorothy J. Nemetz, Mary P. and Lowell Thomas Jr., Clem and Diana Tillion, and Phoebe A. Wood.

THE
HARRIMAN
ALASKA
EXPEDITION
RETRACED

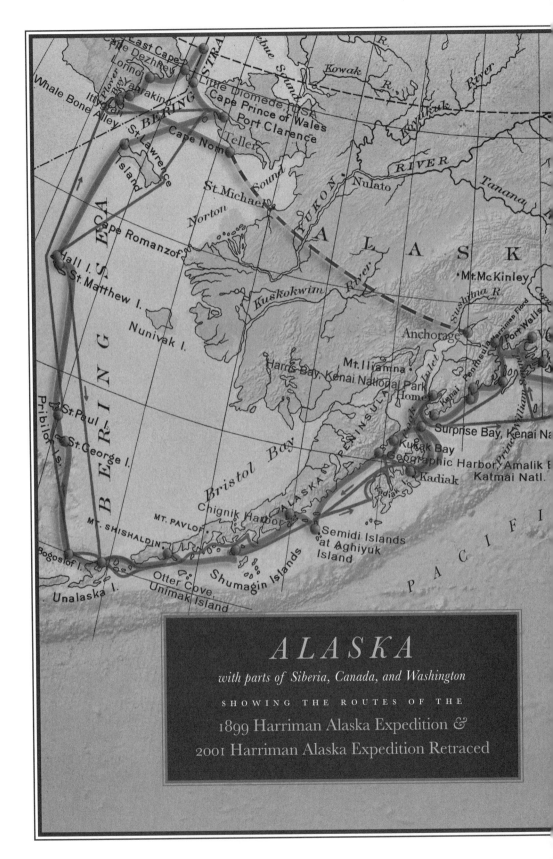

Last Cape
The Dezhnev
Lorino
Plover Bay
Ittygran
Whale Bone Alley
Yarakin
St. Lawrence Island
Cape Nome
BERING STRAIT
Little Diomede, U.S.A.
Cape Prince of Wales
Port Clarence
Teller
Kotzebue Sound
Kowak R.
Noatak River
Koyukuk River

St. Michael
Norton Sound
Cape Romanzof
Nulato
YUKON RIVER
Tanana

A L A S K A

Mt. McKinley
Susitna R.

Kuskokwim River

Anchorage
Cook Inlet
Kenai Peninsula
Harriman Fiord
Port Wells
Prince William Sound

BERING SEA
Nunivak I.
St. Matthew I.
dall I.

Harris Bay, Kenai National Park
Mt. Iliamna
Mt. Redoubt
Home
Kenai
Surprise Bay, Kenai Na
Kukak Bay
Geographic Harbor, Amalik B
Katmai Natl.
Kadiak
Kodiak

St. Paul
St. George I.
Pribilof Is.

Bristol Bay

ALASKA PENINSULA

Chignik Harbor
MT. PAVLOF
MT. SHISHALDIN
Semidi Islands
at Aghiyuk Island
Shumagin Islands

Bogoslof I.
Otter Cove
Unimak Island
Unalaska I.

P A C I F I

ALASKA
with parts of Siberia, Canada, and Washington
SHOWING THE ROUTES OF THE
1899 Harriman Alaska Expedition &
2001 Harriman Alaska Expedition Retraced

Arctic

MACKENZIE RIVER

C A N A D A

Dawson

Pelly River

Ft. Selkirk

Teslin River

L. Bennett

White Pass
Skagway

Glacier Bay

FAIRWEATHER
RANGE

Lynn Canal

Juneau

Taku Harbor

Taku River

Tracy Arm Wilderness

Stikine River

SITKA

Wrangell

Ketchikan

Prince of Wales
Island

Portland Canal

Annette
Cape Fox

Prince Rupert,
BC Canada

Lowe Inlet

O C E A N

Queen Charlotte Islands

Vancouver Island

Vancouver

Victoria

WASH

Seattle

1899 ROUTE

2001 ROUTE

Scale

50   0   100   200   300 Miles

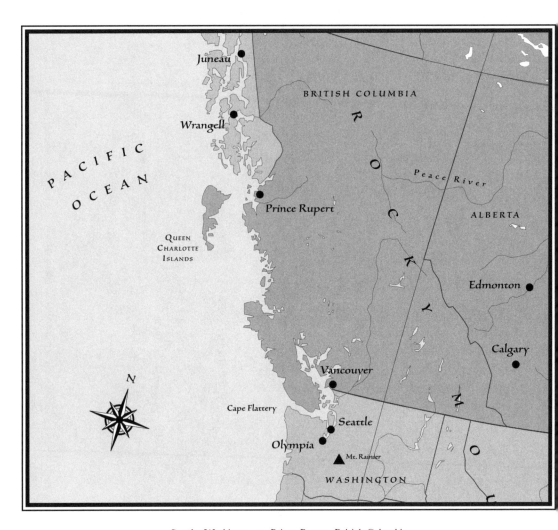

Seattle, Washington, to Prince Rupert, British Columbia

PART ONE

SEATTLE TO PRINCE RUPERT

❧

{Aboard the *Clipper Odyssey*}

A SHIP OF MIRRORS

We sailed on a ship of mirrors
giving us back to ourselves,
a glass tide.
It was easy to watch from inside—
the moon, and even birds—
a voyage of reflection, till certain voices spoke.
In Wrangell Harbor, a Tlingit paddler called:
"From where is this canoe?"
In Yakutat, a Tlingit elder offered:
"Although we are in different boats,
we are in the same river of life."
At Surprise Bay, a tongue of fog
came out to greet us, asking us in;
and the language it spoke was
the clearing of waters and weathers,
the shock of first sight:
a trail of river beauty leading to gold.

— SHEILA NICKERSON

Glaucous-winged Gull

© PATRICIA SAVAGE

CHAPTER ONE

VIEW FROM A SEATTLE
HOTEL WINDOW

꙳

THOMAS S. LITWIN

UNKNOWINGLY, HENRY GANNETT, the 1899 Harriman Alaska Expedition geographer, framed in his report a tension that would confront the United States and Alaska for more than one hundred years:

> There is one word of advice and caution to be given those intending to visit Alaska for pleasure, for sightseeing. If you are old, go by all means; but if you are young, wait. The scenery of Alaska is much grander than anything else of the kind in the world, and it is not well to dull one's capacity for enjoyment by seeing the finest first. . . .
>
> The natural resources of Alaska are enormous. The skins and furs, the fish, the gold, copper, and coal, and the timber of the territory are in value almost beyond calculation, and the mere reaping of this harvest sown and ripened for us by nature will occupy an industrial army for many years. The wealth thus collected will add greatly to the well-being and happiness of our people.

In 1899, Edward H. Harriman and his distinguished party aboard the S.S. *George W. Elder* first brought to light the two Alaskas that our new expedition will be revisiting in just hours—the Alaska that is grand and wild and the one whose "wealth thus collected" would add to our "well-being and happiness."

The idea behind our retracing is quite simple: the 2001 expedition will compare the Alaska of 1899 with the Alaska we find during our voyage in the weeks ahead. What has changed with the passage of a century? With that question, the simplicity ends, and our voyage over Alaskan seas, and through our society, begins. Shortly, we

FIGURE I. *S.S.* George W. Elder.
Credit: Edward Henry Harriman. Source: Harriman family collection.

will sail into a remote land that exists both as an idea and as a place grappling with its own realities.

In the corner of millions of Americans' lives is an Alaskan dream colored by the grandeur that Gannett described. Over time Alaska has become synonymous with the idea of wilderness, of nature free and unspoiled. Although many have seen it only in pictures, they have a deep calling to visit this wild, open land, which seems so removed from the hectic pace of our daily, urban lives. In fact, people around the world dream about visiting Alaska. It is such a powerful dream that this otherwise remote land, separating the North Pacific from the Arctic Ocean, is a leading international tourist destination.

In Alaska communities are isolated, and floatplanes are more common than cars. Winters are long, and temperatures can freeze human flesh rock hard in minutes. Although the idea of the "land of the midnight sun" has romantic appeal, the celestial reality for northern Alaska is that for weeks on end it is dark twenty-four hours a day. This can be a hard land that severely punishes errors in judgment, and it often does. Yet, in the Alaskan dreams shaped from afar, these facts are set aside.

A half dozen scouting trips to Alaska to organize the Harriman Alaska Expedition Retraced and hundreds of conversations along the way have resulted in a richer and more complex story. These preliminary explorations revealed facts, challenged simple conclusions, and transformed Alaska into a place—a place with its own ecology and economies, its own society and people, and the values and visions they hold. Some see an Alaskan wilderness preserved, a wildness uninfluenced by human hands. They say that, minimally, respect for the land should dictate conservation and the sustainable use of Alaska's vast resources. Others press for social justice, cultural freedom, and equity. Homesteaders seek a simpler path and self-sufficiency, away from the crowded world and its rude intrusions. Some of these visions are so strong that they frustrate to wit's end those who have other dreams for Alaska: to develop its landscape, to harvest or mine its resources, or to expand the cruise-ship industry. They bristle at the meddling of outsiders. The tourism posters at Seattle-Tacoma airport don't let on that the Alaskan dream has become very complicated over the last century.

Planning an expedition to explore Alaska has also become more complicated since Harriman and company sailed its coast. They prepared for their voyage in two months; our departure took years of planning, and we had the benefit of satellite communications, computerized data bases, e-mail, and dozens of local Alaskan contacts. We confirmed logistical details, prodded local officials for permits, made agreements with dockmasters, and clarified cultural protocols. Now, as I bide time in nervous anticipation of tomorrow's departure, I find some relief in gazing out my hotel-room window over the expanse of Puget Sound.

Along with countless details turning over in my head, an old saying keeps recurring: "If you want to hear the gods laugh, tell them your plans." My heightened anticipation at this critical moment is well founded. We were to have launched Harriman Retraced a year ago, in 2000, but there was a problem. We had contingency plans for every eventuality—except one. Our ship sank. The expedition vessel chartered for our voyage, the M/W *World Discoverer,* was passing through the Solomon Islands en route to the North Pacific while in Massachusetts we frantically finalized details for our highly anticipated rendezvous, just weeks away. On a sunny Sunday afternoon, the *Discoverer,* while crossing Iron Bottom Sound, just off Guadalcanal, hit an uncharted reef. The first reports were brief. A gash in the hull caused the ship to take on water quickly; soon the hold and the lower two cabin decks were filled with water, and the ship was listing heavily. Crew and passengers were evacuated by lifeboat with only the clothes on their backs; all were safe. The captain, thinking quickly to avoid complete disaster, ran the ship into shallow water and up on a sandbar to avoid its sinking. CNN aired video footage and wire-service reports around the globe. We were thunderstruck when the news reached us: it seemed too surreal to be true. We clearly would not be retracing the 1899 voyage on the *Discoverer.* (On the eve of our new departure, it sits rusting on a Pacific island beach.) Had I listened carefully, I might have heard the gods laughing.

Sinking ships aside, our extended planning efforts offered the first glimpse of how much the world had changed in one hundred years. The 1899 expedition began its planning in late March 1899 and sailed from Seattle just two months later, on May 30. In another two months, on July 30, they returned to Seattle. I can only marvel at the speed and free-spiritedness with which E. H. Harriman and C. Hart Merriam organized their voyage. Merriam, chief of the U.S. Biological Survey, summarized the simplicity of their approach in his introduction in the first volume of the *Harriman Alaska Expedition* series: "The ship had no business other than to convey the party whithersoever it desired to go. Her route was entrusted to a committee so that from day to day and hour to hour her movements were made to subserve the interests of the scientific work." Unlike our 1899 counterparts, we were bound by the legacy of their voyage, historical accuracy, and a world that has grown ever more complex.

In 2001, we could not arrive unannounced at a Canadian, Alaskan, or Russian port with a 340-foot ship, as they did in 1899. Our checklists included immigration and maritime laws; federal, state, and local regulations; international treaties; multiple jurisdictions; and insurance questions that had to be addressed before even stepping aboard the ship. Today, the 1899 expedition would violate dozens of regulations and laws and would have an "unacceptable liability profile." (I can only imagine the response of Centers for Disease Control inspectors if they found in our hold the "eleven fat steer, a flock of sheep, chickens, turkeys, a milch cow, and a span of horses" that John Burroughs described as being brought along on the 1899 expedition.) No doubt we are better off with these protections, but I can't help but lament the loss of the spontaneity enjoyed by the original expedition.

In our planning, we were also keenly aware that the social environment of the United States had evolved rapidly over the last century, with dramatic shifts in cultural values. The ways we currently perceive the social impacts of the early Russian and U.S. fur trade, the whaling industry, salmon canneries, and the Alaska gold rush are vastly different from perceptions in 1899. Although members of the Harriman party recoiled from scenes of human misery that today we too would find shocking and outrageous, many onboard the *Elder* and in the Alaska communities they visited regarded these scenes as a necessary consequence of their society's accomplishments. The seventeenth, eighteenth, and nineteenth centuries saw the construction of global empires and the economic systems to finance them. As they raced to establish strategic claims and vast fortunes, first European governments and later the United States exploited both indigenous peoples and natural resources. The results often included the devastation of native societies.

As 1899 expedition member William Dall observed in his expedition essay, Alaska was no exception: "The history of Alaska is practically the history of exploration and trade along its coasts and within its borders." One hundred years later, we know Dall's observation is correct but incomplete. His shipmate, George Bird Grinnell, helps complete the picture of the land they encountered: "White men, uncontrolled and uncontrollable, already swarm over the Alaska coast, and are overwhelming the Eskimo. . . . In a very short time they will ruin and disperse the wholesome . . . people whom we saw."

Yet this too is a snapshot; the story neither begins nor ends in the decades surrounding 1899. Natives emigrating from Siberia across the Bering Land Bridge were the first to inhabit the Alaska coast nearly ten thousand years ago. These emigrants were North America's earliest natives, and their culturally rich societies were adapted to some of the earth's harshest climates. Their universe would change forever when Russian Tsar Peter I turned his ambitions to the New World. Under his employment, in 1741 the Danish explorer Vitus Jonassen Bering dispatched the first European landing party to the Alaska coast in search of furs. With this event the tumultuous modern relationship between Alaska Natives and foreign governments began. The 1899 expedition could not escape the raw legacy of this 260-year-old event, and we know that we will confront it too in 2001.

From conversations during our scouting trips we could easily identify the cultures that were the winners and those that were the losers in the grand nineteenth-century global geopolitical struggles. Many who ultimately benefited from the society and prosperity that emerged from this era saw our expedition as a wonderful educational opportunity. Educators, historians, and ambassadors for Alaska have embraced our educational mission, believing that the extensive scientific and documentary information gathered by the Harriman Expedition at the end of the nineteenth century is an ideal basis for looking at environmental change over a hundred-year period. In ways the 1899 expedition may not have intended, its reports, essays, and images, contained in the thirteen published volumes of the *Harriman Alaska Expedition* series, provide a benchmark for U.S. society to use in assessing its relationship with the natural world and the resources that support its existence. We can use this information to ask questions about how far we as a society have come in our relationship with nature, to take stock, and to consider where we might be going.

Yet, the same economic system that allowed the 1899 expedition and others like it to be undertaken also enslaved free people and nearly eradicated cultures. For those whose ancestors suffered, Harriman Retraced was a misguided mission, the re-creation of a voyage that symbolized imperialistic aggression. "Why would you celebrate that?" we were asked, in both angry and heartfelt tones. Again, a simple question caused the 2001 expedition's story to grow. As the powerful currents of a larger history and emerging social forces intersected, the gods again laughed. Parts of Harriman Retraced have taken on a life of their own and have broadened our mission independent of any previous plan. We are now grappling with both the environmental and the social changes that have intertwined to shape a history of the Alaska coast beyond that reported by Dall and Grinnell.

Like our 1899 counterparts, though, we too will soon face the challenge of interpreting the world and events that flow past our replacement ship, the *Clipper Odyssey*. We share with them a sense that we are standing at a transitional moment in U.S. history: the close of one century and the beginning of a new era. Our scouting trips have already shown us that our interpretations of the world in 1899 will be immensely influenced by the span of time that separates us from the Harriman party.

In 1899, statehood for Alaska was more than half a century away, World Wars I and II were fifteen and forty years away. Henry Ford's first automobile would not roll off the assembly line until 1903, the same year the Wright brothers would make their first flight. The light bulb and telephone had been available for only two decades, and only one in seven U.S. households had a bathtub. Not for another two decades, until 1920, would women have the right to vote.

In 1899, William McKinley was president of the United States. Since then, seventeen men have served as president, Americans have walked on the moon, and space flight is now common. The Internet links us to the world in seconds, polio has been eradicated, the Soviet Union has come and gone, and world population has grown from 1.6 billion to 6.1 billion. The twentieth century was as momentous as any hundred-year period in human history. And it all happened after the *George W. Elder* returned to Seattle.

Without question, Harriman Retraced will be a voyage through many dimensions of contemporary Alaskan society. In just hours, we will encounter an Alaska alive with passion and change, whose past and future are interwoven with one of the world's most bountiful, awe-inspiring environments. Although our ship will carry us across the water to fixed locations on a chart, our questions will take us across a century and into the history and contemporary life of a society still very much in transition. Soon we will be visiting diverse cultures and communities and the ecosystems in which they exist—all moving and changing through time.

Our greatest assets in understanding the great mix of issues we will encounter are the people of Alaska. It is crucial to the success of the 2001 expedition that we meet with as many Alaskans as possible, on their terms, in their own environments. To understand the complexities of the modern Alaskan dream we need to speak with mayors, teachers, tribal leaders and elders, children, business owners, and conservationists. Our goal is to share in the community's life as it is, not as it appears on those airport posters and in tourism brochures. Plans for meeting with communities evolved naturally during the scouting trips. It was a wonderfully messy process, from which we always emerged with our heads and notebooks packed with information. Through conversations in coffee shops, clan houses, corporate offices, and government headquarters, I got to know the people and communities we will soon be visiting. Many were not at all bashful about sharing their views of the Alaskan dream, past and present; almost everyone had an opinion or story to tell. When the conversations were over, we had arranged meetings, gatherings, and meals with more than eighteen communities. This approach, we were told, was unusual: many said that ships often came to their communities, but few, if any, invited the community aboard for a visit, much less to share opinions and a meal. Starting tomorrow, we will be visiting, talking, debating, and sharing ideas along the length of the vast Alaska coast.

Although reaching out to communities was critical to our goals, it gave our planning team chronic heartburn. The community groups I met with were often a mix of staff and volunteers—all good, independent-minded Alaskans with ideas of their own. The contrast of a community group's world-view with that of a disciplined and professional ship's crew made for many interesting conversations. Throw into the mix twenty-five traveling academics and artists, and you quickly test the managerial limits of professional sailors. In recounting the 1899 expedition, conservationist John Muir made a timeless observation: "Scientific explorers are not easily managed, and in large mixed lots are rather inflammable and explosive, especially when compressed on a ship."

Although the final plan is a bit unorthodox, it reflects strong logistical planning, strict attention to operational details, and safety standards beyond reproach. With this plan and an open mind, we are ready to launch what they called in 1899 the "floating university." Like the members of the 1899 expedition, we too will soon feel the tension between the brevity of our visits and the volumes of information we want to gather. But one hundred years has brought an important change that works directly to our advantage. Today, Alaska has a flourishing university system and a population that includes scholars, writers, and artists. As we board the ship tomorrow, we will have in our party many Alaskan scholars who will share both their academic expertise and their knowledge of their homeland with the visitors from "away."

This local knowledge will be invaluable as we set off into an Alaska whose politics have become complicated. In preparing for our voyage, we saw that how Alaskans interpreted Harriman Retraced had as much to do with the economic, cultural, or political persuasions of the observers as it did with the actual goals of the voyage. The values that different Alaskan community members attached to the retracing convinced us that a century had not in the least mellowed debate over Alaska's future. In fact, with policy decisions on the horizon dealing with oil drilling in the Alaska National Wildlife Refuge, Native hunting and fishing subsistence rights, wolf hunting, logging in national forests, cruise-ship pollution, and commercial fisheries' catch rates, the intensity of debate is at historically high levels. The most recent gubernatorial election was, in effect, an impassioned referendum on the future of the state, its people, and its natural resources. Unlike one hundred years ago, when alternative views regarding resource extraction or Native rights were in their infancy or nonexistent, during the period before the election, newspapers, television, and Main Street were alive with proposals and counterproposals, agitation and consternation—some of it generated by no less than two funded, organized, media-savvy political parties.

This turbulence around environmental issues is precisely the reason for retracing the 1899 expedition. Alaska presents a microcosm of the natural resource and social issues that people are facing around the world. Its complex policy problems concern those inside and outside the state. And, because of its vast undeveloped land area, Alaska is a remarkable environmental laboratory with countless incomplete experiments under way. Debates involving Alaska's problems may provide answers to questions that arise well beyond its own borders. Looking for these opportunities is the basic justification for retracing a somewhat zany Victorian-era expedition. With satellites

routinely scanning even the most remote areas of the globe's surface, the most important discoveries for the future of the planet may be at busy social interfaces.

This is an exciting moment. As I stand watching the sun sink into the horizon
beyond Puget Sound, scientists, writers, and artists are converging on Seattle for a
single purpose. Tonight we will meet, many of us for the first time. It is also a sobering moment. Despite the years of planning, scouting, and sweating the details, I know
there is still uncertainty and much to learn. Standing at a hotel window, I have unceremoniously discovered the point where planning ends and exploration begins. It is
time to go, time to catch up with Mr. Harriman and his party.

CHAPTER TWO

FOR THE BENEFIT OF OTHERS:

The 1899 Harriman Alaska Expedition

✦

KAY SLOAN

The expedition . . . was originally planned as a summer cruise for the pleasure of my family and a few friends. . . . Our comfort and safety required a large vessel and crew, and preparations for the voyage were consequently on a scale disproportionate to the size of the party. We decided, therefore[,] . . . to include some guests who, while adding to the interest and pleasure of the expedition, would gather useful information and distribute it for the benefit of others.

– *Edward H. Harriman, Preface, in vol. 1 of* Harriman Alaska Expedition

MORE THAN TWENTY YEARS AGO, my desk at the University of Texas at Austin held stacks of the diaries, letters, memoirs, and scientific reports left behind by members of railroad tycoon Edward Henry Harriman's famous nineteenth-century expedition to Alaska. As my colleague William H. (Bill) Goetzmann and I wove together their daily adventures for our book, *Looking Far North: The Harriman Expedition to Alaska, 1899,* I could imagine being onboard the steamship *George W. Elder* exploring Alaska. Along on the voyage were some of the nineteenth century's most accomplished citizens: the renowned naturalist John Muir, the government geologist Grove Karl Gilbert, the photographer Edward Curtis, and two dozen other illustrious scientists, writers, and artists. In the decades following publication of our book, I imagined from time to time that, someday, someone would re-create Harriman's magnificent voyage. When I was invited to join the Harriman Alaska Expedition Retraced, a historian's fantasy—this historian's—came true.

With great anticipation, I flew to Seattle in late July 2001 and on to Prince Rupert, British Columbia, where I boarded the *Clipper Odyssey*. At that moment, it became real—twenty-two other scholars and I were about to retrace the last grand expedition of the nineteenth century, visiting the sites and exploring the issues that had confronted the travelers of one hundred years before.

In 1899, Harriman accomplished a remarkable feat: he masterminded the most unlikely scientific expedition in U.S. history. The extensive documentation of that voyage now allowed us to look back across a century. How much did the Alaskan wilderness and Alaskan society change in that time? How relevant would the issues raised on that voyage be? Could a hundred years of history provide any guidance as we moved into the twenty-first century?

In March of 1899, the Harriman paid an unannounced visit to C. Hart Merriam, chief of the U.S. Biological Survey in Washington, D.C. Merriam had no idea who this Harriman fellow was or why he was now standing before him. Harriman, the newly appointed chair of the Union Pacific Railroad, proposed to a skeptical Merriam an all-expense-paid scientific expedition to Alaska. Merriam queried his colleagues and, to his astonishment, learned who Harriman was and that he was quite capable of underwriting such an expedition. Merriam contacted Harriman immediately, and they met that evening to begin planning. It didn't take Harriman long to advance his plan. The next day Merriam met with two experienced explorer-scientists, William Healey Dall and Gilbert. Dall, considered the leading expert on the region, had already made a number of trips to Alaska. Gilbert was renowned for his explorations of the American West. Harriman authorized the scientists to proceed with planning, and they quickly assembled twenty-three scientists representing twelve disciplines. Only two months after Harriman's first conversation with Merriam, they left for Alaska.

In May, a private train of Pullman "palace cars" departed from New York City with a party of some of the nation's top scientists, artists, and writers, graciously hosted by Harriman. They chugged across the continent to Seattle, where they embarked on the most luxurious scientific expedition ever known—with the goal of exploring the country's most tantalizing, exotic wilderness. Onboard the *George W. Elder* were 126 people, including Harriman's family and staff. His son, Averell, was eight years old when he boarded the ship. Averell would return to the Bering Sea four decades later as U.S. ambassador to the Soviet Union.

Never before had there been such an extraordinary expedition (and there hasn't been one since). In Seattle, the *Elder*'s coal bunkers were filled. Hunters joined the expedition; during the trip they provided fresh meat and even helped Harriman shoot a bear. In addition, there were physicians, stenographers, taxidermists, and a chaplain, as well as an animal menagerie intended to feed the crew and to provide transport. John Burroughs, a well-known nature writer from New York, wrote, "The hold of the ship looked like a farmer's barnyard. . . . We heard the mellow low of the

FIGURE 2. *Harriman Expedition party just prior to boarding.*
Credit: Edward S. Curtis. Source: Harriman family collection.

red steer even in the wilds of the Bering Sea." As the *Elder* cast off its lines and made its way into Puget Sound, large crowds cheered its departure, and newspapers across the nation ran front-page stories on the event.

It must have been an extraordinary moment for Harriman, whose prominence had not come to him easily. In 1899, Harriman was at a turning point in his career. His dramatic emergence as the leader of the Union Pacific Railroad commanded national attention. The public discovered him, seeing Harriman as a visionary entrepreneur and a masterful railroad builder. At age fifty-one, he was a self-made man with a drive and ambition that had revealed themselves early in his life. The son of a Long Island Episcopalian minister, he began his career at age fourteen as a quotations runner on Wall Street. Later, as a stockbroker, he began accumulating the wealth required to become an influential banker and deal maker.

Harriman skillfully turned his financial power into a railroad empire. He used his role as chair of the newly acquired Illinois Central Railroad to position himself for a deal that would launch him into prominence. In 1898, he successfully outmaneuvered his competitors in a power struggle that led to his takeover of the Union Pacific Railroad and his triumphant ascension to the chairmanship of the board. Newspapers referred to him as "the most powerful man in America." However, his triumph exacted a toll, even if only his family saw it. Harriman was facing exhaustion when his friend and physician, Lewis Rutherford Morris, ordered him to take an extended, restful vacation.

To revitalize the ailing magnate, the Harriman family chose a newly fashionable pursuit among New York society: tourism. Yet Harriman, who was brilliant at both conceptualizing and implementing grand ideas, clearly was not going to spend his vacation in a lounge chair in the Catskills. Instead, he orchestrated the Harriman Alaska Expedition. In his 1911 *Biography of E. H. Harriman*, Muir wrote: "Mr. Harriman was . . . taking a trip for rest and at the same time managing his exploring guests as if we were a grateful, soothing, essential part of this rest-care. . . . He kept us in smooth working order."

Although his health played a part, Harriman's motivations for undertaking the expedition were undoubtedly complicated. Spurred on perhaps by fellow New Yorker Theodore Roosevelt's big-game exploits, Harriman wanted to hunt the famous Kodiak bear. The skin would make an admirable trophy back in status-conscious New York City. Possibly he was also inspired by reports from the ongoing gold rush in the Yukon Territory that a small railroad had been constructed to carry gold-crazed

FIGURE 3. *Officers and deck crew of the* George W. Elder. *Captain Peter Doran center, right of binnacle. Credit: Edward S. Curtis. Source: Harriman family collection.*

FIGURE *4. Edward Henry Harriman, circa 1890. Source: Library of Congress.*

prospectors up the steep White Pass Trail. This curious railroad through such rugged terrain—with its implications for a greater trans-Siberian rail line—may have caught Harriman's entrepreneurial eye. Or perhaps the expedition was Harriman's way of celebrating his newfound power as a winner among the boardroom barons of the nation's brutally competitive railroad industry.

The close of the nineteenth century was the great age of philanthropy, and Harriman was surely aware of his colleagues' charitable activities. With Andrew Carnegie's and John D. Rockefeller's contributions to the country's welfare taking the form of endowments to libraries and universities, Harriman may have been seeking a more distinctive, individual statement. By leading an expedition of the nation's top scientists, he saw himself making a lasting contribution to science and exploration—an expansive, well-documented reconnaissance of Alaska's vast wilderness coastline and its inhabitants.

To this day, the Harriman expedition stands as one of the most unusual scientific expeditions in history: a blend of research and pleasure, of intellectual depth and occasional silliness. Merriam referred to the ship as a kind of "floating university," where lectures and debates, mixed with firsthand experience and discovery, took place in luxury unknown in previous scientific expeditions. Burroughs confided in his journal: "I am the most untraveled man in the crowd[;] . . . they are fearfully and wonderfully learned. The botanists and zoologists talk in Latin most of the time, and the geologists have a jargon of their own. I keep mum lest I show my ignorance." Likewise, the poet Charles Keeler felt somewhat of an "outsider," occasionally wondering exactly what role he was expected to play. Nonetheless, he managed to enjoy himself; as he wrote his wife from Kodiak Island: "We only go to sea in fine weather when the ocean is like a millpond and . . . everything is done in the most luxurious manner possible." When the *Elder* arrived back in Seattle, its passengers had sailed nine thousand miles in two months and had accumulated volumes of field notes, more than a hundred trunks of specimens, and five thousand photographs and illustrations.

Harriman could not have known the full repercussions of his enterprise when he began planning his Alaska "vacation." By contemporary standards, the expedition's planning was highly unorthodox. Geologist Gilbert interpreted their mission as a study of what they had "eyes to see." Its open-ended itinerary gave the scientists freedom to suggest a destination or to remain at a site for their own research; the very promise of such freedom attracted to the expedition a remarkable group of individuals, a who's who of late-nineteenth-century science, art, and literature.

Merriam was a pioneering scientist in his own right. At just sixteen years of age, he participated in the Smithsonian Institution's Hayden Survey of Yellowstone and the western territories. After graduating from Yale, he went to Columbia University to become a medical doctor. He returned to his first love, natural history and the study of mammals, after six years of practicing medicine. By age thirty, he was chief of the U.S. Biological Survey, the predecessor of the U.S. Fish and Wildlife Service. In addition to his organizational skills and large scientific network, Merriam the biological scientist revolutionized the collecting of field samples for the creation of systematic mammal collections. Harriman clearly knew who he was looking for before he entered Merriam's office.

After meeting Harriman, Merriam began making contacts. Florence Merriam, his younger sister and a Smith College graduate, recommended the up-and-coming bird artist Louis Agassiz Fuertes. Fuertes had illustrated Florence Merriam's book *A-Birding on a Bronco,* and she knew young Fuertes was right for the expedition. Her brother agreed, and Fuertes began a career that would modernize natural history illustration. Merriam then contacted another longtime colleague, George Bird Grinnell. As a young naturalist on George Custer's Black Hills expedition, Grinnell had developed a lifelong interest in Native American culture. At age twenty-seven, he was editor of the leading outdoor and natural history magazine, *Forest and Stream.* Founder of the Audubon Society and Boone and Crockett Club, he was also an advisor to Presidents Theodore Roosevelt and Grover Cleveland on Indian affairs. Grinnell had just published two volumes of Indian lore when Merriam extended his invitation.

Serendipity struck again. Years before, Grinnell had been hiking Washington's Mount Rainier when he and his party became lost. They came upon a young portrait photographer from Seattle shooting landscapes, and he agreed to lead them off the mountain. This chance encounter was on Grinnell's mind when he recommended this photographer, Edward Curtis, to Merriam. Grinnell became Curtis's mentor on the expedition. The commitment Curtis formed on the voyage to documenting what he called a "vanishing race" led him to spend the rest of his life photographing Native Americans and recording their rich cultures.

Then there were "the two Johnnies"—Burroughs and Muir. At Harriman's request, Merriam stepped outside his circle of scientists and invited John Burroughs, the sage of the bucolic Catskills landscape. At this point in his career, the sixty-two-year-old Burroughs, who published a book about every two years, was well known as a writer of "nature essays." Harriman wanted him to write the official, popular narrative of the expedition. Burroughs completed the task in his characteristically romantic, sometimes sentimental, style, but not without angst. He did not travel well, and, in Alaska's immense, rugged landscape, he felt homesick for the pastoral scenes of rural New York. To make matters worse, he was constantly seasick aboard what the expedition members renamed the "George W. Roller." Unable to bear the thought of entering the Bering Sea, Burroughs packed his bags and attempted to jump ship in Dutch Harbor. With Keeler, Muir confronted Burroughs as he strolled down the gangplank. "Where are you going with that grip, Johnny?" he asked. Assuring his gentle companion that the Bering Sea was "like a millpond," Muir escorted the reluctant Burroughs back onto the ship, with Keeler carrying his valise.

Muir's comments were often barbed with wit when he targeted the elderly naturalist. Just a year younger than Burroughs, the founder of the Sierra Club and tireless wilderness advocate was no newcomer to Alaska. The opinionated, garrulous Muir had traveled to Alaska on extended expeditions in 1879–1880 and again in 1890. By the time he joined the 1899 expedition, he was a recognized authority on glaciers, with one of the largest in Glacier Bay named after him. This expertise in glaciology as well as his broad background in nature study prompted Harriman's invitation. Muir's bunkmate, Keeler, found Muir's expertise so complete that he often held back his own opinions in the face of Muir's pontifications. For Muir, the greatest joy of the trip lay in experiencing the wonders and mysteries of the wilderness.

This unlikely mix of well-established professionals, young artists, and professors up and coming in their fields contributed to the expedition's success. Harriman's voyage yielded thirteen published volumes of essays and scientific information, complete with illustrations by Fuertes and Curtis. It took Merriam ten years to edit and assemble the volumes that presented new ideas about glaciation and the geologic significance of volcanoes. Consumed with a decade of editing the *Harriman Alaska Expedition* series, Merriam never completed volume 6, on Alaskan mammals. Although the volumes in the series were numbered 1–14 to include his contribution, only thirteen volumes were published. The scientists reported finding thirteen genera and six hundred species new to science, as well as thirty-eight new fossil species. Extensive collections of birds, mammals, plants, and insects were catalogued and studied back at the finest institutions in the United States. For the geographers and adventurers aboard, a highlight was the exploration of Prince William Sound, where the expedition members named newly discovered glaciers after their prestigious alma maters and the Seven Sisters colleges: Harvard, Yale, Amherst, Radcliffe, Smith, Bryn Mawr, Vassar, and Wellesley. If that was a highlight, their triumph was being the first Western navigators to discover Harriman Fjord. As part of their exploration, expedition members mapped and named the enormous glaciers at the terminus of the fjord; henceforth, this site was called Harriman Glacier.

IN JULY 2001, I stood at the *Clipper Odyssey*'s rail, taking in the forested vistas beyond the Prince Rupert dock, when the engines started. As the lines were tossed and the space grew between the ship and the massive pilings, my role on the voyage seemed richly ironic. As a historian, I have focused my work on the past. The details of the 1899 expedition were neatly stacked in my mind, ready to be recalled. At this moment, though, as the deck shuddered under the increasing power of the ship's engines, we were starting on a journey into the future.

The focus of my journey, my reference point for understanding all the tomorrows that were about to unfold on this trip, would surely rest in what Bill Goetzmann and I called the "two Alaskas." Each day my fellow passengers and I would see the Alaskan grandeur celebrated by Muir and the seemingly infinite, exploitable resources of ocean and wilderness. This was our kinship with the original Harriman expedition members who had the "eyes to see" the two Alaskas of 1899—one of rich economic resources ripe for exploitation and the other of pristine glaciers and mountains, a sight Muir felt was akin to a mystical experience, a holy wilderness.

Significantly, this voyage evoked questions for me that were just beginning to take shape in 1899. Since Bill Goetzmann and I wrote *Looking Far North* in 1982, an older history, that of the "first Alaska," has come into sharper focus within the evolving historiography of the United States. It is a history of an ancient people with ways of life dependent on and interwoven with their natural environments. The economies and societies ranging the globe in search of resources, wealth, and power crashed headlong into the rich cultures and religions of these Native peoples.

Into this now century-old collision, the 1899 expedition sailed. On Annette Island, at Metlakatla, the expedition members witnessed the religious experiment of the Scottish Reverend William Duncan to Westernize the Haida people, whose villages were destroyed and culture was outlawed. Farther along, some saw the forced labor of Natives in the salmon-canning industry as efficient and productive. Others, like Grinnell and Muir, were appalled at the terrible exploitation they saw at the Orca cannery. Muir shook his head sadly at the sight of the laborers there. "Men in this business," he wrote in his journal, "are themselves canned." As the expedition sailed west into the land of the Aleuts and Eskimos, Grinnell observed the grim circumstances of these ravaged people. The tension between the two Alaskas that began with the Russian fur industry in the eighteenth century enveloped Alaska's Native peoples in often disastrous ways. Their cultures, on the brink of extinction, were the ones Curtis rushed to document. On my first night aboard the *Clipper Odyssey*, I couldn't avoid thinking of the irony of our first stop the next morning. We would wake up at Cape Fox Village, the scene of an infamous looting during the 1899 expedition that exemplified those two Alaskas.

Near the close of Harriman's grand voyage, a gold miner told the artist Frederick Dellenbaugh about an intriguing village abandoned by the Native inhabitants and even sketched a crude map, placing it near "Foggy Bay." Because of this chance encounter the Harriman expedition landed at Cape Fox Village, on a sandy cove containing rows of houses and nineteen beautifully carved and decorated totems. They found no signs of recent habitation. They spent the day exploring the village while deck hands loaded the totems, along with other spiritual objects found in the homes, onto the ship. Some of the scientists, including Keeler of the California Academy of Sciences and Daniel Elliot of the Chicago Field Museum, saw the value of placing the objects in their museums and other institutions around the country. In such institutions, accessible to curators and anthropologists, they could be preserved and studied. Others cringed at the apparent desecration. Muir watched in disgust as the crew strained to dislodge the totems. Describing an earlier trip to Alaska, in 1879, in his book *Travels in Alaska,* he called it a "sacrilege" when a totem pole was cut down "to enrich some museum or other."

In one of the most powerful moments of our expedition, we arrived at this same sandy cove and returned the ancient house totems and other sacred objects, brought from museums across the country and in pristine condition, to the Tlingit people. No doubt, the original expedition members never imagined such an event. In July 2001, on the first day of the contemporary expedition, I experienced a rare event: the rewriting of history.

Parakeet Auklet

Seattle to Prince Rupert
22 July 2001

At 6:30 A.M., PDT, members of the Harriman Alaska Expedition Retraced party gathered in the hotel lobby. Cups of coffee, sleepy stares to nowhere, quiet conversation, and anticipation were all part of the early-morning mix as our luggage was loaded into the belly of our awaiting bus. With gentle urging, the individuals scattered around the lobby coalesced first into a group, then a line, to board the bus taking us to the SeaTac airport.

By this point in 1899, most of the Harriman Expedition members had been together for eight days traveling on one of Edward Harriman's own trains, composed of Pullman "palace cars." In Gilded Age luxury, they continued planning their expedition while the United States glided by their windows—the long-tamed pastoral East, Midwest farmland, the jagged, uplifted Rockies, and the West still in ecological and social transition. John Burroughs's favorite recollection of the train trip was his ride on the cowcatcher: "In this position one gets a much

more vivid sense of the perils that encompass the flying train than he does from the car window. . . . How rapidly those slender steel rails do spin beneath us. . . . And how inadequate they do seem to guide this enormous throbbing and roaring monster which we feel laboring and panting on our backs."

By all accounts, most of my colleagues who converged on Seattle just yesterday saw the landscape from a less-intimate thirty thousand feet. Fewer than twenty-four hours after their arrival, we had them on another jet bound for Prince Rupert, British Columbia. This second departure from the 1899 expedition's itinerary was a response to the Jones Merchant Marine Act of 1920. Simply put, any ship transporting cargo between two U.S. ports must be built in the United States and be owned and crewed by U.S. mariners. Although we know perfectly well that in 1959 Alaska joined the Union as the forty-ninth state, the vast distance separating "the great land" from the Lower Forty-Eight somehow allows us to see Alaska differently. The Jones Act dispassionately reminds us that Seattle, Washington, and our first port of call, Cape Fox, Alaska, are, geography notwithstanding, two U.S. ports. Because our ship, the M/V *Clipper Odyssey*, flies under a Bahamian flag, with Nassau as its port of registry, we were off by jet to a "foreign" port in Canada.

Technology again compressed time as we traveled in eighty minutes a distance that the *George W. Elder* took four days to achieve. As we awaited our beverage service, with Vancouver Island and the Canadian Coast Mountains racing by below us, I took comfort in knowing we had at least postponed experiencing a malady the 1899 travelers had encountered in these waters: seasickness. Burroughs, the principal narrator of the expedition and a self-described "dreamer" aboard the *Elder*, was perhaps the worst plagued, almost from the start of the voyage: "On this second day we begin to feel the great pulse of the Pacific around the head of Vancouver Island. . . . For three hours the ship rolls as upon the open sea, and to several of us the 'subsequent proceedings' that night were void of interest."

With touchdown in Prince Rupert, anticipation and excitement were high. In just over an hour the jet had carried us into a different world altogether; the 2001 expedition had begun. Urban Seattle seemed incredibly distant as we stepped into the mist of coastal British Columbia's temperate rainforest. Ecosystem boundaries still prevail here; the Douglas fir, western hemlock, Sitka spruce, and cedar surrounding us ignore international boundaries. The rainforest will now be with us along four hundred miles of coast, until we leave Alaska's Inside Passage at Glacier Bay.

With all that lay ahead, I was eager to find my way to the docks for the first, long-anticipated look at the M/V *Clipper Odyssey*. I could hardly grasp that the concept of retracing an expedition that took place 102 years ago was about to be transformed into a current event. As a temporary steward, I watched nervously as crated Tlingit house posts and totems taken from Cape Fox by the 1899 expedition were carefully lifted by a cargo crane and lowered onto the *Odyssey*'s aft deck. Oddly, as I stood on the dock admiring the long graceful curve of the *Odyssey*'s bow, I thought of the bedraggled *World Discoverer* rusting on a South Pacific beach. On this auspicious day, standing on a dock surrounded by the North Pacific, the tallest trees on earth, and the deep fjords of the Coast Mountains, I knew that we had already traveled a great distance.

In reality, ships are a collection of engineered parts and mechanical systems assembled in a precise way, which allows them to float on water. Nothing romantic about it. In fact, the *George W. Elder* started out as an unadorned iron-hulled steamship owned by Harriman's Oregon Railroad and Navigation Company. Before the *Elder*'s extensive conversion into Mr. Harriman's luxurious floating university, it had the routine life of a packet delivering freight up and down the Pacific Coast. By contrast, the *Odyssey* is a feat of modern marine architecture, designed with a single purpose: to sail the oceans of the world. This vessel was built in Tokyo and launched in 1988. It is 338 feet long, has a 51-foot beam, and draws 15 feet of water. Its shallow draft allows the ship to explore the bays, coves, and fjords of the world's coastlines. A small fleet of Zodiacs, a nearly indestructible, inflatable boat invented by Jacques

Cousteau, would provide transportation to and from the mother ship. The *Odyssey* requires 104 feet of clearance from the surface of the water to the highest point of the satellite antennae. Equally important are the 358 tons of fuel that is carries in five tanks; this fuel gives the ship a seven-thousand-mile range at a cruising speed of sixteen knots. Power is provided by two Wartsilla three-thousand-horsepower diesel engines that drive two controllable-pitch propellers. The *Odyssey* can desalinize 70 tons of water per day, closely matching daily use. In addition, 275 tons of water are stored within the ship.

All these systems have come together to create an extraordinary base of operation for our journey. Yet, invariably, along the way a transformation will occur as all the parts mingle with saltwater, wind, tides, storms, and dramatic sunsets. We will find that as a ship takes you deeper into the constantly changing marine environment, its rhythms and ways begin to shape the routines of your own life. Soon the onshore world becomes a place to visit; the ship is where you live.

And here we were, at the beginning of this magical transformation. With all passengers onboard and settling into their cabins, Captain Michael Taylor signaled his crew at 6:00 P.M. PDT to cast off the *Odyssey*'s lines and steer into Chatham Sound, heading northwest toward the Canadian-U.S. border. About midnight, we will cross the border and sail into the two Alaskas.

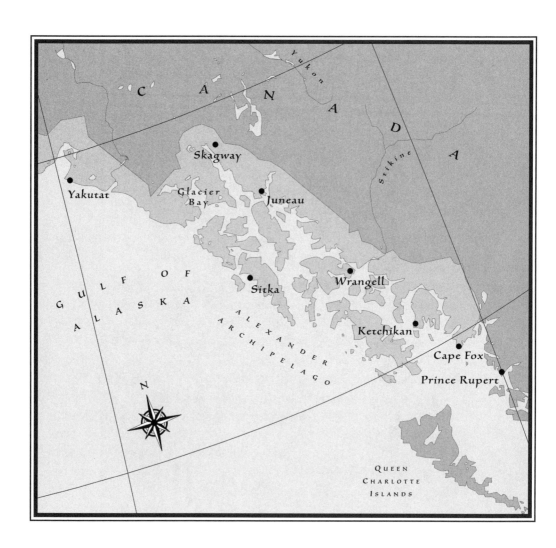

The Alexander Archipelago, Prince Rupert to Glacier Bay

PART TWO

INSIDE PASSAGE

❧

{On the Beach, Cape Fox}

REPATRIATION BEGINS

We came to make amends.
First, we offered food to the flames,
then, with permission, entered
the woods to look for what was lost.
Some found posts and foundations,
but there were no doors,
and walls had fallen back into trees.
Here in this village of epilogue
we began to address the ghosts,
inviting them out of bark and leaf
and moss. Green children all, we
filed back to our ship with its cargo
of totem faces taken from twilight,
the craft of the Real People.
We rode on to Metlakatla with stories
rising, the Tongass swelling as if to speak.

— SHEILA NICKERSON

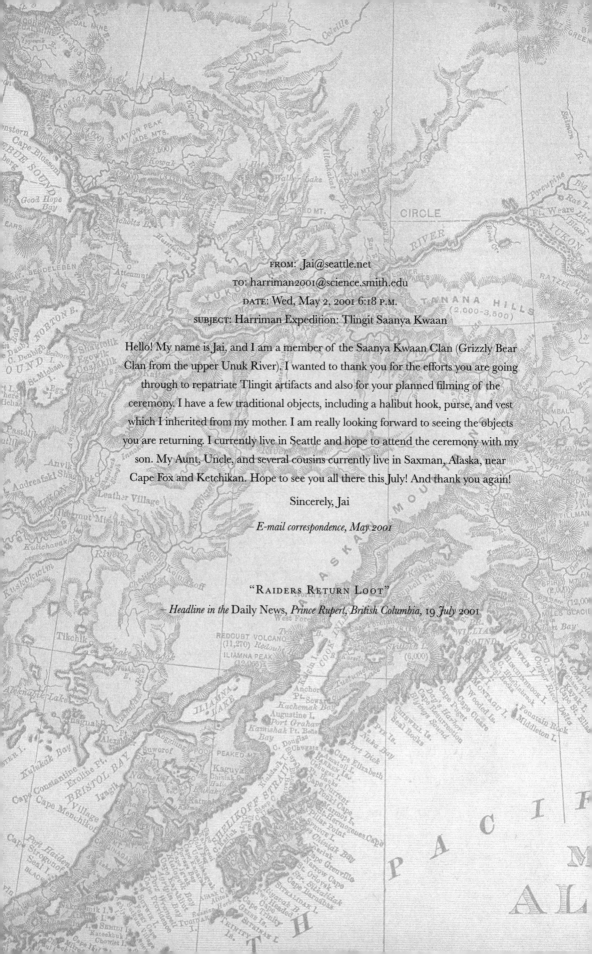

FROM: Jai@seattle.net
TO: harriman2001@science.smith.edu
DATE: Wed, May 2, 2001 6:18 P.M.
SUBJECT: Harriman Expedition: Tlingit Saanya Kwaan

Hello! My name is Jai, and I am a member of the Saanya Kwaan Clan (Grizzly Bear
Clan from the upper Unuk River). I wanted to thank you for the efforts you are going
through to repatriate Tlingit artifacts and also for your planned filming of the
ceremony. I have a few traditional objects, including a halibut hook, purse, and vest
which I inherited from my mother. I am really looking forward to seeing the objects
you are returning. I currently live in Seattle and hope to attend the ceremony with my
son. My Aunt, Uncle, and several cousins currently live in Saxman, Alaska, near
Cape Fox and Ketchikan. Hope to see you all there this July! And thank you again!

Sincerely, Jai

— *E-mail correspondence, May 2001*

"RAIDERS RETURN LOOT"

— *Headline in the* Daily News, *Prince Rupert, British Columbia, 19 July 2001*

The First Morning, Sunrise at Cape Fox Village

23 July 2001

After dinner last evening, Rosita Worl, Tlingit leader, anthropologist, and Harriman Retraced scholar, prepared us for the many issues and emotions that would soon face us as the repatriation of the Saanya Kwaan's sacred objects unfolded. We all had studied the contributions of the 1899 participants with an objective historical distance; no body language or glances, politics or emotions to complicate the picture. In our first hours aboard the *Odyssey*, I realized how much information was missing from these inanimate portraits. This night, we watched Rosita Worl carefully step out on a cultural high wire that spans 102 years of turmoil, anger, and hope. Remarkably, she was attempting to take us across with her. As discussion wound down, some drifted off to their cabins, others to the deck for a moment of quiet. An interesting mixture of exhaustion, uncertainty, and excitement was in the air.

At first light today, we awoke anchored off old Cape Fox Village beach on Kirk Point. At this quiet moment, we could not have imagined the emotional and powerful day that was ahead. I made my way to the *Odyssey*'s bridge at 5:45 A.M. ADT and looked over the charts. We were at the southern end of the 2.3-million-acre Misty Fjords National Monument and less than eight miles from the Canadian border. Scanning Kirk Bay with binoculars, I could easily see why the Saanya Kwaan had located a village here. The village, called Gaash in Tlingit, sat above a crescent-shaped beach with a large, protective cove. No large boulders or rock faces blocked access to the gently sloping beach, which easily stretched a hundred yards or more from the low-tide line to the wrack line. Salmon purse seiners working southeast of the ship were testament to a local supply of fresh fish. On the cape itself, a young spruce forest had grown up over the years, clearly separating the sand beach from the now wooded uplands. The young forest had consumed the old village site that arriving boats would have easily seen a century ago.

FIGURE 5. *Cape Fox Village.*
Credit: Edward S. Curtis. Source: Harriman family collection.

By 6:30 A.M. we were scanning the horizon for the stevedore boat that was bringing to the ship members of the Saanya Kwaan, members of the Harriman family, and museum representatives. Just as we spotted their boat, the radio sounded, telling us that they had sighted the *Odyssey*. The electricity of this moment could be felt among all who had gathered on the bridge. Time speeded up; soon the stevedore boat was alongside the ship's pilot door with its passengers stepping aboard. Rosita Worl, in Tlingit regalia, was there to greet the party. Saanya Kwaan representatives Irene Shields Dundas and Eleanor Hadden, deck crew, and expedition members all stood in the confined space of the pilot-door entry. For Irene, this day was the culmination of many years of effort to bring her clan's property home. Hugs were interspersed with greetings and introduc-

tions as the delegation moved into the open space of Deck Three.

In the gathering stood Edward H. Harriman's great-great-granddaughter, Margaret Northrop Friedman, and her husband, Peter Friedman. Margaret's great-grandfather, Roland Harriman, was six years old in 1899 and the expedition's youngest participant. Fulfilling this historical role, asleep in an infant pack, was four-month-old Ned Northrop Friedman, great-great-great-grandson of Edward. It was not clear until about two weeks before we departed whether a member of the Harriman family would join the repatriation; Margaret and Ned's presence today was significant. Until we had known that they would be with us, our repatriation planning had focused on a ceremony, One Hundred Years of Healing, in memory of the clans and houses of Teiwedi (Brown Bear), Neix.adi (Eagle, Beaver, Halibut), and Kiks.adi (Frog). Through the healing ceremony, the clans' property could be returned, but, without a Harriman present, the dispute could not be settled, and the hundred-year-old controversy about the removal of clan property without permission would have remained a bitter, open wound. With Margaret's and Ned's participation, the event could now become one of the Tlingits' most important events, a potlatch—in this case, a form of potlatch used for settling disputes. This meeting of clan leaders with Margaret and Ned allowed for the return of the property and the resolution of the dispute.

Watching Irene, Eleanor, and Margaret quietly talking in the midst of the excited crowd, I recalled the simple notion that had helped to move the contentious repatriation discussions forward: building a bridge to the future. This phrase came to represent our understanding that there were longstanding grievances, misunderstandings, and powerful feelings, but if we were to make progress on behalf of future generations, they would have to be set aside. Here were these three young women and a baby, sent as their clans' representatives, helping to construct that bridge to

the future. Moreover, they were the first to cross it. The unassuming strength and courage they demonstrated were important ingredients of the day's success. This was also an important day for the delegates from the Burke Museum of Natural History and Culture, the Smithsonian's National Museum of the American Indian, the Chicago Field Museum, Harvard's Peabody Museum of Archaeology and Ethnology, and Cornell University. By the end of the day, these institutions had officially returned clan objects that had left this cove 102 years earlier.

Within the hour, the group moved to the *Odyssey*'s stern, and the first Zodiac was launched toward the Saanya Kwaan's ancestral village. Irene and Eleanor, now in ceremonial regalia, were the first to step ashore—this was their homeland, and it was required that they meet the visitors looking to land at this beach. As the other boats made their way to the landing, Irene, Eleanor, and Rosita moved to the upper beach and built a ceremonial fire. The three figures, dressed in red, black, and yellow robes set off by the dark-green tree line, marked the spot where a long journey was coming to an end.

Sea Otter with Urchin

© PATRICIA SAVAGE

CHAPTER THREE

STANDING WITH SPIRITS, WAITING

❧

R O S I T A   W O R L

HISTORICAL ACCOUNTS OF the 1899 Harriman Expedition tell us that some of its members justified the questionable taking of Saanya Kwaan property by choosing to believe that Cape Fox Village was abandoned and that they were acting on behalf of science. Without thought as to who the owners might be, they took what they perceived to be merely inanimate objects or scientific specimens. Other members of the expedition, like John Muir, watched the taking in disgust. The ship was loaded with the magnificent works of art, including totem poles, house screens, and masks, that would ultimately come to rest in major museums around the United States.

A hundred and two years later, three Tlingit women dressed in ceremonial regalia stood silently on the beach, their eyes riveted on the small fire that they had just finished building. The fire was necessary to transport their offerings to the Spirit World and to their ancestors. They had come to the ancient Saanya Kwaan village site of Cape Fox as part of the 2001 Harriman Alaska Expedition Retraced. Two of the women, Eleanor Hadden and Irene Shields Dundas, had direct ties to the Saanya Kwaan, the Tlingit clan that originally inhabited the southern coastal region of the Tlingit homeland in Southeast Alaska.

I was the third, joining them not in my capacity as a Harriman Scholar but as a Chilkat Tlingit from our homeland's northern region. All of us were familiar with the history of the expedition of 1899, and we struggled with our embittered emotions about its removal of sacred clan objects owned by the Saanya Kwaan. However, we knew that we could not be overcome by these hostile feelings because we had a greater task at hand.

FIGURE 6. *Clan objects await loading onto the* Elder *at Cape Fox Village.*
Credit: Edward S. Curtis. Source: Harriman family collection.

Not one word was spoken, but tears streamed down our faces as we thought about the ancestors whose spirits resided in the sacred clan objects that we identify as *at.óow* in our language. Sorrow and grief overcame us as we traveled back in time to 1899, imagining the flurry of activity that resulted in the removal of the clan objects. To the Tlingit, clan objects are not mere works of art; they are sacred and tangible links to their ancestors and clan histories. They embody the essence of who the Tlingit are and mark their path into the future. Slowly, the youngest woman began to beat the drum she was carrying. It was time for us to make offerings and to apologize to the ancestors for allowing the clan objects to be removed from their homeland and transported to foreign places.

Based on their ancient belief of Haa Shagoon, present-day Tlingits acknowledge their role, their complicity, in the loss of the Saanya Kwaan *at.óow*. The teachings of Haa Shagoon tell the present generation of Tlingits they are one with their ancestors, just as they—the present generation—will be united with future generations of Tlingits. Thus, they are just as responsible for the actions of one hundred years ago as were their ancestors, who allowed the removal of clan objects. As we three women reflected on the significance of the returning Saanya Kwaan *at.óow* and finished the ancestral offering, we felt our grief dispersing and a somber mood transformed into joy. We welcomed the ancestors back to their homeland with a song.

Then we discussed whether to invite expedition members, who were respectfully waiting at the shoreline, also to make offerings to the ancestors. In the group were direct descendants of the original expedition leader, Edward Harriman's great-great-granddaughter and her four-month-old son. One woman quietly said to the others that the first expedition took the Saanya Kwaan *at.óow*, but the new expedition was assisting and celebrating the return of the clan objects, now awaiting us on the *Clipper Odyssey*'s decks. This simple statement ended the discussion. It was time to begin the healing process and lay our anger to rest. The drummer beckoned the visitors to enter the ancient village site of her ancestors. As we chanted, members of the expedition walked in a solemn procession, each stopping by the fire to make an offering to the ancestors.

As I stood at this sacred site, surrounded by relatives, ancestors' spirits, and white people, I knew this day was special, but in many ways it reflected our everyday world and the emotions we hold. The emotions and power I felt on that beach came from both the importance of the day and the centuries of experience that have shaped our modern world. They grew from the land and a heritage that has sustained our people since ancient times.

For thousands of years, Tlingit Indians have inhabited the rich coastal environment of Southeast Alaska. Before the arrival of Westerners, the Tlingit population numbered about ten thousand, and we maintained absolute control over our homeland. This territory stretched six hundred miles along a narrow strip of the coastal mainland and included the adjacent islands from Portland Canal, British Columbia, to the Copper River Delta. The Stikine, Taku, Chilkat, and Alsek rivers provided access through the otherwise impenetrable steep and rugged coastal range into the interior region, where a smaller group of Inland Tlingit established themselves among the Athabaskans.

The warm Japanese Current brings moderate temperatures and heavy precipitation to Southeast Alaska, nourishing an environment rich in natural resources. Dense stands of rainforest spruce, hemlock, and yellow and red cedar cover all but the mountain peaks. The thick underbrush provided the Tlingit with a variety of berries, plants, and roots used for food and medicine. The sea was the source of their greatest riches, teeming with five species of salmon, halibut, smelt, cod, seal, and sea lion. Herring gave stores of spawn, and sea otter provided pelts. Shellfish, sea urchins, and seaweed supplemented the Tlingit diet. Waterfowl and gulls provided meat and eggs.

The abundance of natural resources contributed directly to the development of a traditional economic system and efficient technologies within Tlingit society. The natural bounty enabled the Tlingit to fulfill their own needs while accumulating a surplus of goods that could be traded and transformed into greater wealth. At first, they traded among themselves—island marine resources in exchange for mainland goods. Over time, trade was extended to neighboring interior tribes in the region now called Canada. Tlingits traveled the coast southward in large wooden canoes to trade with the Tsimshian and northwestward to trade with the Eyak and Athabaskan.

Through commerce, they obtained a range of goods not available in their homeland, including furs, copper, dentalia, walrus ivory, and hides from the Bering Sea Inupiat Eskimos, Haida canoes, and Tsimshian carvings. Contemporary Tlingit are not proud that their ancestors supported slavery, but slaves were central to their society and trade. Slaves significantly increased economic production and Tlingit wealth through their labor and their value as major items of both import and export exchange. During their ten-thousand-year occupation of the region, the Tlingit developed a rich and socially complex culture rarely found among hunting-and-gathering societies.

With an abundance of resources and the goods obtained through trade, the Tlingit created a rich material culture and aesthetic that reflected their worldview and relationship with nature. They fashioned a form of art that brought them international recognition and renown. Foremost were their highly developed woodworking skills. These skills are evident in the mortuary and totem poles and in the large plank houses containing elaborately carved and painted posts and wall screens. From wood the Tlingit manufactured highly decorated ceremonial and utilitarian objects including hats, masks, dance paddles, box drums, storage boxes, bowls, and canoes. Hats and baskets were made from roots and barks. Their woven textiles include the famous mountain goat–wool Chilkat blanket.

Tlingit art was highly developed, and it was coveted by Westerners for its beauty and craftsmanship. In fact, the quality and allure of this art brought the Harriman Expedition to old Cape Fox Village in 1899, an episode that was to be woven into Saanya Kwaan history with pain, anger, and sorrow. Tlingit artistic talent and economic production, combined with an established trade network, provided the Tlingit with a degree of luxury rarely experienced by other Natives of Alaska.

These characteristics both contributed to and resulted from the complex, highly organized Tlingit society. United by a common language and a culture, members of this society are divided into two groups, or moieties: the Eagles and the Ravens. These moieties are further divided into clans, which are in turn subdivided into house groups. Clans, the most important social units, are dispersed throughout Southeast Alaska into geographical units called *kwaan,* such as the Saanya Kwaan, who lived in the Cape Fox region. Marriage is not permitted within a single moiety, so an Eagle may marry only a Raven, or Raven an Eagle. Descendance is matrilineal, with children being members of their mothers' moieties, clans, and house groups. Although this system could divide us, we are unified through an enduring rule that requires social and spiritual reciprocity and balance between Eagle and Raven clans in all activities in order to ensure harmony.

The Southeast Alaska Indians knew their wealth stemmed from the abundant natural resources surrounding them, and they were fully prepared to protect their homeland against any encroachments. The Tlingit were expanding their northwestern frontier across the Gulf of Alaska when in the late 1700s they encountered the Russians, who were extending their sea otter enterprise eastward along the Gulf of Alaska to the southeast region. The Tlingit aggressively defended their territory from the Russians, beginning with their earliest encounters. Concluding that they could not defend their lands as separate, independent clans, they looked to unification as a way to resist the Russians' efforts.

Later, in the nineteenth century, with the arrival of the Americans, Tlingit military power proved incapable of protecting coastal villages from U.S. corporate and military actions. The U.S. Navy's bombardment of Angoon, Kake, and Wrangell villages in the late 1800s made it clear that a new strategy would be required if Tlingit culture was to survive. With this realization, our ancestors hired a lawyer and began to focus on the political and legal arenas. A clan leader traveled to Washington, D.C., to voice Tlingit objections, but no written response or tangible outcome resulted.

By the time the 1899 expedition landed on the shores of Tlingit territory, the once-powerful Tlingit had been brought to their knees by U.S. colonial expansion. Diseases introduced by Westerners reduced the aboriginal population by half. In increasing numbers, colonialists invaded the Tlingit homeland, ignoring landownership rights that had been safeguarded for centuries.

Undaunted, the Tlingit continued their political unification efforts to reclaim their heritage and land. Shortly after the 1899 expedition, the Tlingit allied themselves with the small group of Kaigani Haida Indians, who had migrated from Canada into Southeast Alaska shortly before the arrival of Westerners in 1741. In 1912, they organized the Alaska Native Brotherhood (ANB) with the objective of protecting their civil rights. In 1929, the ANB expanded its mission to include settlement of the aboriginal land claims of the Southeast Indians. The Tlingit and Haida expanded the alliance to include the Tsimshian, who were brought from British Columbia to Southeast Alaska's Annette Island by Scottish missionary William Duncan in 1887. Although the Tsimshian participated in the alliance, they maintained a separate governing structure. The alliance continued to assert its land claims until finally, in 1967 and 1971, the U.S. Court of Claims and Congress recognized Tlingit aboriginal title and settled the outstanding claims.

The settlements contained one significant change from tradition. Up to this point, land was held by separate clans, which governed the social order. With the new settlements, portions of clan aboriginal lands and assets were transferred to the newly created Central Council of Tlingit and Haida Indians of Southeast Alaska and native corporations created by Congress in 1971. The political unification of the Tlingit and Haida was solidified in 1968, when they were awarded $7 million to settle the taking of the sixteen million acres that formed the Tongass National Forest. For the first time in their history, they held the asset as a unified group under a newly formed tribal government. Ironically, this limited victory came at the expense of the clans—the traditional property-holding units.

Regional unification was further reinforced with the enactment of the 1971 Alaska Native Claims Settlement Act (ANCSA), which resolved the remaining Tlingit land claims. This settlement was unprecedented in that both Congress and the Alaska Native leaders rejected use of the reservation system, which had been routinely used in the Lower Forty-Eight. Under the reservation system the land is held in trust by the federal government through the Bureau of Indian Affairs (BIA). Many Natives, particularly in the Southeast Alaska region, opposed this system and wanted complete control of their lands and resources. They attributed the failure of their commercial fishery enterprises to dictatorial governmental controls that reflected little knowledge of regional fisheries and their business operations. Southeast Natives were adamant in their rejection of BIA oversight.

Under ANCSA, Congress mandated that transferred lands were to be held by a regional, Native, for-profit corporation designed to advance the social welfare of Native peoples. The Tlingits established the Sealaska Corporation for this purpose. Although a relatively small portion of the original Tlingit territory was involved, it was now under Tlingit and Haida control. The act also created eleven Tlingit and Haida village corporations, each receiving twenty-three thousand acres. Unfortunately, five communities did not receive land. In 1987, the "Landless Communities" initiated efforts in Congress to obtain a land entitlement, but to date they have not been successful, largely because of opposition by environmental groups.

During the last one hundred years our struggle to save the Tlingit way of life has met with many challenges. With the expansion of Western-style schools and institutions, Tlingit society was forced to accept dramatic cultural and economic changes. Missionaries and educators were ruthless in seeking to repress Tlingit language and culture. Tlingit land was taken.

In 2001, as the *Clipper Odyssey* sailed through the Inside Passage, the Southeast Alaska Indians were united under two major Native regional entities, the Central Council of Tlingit and Haida Indians of Southeast Alaska and Sealaska Corporation. After their aboriginal land claims were resolved, the Tlingit had begun to focus on cultural revitalization. In 1980, the Sealaska Corporation sponsored a meeting of regional elders. In quiet and deliberate terms, the elders discussed their history and the status of their culture: they likened their culture to a blanket. They poignantly stressed that their hands were growing weary of holding on to their culture, and they symbolically transferred the blanket to Sealaska Corporation. Although they did not want to abdicate their obligations, the elders realized that, in a rapidly changing world, new methods and technologies would be required to preserve their culture for future generations. In response, the Sealaska Heritage Institute was established and was dedicated to the preservation of Southeast Alaska Native languages, cultures, and sacred sites.

These efforts set us on the historic path to Cape Fox Village on July 23, 2001. According to anthropologist Douglas Cole, the zenith of anthropological collection on the Northwest Coast occurred within a fifty-year period, beginning in 1875. In *Captured Heritage,* Cole wrote about the enormous outpouring of capitalist philanthropy that supported the expansion of museums devoted to collecting and exhibiting scientific and artistic objects. He could have been describing the 1899 expedition's visit to Cape Fox when he described the process of acquisition: "A staggering quantity of material, both secular and sacred—from spindle whorls to soul-catchers—left the hands of their native creators for the private and public collections of the European world. The scramble for skulls and skeletons, for poles and paddles, for baskets and bowls, for masks and mummies was pursued sometimes with respect, occasionally with rapacity, often with avarice."

To help undo a century of Westerners' collecting of Native objects, Native Americans were successful in convincing Congress to pass the Native American Graves Protection and Repatriation Act of 1990 (NAGPRA). One of the only federal laws that provides enforceable protections for Native American cultures, NAGPRA enabled the Tlingit to seek the return of human remains and certain cultural objects held by museums. Soon after the law's passage, clan leaders and elders assembled to learn about the mechanics of the law. They learned how to pronounce "repatriation" and assessed how "cultural patrimony" compared with their concept of *at.óow.* Ironically, as one Tlingit elder quoted by Cole lamented, "They ridiculed us in saying we were pagans and worshiped idols, yet they took these idols that they called our sins and brought them to their great museums!"

The Tlingit began to file repatriation claims for their sacred *at.óow.* The Saanya Kwaan, the descendants of the inhabitants who lived at Cape Fox, or Gaash, as it is also called, were among the first to submit claims. Their village corporation, the Cape Fox Corporation, submitted claims to several museums, including the Smithsonian National Museum of the American Indian, the Harvard Peabody Museum of Archaeology and Ethnology, the Burke Museum of Natural History and Culture at the University of Washington, Cornell University, and the Chicago Field Museum.

Although Westerners had been satisfied that the property had been "abandoned," the Saanya Kwaan's experience was very different. In approximately 1892, Cape Fox Village was struck with a smallpox epidemic. As large numbers of relatives died, villagers thought that they had been subject to a witchcraft spell, and they immediately left the village to protect the relatives still alive. In 1894, they established themselves together with members of the Tongass Tlingit in Saxman, not far from Ketchikan. The new village was named after a Presbyterian missionary who, along with others, had been sent to Christianize and civilize the Tlingit. The Saanya Kwaan never doubted that they retained ownership of their property when they left Cape Fox—under traditional Tlingit law the ownership of clan property remains with the clan, absent or not.

Then the Harriman Expedition arrived and departed with the sacred objects. That day, and the emotions surrounding it, were remembered for generations. Remarkably,

FIGURE 7. *Elizabeth Averell and Dr. Lewis Rutherford Morris, members of the expedition, pose with Tlingit carvings and masks at Cape Fox. Credit: W. B. Devereaux. Source: Harriman family collection.*

a new law, changing attitudes, and a new expedition brought together on Cape Fox beach the descendants of the Saanya Kwaan and of Harriman. Later in the day, a potlatch and repatriation ceremony were held in Ketchikan. Waiting on Ketchikan's dock were several hundred Tlingit and Haida, there to welcome the *Clipper Odyssey* and the sacred clan objects brought on its deck. I found myself at that moment between two societies, in the role of cultural broker. I was a member of the 2001 expedition, and, according to tradition, I shouted my greetings from the ship to the hundreds of Tlingit standing on the dock as if I were a stranger. As a Tlingit—knowing and sharing their mixed feelings—I shouted to them, "Take courage, Noble People of the Land!" As I looked down from the ship, I saw many of my friends and colleagues. I saw many with whom I had grown up. I responded to several who called to me, *"Ax̱ léelk'w!"* They were grandchildren of my clan, and they called to me, "Grandmother!"

Soon after we docked, the Saanya Kwaan leaders and representatives boarded the ship to inspect their clan treasures. Next, they wanted to meet with the great-great-granddaughter of Edward Harriman and with the organizer of the 2001 expedition. Emotions were high. Slowly, one after another, the leaders spoke, directing their remarks to the young woman who stood straight and tall holding her son. Perhaps she was somewhat nervous, judging by the way she grasped her husband's hand. The leaders spoke of their joy in the return of their *at.óow*. Some spoke in low, deliberate tones of their anger over the loss and absence of clan property but then expressed gratefulness that it had been preserved. They thanked the great-great-granddaughter for caring for their sacred objects. They expressed their gratitude to the leader of the expedition for his role in transporting their objects home.

For the Tlingit, it was a day of sadness, a day of bitter memories of a "captured" heritage, a day of anger about the colonialists' attitude of superiority, which perpetuated the infamous mistreatment of the Tlingit in the previous century. Yet, it was equally a day of triumph—the triumph that came from knowing that their ancestors, grandparents, and parents had been successful in their struggle to regain title to their land, respect for their culture, and honor and pride for succeeding generations.

For those Tlingit standing on the Cape Fox beach and those who joined in the celebration that continued through the night in Ketchikan, it was also a day of great joy and reconciliation. It was a time to resolve the contradictory feelings of anger and joy that overwhelmed their bodies and spirits. It was a time to apply the teachings of their traditional Peace Ceremony: to lay aside their differences, to try to understand the ways and thinking of the ancestors and members of the Harriman Expedition. It was a day to stamp out their hostility as they did in their Peace Ceremony.

The events surrounding the Harriman Expedition Retraced in many ways embodied the century of change that had occurred among the Tlingit of Southeast Alaska. The Tlingits, in their own voyage through a century, organized themselves politically to settle their aboriginal land claims and to secure the civil rights once denied them. During this period they initiated many initiatives to protect and restore elements of their ancient culture.

Yet one of the greatest challenges that the Tlingit faced—changing attitudes and practices toward Native peoples—could not be met by them alone. Native cultures were once repressed and viewed as dying, vanishing. With time, many in the non-Native society have altered their views. Some have become friends and accept that Native cultures should be protected. And when we Tlingit are at our best, we agree that cultural diversity and cultural pluralism can be a strength of Alaska and of the United States. This new attitude is exemplified in NAGPRA and in the Harriman Expedition Retraced, which respectfully brought non-Native and Native peoples and their cultures together.

Repatriation Unfolds, Metlakatla to Ketchikan

23 July 2001

S mall groups stood talking on the beach, then made their way to the tide line, where the Zodiacs waited for the trip back to the ship. Although time seemed suspended, we had spent about two hours at Cape Fox. With most of the day still ahead of us, the ship weighed anchor and set a course, by way of Nichols Pass, for Metlakatla on Annette Island's west coast. The charts confirmed that since leaving Cape Fox, we had been sailing within the Tongass National Forest's lush temperate rainforests, which cover the dozens of islands making up the Alexander Archipelago.

Our stop in Metlakatla starkly underscored the emotions and issues that Irene, Eleanor, and Rosita had placed before us. Father William Duncan's 1887 settlement of "New Metlakatla" received considerable attention from George Bird Grinnell in the 1899 expedition's report. Grinnell's matter-of-fact observations reflect a widely held attitude that for more than a century helped repress Tlingit culture: "It took many years

for Mr. Duncan to change these Indians from the wild men that they were when he first met them, to the respectable and civilized people that they now are[,] . . . teaching them to live as the white man lives." Highlighting the cultural chasm that existed at the time, these are words spoken by someone considered sympathetic to the plight of Natives and an early advocate for their human rights.

Sympathy notwithstanding, Grinnell and his colleagues admired Father Duncan's efforts, including his successful congressional petition in 1891 to turn Annette Island into an Indian reservation. It is the only reservation ever established in Alaska, before or after statehood. After the passage of one hundred years, Father Duncan's efforts seem an odd mix of good intentions and cultural arrogance, a curious, benign form of racism. At a time when Tlingit and Tsimshian communities were being devastated by other Western influences, Father Duncan provided a haven for disenfranchised community members. Although his intentions may have been good, his stern and restrictive methods of "civilizing" them led to a successful revolt in 1915 by the Native community.

Making our way back to the ship, we grappled with the history that the Father Duncan Museum represented, struggling to reconcile our contemporary views. In 2001, praising Father Duncan's efforts is not simple. The values we brought to this village were different, but they are also products of their time and raise their own nagging questions. Were we being politically correct, revising history to satisfy current sensibilities? A fundamental question taunted this academic query: How does a society become comfortable with an economic justification for treating another culture in this manner?

An immediate challenge was understanding the role that Harriman Retraced played within this history. Some colleagues worried that we were being used to further a broader Native political agenda. I relied on my earlier visits with Saanya Kwaan leaders and elders for guidance. The tears, anger, outrage, hurt, and sorrow that I had witnessed, and the scoldings I had received, were real: "Do you understand, Tom, that 'the Harriman' took away our history: I can't tell my grandchildren who we are; the stories are lost." The real trap was seeing the world as one-dimensional: the tears and the broader political agenda were both real and very much part of an unfolding historical era. We, with our 340-foot-long ship transporting cherished objects, sailed into the midst of it.

The appearance of Pennock Island signaled our approach to Ketchikan and the off-loading of the clan objects on the *Odyssey*'s decks. From the bridge we could see a busy port. In 1991, fifteen cruise ships visited Ketchikan. Today, on average, 480 ships visit each year, bringing three hundred thousand visitors. Quite a change for a place that began as a Tongass and Cape Fox Tlingit fishing camp on the Ketchikan River. The concentration of red and black Tlingit robes, TV cameras, and onlookers made it clear that the berth in the center of the city dock was reserved for our ship. It also became apparent that we were now in a fishbowl; our actions, from how Captain Michael Taylor handled his ship to how we conducted ourselves, would be scrutinized in this emotionally powerful situation. The quiet of Cape Fox beach seemed a long way away. The tension came from knowing the importance of this day but not knowing how it would unfold. With no precedent to follow, we would be relying heavily on instinct and goodwill. The smiles and waves from well-wishers and friends standing on the crowded dock were reassuring.

The best way to describe the rest of our visit to Ketchikan is as the touching of parallel universes. In many ways the Tlingit culture is now embedded in Western culture, and the lines between the two blur. On this day, though, the two universes seemed more separate than usual. We brought our culture on an internationally registered ship with its passengers, captain, crew, and shelves full of protocols, rules, and guidelines, which governed our every action. On the dock were Tlingits from throughout Southeast Alaska, hosted by the Saanya Kwaan, who were determined to respect their own ancestors, heritage, and cultural traditions. They were simultaneously grappling with deep emotions surrounding the hundred-year absence of their objects and the elation and celebration of their return.

FIGURE 8. *Tlingit carved house posts removed from Cape Fox in 1899 were returned from the Burke Museum of Natural History and Culture, University of Washington, aboard the* Clipper Odyssey *in 2001. Credit: C. Hart Merriam. Source: Harriman family collection.*

Although we sympathized with the Saanya Kwaan, I am not sure we all understood that many of them saw us as cultural delegates responsible for the removal of the objects in 1899. The people who removed the Saanya Kwaan's property in 1899 were our people, and we were obligated, within Tlingit culture, to assume responsibility for their actions. Respect is a fundamental and important Tlingit value, and the removal of property from Cape Fox without permission was a serious display of disrespect. That it had occurred a century ago didn't matter. When we created Harriman Retraced, we created a repository for an obligation in search of a home. In earlier meetings in which clan elders had scolded me, E. H. Harriman was standing right next to me. It was not important that he had passed away ninety years earlier.

Suffice it to say that our historic, albeit unscripted, meeting lurched forward through a series of huddles, consultations, exchanges of messages, and overarching goodwill. In fits and starts, the large crated objects were craned off the ship to an awaiting flatbed truck. With the loading complete, we boarded waiting buses and joined a long procession of cars and trucks that followed the flatbed, now adorned with a dozen young Tlingits sitting atop the crates. Tourists stopped and stared. State police cars, their lights flashing, blocked the intersections. We made our way through Ketchikan to Saxman, home of the Saanya and their clan houses since they left Cape Fox in 1893. Protocol required that the long-missing objects pass before the clan houses so ancestor spirits could be rejoined.

The long, unwieldy procession wound though a neighborhood and stopped—for coffee and cake—at a clan house and home of a respected clan elder. Honored by the invitation, we gathered under a party tent set up on the front lawn and shared in the pronouncements regarding this day's importance. This calm center was surrounded by dozens of people, buses, cars, and clogged intersections. As the procession continued, cars that happened upon it joined in, and others dropped out. Horns honked, people shouted from their cars, and bystanders waved and whistled. One moment I thought I knew what was going on, the next I didn't have a clue—this was an honest-to-goodness happening. Irrespective of anyone's organization structure or cultural perspective, we were going with the flow. If there ever was a time that parallel universes bumped, this was surely it.

The procession ended with our arrival at the Ketchikan Civic Center and potlatch. By this point I had lost all track of time, except that I could see it was getting dark. The large hall was filled with hundreds of people—adults, children, babies, teens, elders—standing, sitting, walking, talking, hugging, shaking hands. This was not just a community event, it was the community. Laid out in the middle of the hall were the newly returned totems, house posts, and house front. People gently touched them. Some stared, some quietly wiped away tears, others expressed joy. Children stood on tiptoe to see over the sides of the crates. Into this gathering, "the ship people" melted. Reactions, conversations, and interactions were as varied as the people filling the crowded space we suddenly shared. Some community members were happy to see us, others were shy. Some were politely cool; a grievance that had been building for a hundred years was not going to disappear in a day, if ever.

The scene shifted to the stage where the official repatriation transfers were taking place. One by one, the Saanya Kwaan took possession of the sacred objects as each museum or university signed the transfer documents. Then the most uncertain moment of all arrived. All eyes fixed on Margaret Northrop Friedman, Edward Harriman's great-great-grandchild, as she stepped out of the group, moved to center stage, and met the waiting clan leaders. In a natural, unassuming manner she extended to the Saanya Kwaan the Harriman family's greetings and expressions of friendship. Before an audience of hundreds, she spoke in recognition of the importance of this day and of her family's happiness that the clan's property was returning home. The clan leaders carefully watched, carefully listened. Her words, and how she said them, were crucial. Margaret finished by unfolding a quilt that had been in her family since 1895, and she presented it to the Saanya Kwaan leadership. They nodded solemnly, shook hands, and accepted the Harrimans' gift of reconciliation and friendship. In this brief exchange, judgments and final decisions crystallized, and the circle was completed.

Where the day's events would lead was less clear. It was a curious moment: one powerful set of circumstances had gone away, but it was too soon for new understanding and purpose to fill the space. It was truly a moment suspended in wonderment, evoking the simple thought, "Now what?" The formalities subsided, and traditional dances and celebrations arose as the evening turned to night, then to early morning.

In this state, infused with exaltation and exhaustion, I was concluding a last interview, at midnight, with TV2-Anchorage. Behind the camera I could see a member of the expedition team patiently waiting to get me on the last van back to the ship. The hallway filled with good-byes and expressions of relief, with little concern at this moment for what lay ahead. We were met at the ship's gangway by an agitated crew member who reported that one of our expedition team was still missing: Rosita Worl. With a ship itching to leave port, this was a serious matter for the captain and officers. Without boarding the ship, we turned around and went back to the potlatch, now as a search party. Back through the crowd, into the side rooms, through the parking lots: no Rosita. We gave up and returned to the ship, where a note was waiting for me: "10:20 P.M.—Rosita said she is jumping ship and will meet us in Juneau." Of course, she would stay with her Tlingit relatives on this important ceremonial and historic occasion. Of course, the rules clearly stated that all expedition members had to be onboard before departure. Bump go the universes.

Into the Rainforest, Wrangell-Wrangell Narrows

24 July 2001

The *Odyssey*, less one expedition member, steered away from the dock shortly after midnight. With the ending of a day that spanned eighteen hours or one hundred years, depending on your point of view, understandably the ship was quiet. Slowly the ship left Ketchikan harbor on the east side of Gravina Island and began its sail northwest through Tongass Narrows. We were on our way to Wrangell, about one hundred miles away, through the Inside Passage. Sleep came to this weary passenger as the ship cleared the Narrows and joined Clarence Strait, moving deeper into the Alexander Archipelago.

On deck at first light, I walked directly into John Burroughs's words, "We are steaming over a vast irregular body of water— Clarence Straits[;] . . . far-off snow-capped mountains roll up against the sky like thunderheads. Nearer by are small spruce-tufted islands and low dark shores. Etolin Island is ahead of us, and Prince of Wales Island on the west." Prince of Wales is just one of eleven

hundred islands in the archipelago, but at 2,350 square miles, it is the largest. It is, in fact, the third-largest island in the entire United States, and so it was not surprising that its unfolding shoreline had been with us throughout the night.

It would be interesting to know how 1899 expedition geologists Grove Karl Gilbert and Benjamin Emerson explained this land- and seascape to their shipmates. Today we take for granted an idea that was not part of their theoretical "kit" when they made their geologic explorations at the end of the nineteenth century: the theory of plate tectonics. In its simplest form, the theory describes the drifting and colliding of pieces of the earth's crust. As the *Odyssey* made its way through the archipelago, the islands surrounding us were not what they seemed to be.

The forested islands we were sailing among in actuality are hundreds of mountaintops, part of a mountain range that begins with the Cascades in the northwest United

States and runs up through British Columbia's Coast Mountains into Alaska. Contrary to our political maps, Alaska is very much connected to the Lower Forty-Eight. For over one hundred million years, the Pacific Plate of the earth's crust has been moving north, inch by inch. As it slipped and ground its way beneath the North American Plate, massive areas of the earth's crust were forced up and became the mountain chain through which we were sailing. Over grand expanses of time that bear little relation to the numbers on our watches, change kept coming.

These mountains would have been more obvious fifteen thousand years ago, at the end of the last ice age. So much of the earth's water was tied up in the continental ice sheet that sea level was about 450 feet lower—about the height of a forty-story office building—than it is now. Many of the islands we admired from the deck of the ship were then fully exposed mountains connected by fjord-like valleys. Thousands of miles to the west, the Bering Land Bridge protruded from the shallow waters of the Bering Strait, connecting Asia and North America. Siberian peoples of the Chukchi Peninsula explored the land bridge and over time made their way across to North America. With the passage of millennia, some of their descendants would settle in the new ecological landscape of Southeast Alaska and come to be known as Tlingit and Haida.

As these mountaintop islands confirmed, before the environment was ready to sustain these Native cultures, it underwent profound changes. How this transformation came about—the sweeping ecological changes occurring over expansive geological time frames and coinciding with the emergence of human cultures—defies simple explanation. Forests, rivers, and wildlife habitat were first plowed

by and then buried under thousands of feet of ice for thousands of years. When the ice sheet finally retreated, it left behind a scoured landscape. Wildlife, plants, and trees long displaced by ice and cold slowly made their way back to the raw landscape. A few plants and animals gradually grew into populations; populations melded into ecological communities. Wild communities depending on similar environmental conditions emerged as ecosystems. To transform barren soil into the ecosystem we now saw required time, vast amounts of time. The climate warmed, the ice sheet continued to melt, and the sea level rose. The mountains formed by the ancient collisions of the plates of the earth's crust intercepted warmer air off the Pacific Ocean, turning it into one hundred to three hundred inches of rain a year. All, highly improbable.

The ecological stage was set for the growth of a temperate rainforest that eventually stretched from California to Southeast Alaska. In Alaska, it came to be filled with an incredible richness of life: 54 species of mammals, 230 species of birds, 5 species of salmon, and some of the largest trees on earth. Ancestors of the Tlingit and Haida migrated to the region, settled, and prospered. The same bounty attracted immigrants from Europe and, later, U.S. citizens, including the members of the 1899 and 2001 Harriman expeditions.

Most of the *Odyssey*'s party was on deck as the ship set a northeast course off Clarence Strait into Stikine Strait. As we emerged from between Zarembo and Woronkofski islands and approached Wrangell, the sight that met us was dramatically different from the one that had met the 1899 expedition. By 1899, the quest for gold had left Wrangell a wreck. Burroughs barely mentions visiting the place: "We spent a few hours on shore looking at totem poles and viewing the shabby old town."

Its fate driven by geography, Wrangell sits at the mouth of the Stikine River, whose headwaters rise from the ground in British Columbia. Its abundant salmon runs became a footnote after its conversion into a transportation hub for the miners who flocked there during three separate gold rushes: one in 1861, another in 1872, and the third in 1897. During the 1897 "Klondike" gold rush, the services of Marshal Wyatt Earp were retained to maintain order. A short time later, the Harrimans found a community that had been built to serve the gold-rush frenzy and was discarded when the dream of quick fortunes collapsed.

Our experience at Wrangell could not have been more different. As we approached the Wrangell harbor dock, we found ourselves in a remarkable situation: a party of Stikine Tlingits in a traditional dugout canoe paddled up to our looming ship to challenge its approach to their homeland. Equally remarkable for them, judging by their quizzical looks, which turned to smiles, was my call of greeting from the deck, "*Haa deí!*" The Stikine scouting party wanted to know who we were and why we had come. Based on our reply of goodwill and friendship, we were invited to dock: "*Gunalcheesh, ho, ho*" (thank you very much). We re-

ceived a warm welcome in Wrangell, a small, friendly community whose economy today is built on tourism, sport and commercial fishing, outdoor recreation, a modest gold-mining industry, and forestry. We would discover this pattern repeated throughout Southeast Alaska, where cultures, economies, and natural resources converge on a landscape that has been changing since ancient times.

At noon we left Wrangell, heading west, ducking under Vank Island into Sumner Strait. At Point Alexander on Mitkoff Island, we steered north into Wrangell Narrows, and the discussion turned from extracting gold to harvesting trees. Before us, we could see large geometric patterns cut from the island forests of the Alexander Archipelago. The giant rainforest trees removed for lumber from the island mountaintops were ecologically priceless. Some of the largest had grown on limestone soils that began as coral reefs near the equator. For the community of Wrangell, these trees clearly had a price and played a fundamental role. This price became obvious in 1994, when the Alaska Pulp Corporation closed its mill and 225 members of a small community lost their jobs. As we scanned a ragged-stumped clear-cut with our binoculars, forest ecologist Paul Alaback reminded us that, in 1899, there was considerable debate about whether these forests had any value at all.

CHAPTER FOUR

FERNOW'S PREDICTION

and the Search for a Sustainable
Timber Industry in Southeast Alaska

꜠

PAUL B. ALABACK

In addition to the small value of these woods and their comparatively unsatisfactory development, the conditions under which lumbering on the rugged slopes would have to be carried on are extremely difficult; add to these detractions the distance from market, and we may readily see the reasons why this reserve will, for an indefinite time, be left untouched except for local use.

   – *Bernhard E. Fernow, "Forests of Alaska," in vol. 2 of* Harriman Alaska Expedition

A CONTINUOUS MIST, interrupted by pulses of rain, cloaked the lush, dark-green woods around us. Even the first-time visitors on the *Clipper Odyssey* knew this was a rainforest. From the deck we got intermittent glimpses of bright green rectangles, their angled edges contrasting with the soft curves of mountains and dark forest. As our ship made its way into the Wrangell Narrows, these geometric shapes came into focus in a column of sunlight: they were carpets of young, fast-growing trees, each one swallowing up a sea of stumps and rotting logs. Each rectangle was surrounded by a dense, dark wall of old-growth forest, 140 feet tall. We were getting our first close look at a clear-cut.

   At that quiet moment, it was hard to fathom that these clear-cuts triggered one of the loudest, most bitter environmental controversies of the twentieth century in the United States. The Tongass National Forest, which now surrounded us, has been at the center of a sustainable-development versus rapid-exploitation debate that has gripped Southeast Alaska for the better part of the past century. Most of the coastal forest in south-central and Southeast Alaska has been a part of the Tongass and Chugach National Forest since 1907. Over the twentieth century, the Tongass was transformed—from a forest with only small, localized logging and wood-processing facilities to a region heavily influenced by national and foreign interests, an area where multinational firms ran huge, industrial-scale pulpwood and sawmill operations.

The thinking about the forest has also changed dramatically. Once the Tongass was widely thought to be resilient to any negative effects of logging; it was so vast that it was considered essentially inexhaustible. Today the discussion has become more nuanced, with consideration given to wilderness preservation, watershed and wildlife protection, local communities, and ecological balance. An area that was once the domain solely of entrepreneurs and loggers now faces intense public scrutiny any-time road-building, mining, or logging operations are proposed. The high pitch of today's controversy would probably surprise Bernhard Fernow, the Cornell forester on the 1899 Harriman Expedition, but the underlying economic problems of logging in Southeast Alaska certainly would not.

Fernow is considered the father of North American forestry. During the 1899 expedition, he made detailed observations of the ecology and the possibilities for management of the vast Alaska coastal forests. Given the limited understanding of ecological science at the time, his field notes on these unstudied forests were a valu-able contribution. But the best remembered parts of his expedition writings are the controversial sections: his views regarding the quality and economic value of Alaska's forests. Fernow wrote that "the Alaska forest lacks the most important timber of the Pacific coast [Douglas fir]." The general quality of the timber, he wrote, was poor. With only a limited number of commercial markets, all at a healthy distance from Alaska, Fernow dolefully predicted, "the prospect of reliance upon its stores [is] by no means cheerful."

From the beginning, many, including a fellow expedition member, geographer Henry Gannett, disputed Fernow's assessment. And the fact that a significant timber industry did develop in Southeast Alaska seems to prove Gannett's view correct. But this assessment is not as simple as it seems; in fact, history may already have proved Fernow right. As we lined up along the *Clipper Odyssey*'s rails to gaze at the high-profile clear-cuts staring down from the mountainsides, we struggled to understand this apparent contradiction.

Fernow was clearly influenced by what he saw of the fledgling timber industry in the Pacific Northwest. After the settlement of the West and the establishment of Seattle as a commercial nexus, the northwestern timber companies had grown rap-idly from 1880 on. The wood resources in the area were vast—so vast that only a decade before factual reports of the size and stature of the Pacific Northwest forests had been branded mythical. Timber supplies around Puget Sound alone were seen

FIGURE 9. *Forester Bernhard Fernow examines a Sitka spruce near Sitka, Baranof district. Credit: G. K. Gilbert. Source: National Archives, USGS collection.*

as inexhaustible. One year after the Harriman expedition, Frederick Weyerhaeuser bought nine hundred thousand acres of the best timberland in the country around Puget Sound for five dollars an acre. Western logging was already in full swing (without, of course, much concern for conservation).

What Fernow did not foresee were both the voracious appetite that the rapidly expanding U.S. population would soon develop for lumber and the pressure on northwestern forests that would result. Entrepreneurs would need to find new sources of raw materials, and Alaska was just a packet-ship sail away. But, as Fernow predicted, they would not find the quality or quantity of timber required by large commercial lumber markets.

In 1889, only eleven sawmills were in operation in Southeast Alaska, and they provided lumber primarily for local use. Wood was used for the construction of homes and in businesses, especially canneries and fishing; a major use was boxes for shipping salmon. Logging was done by hand and only the largest and most valuable trees were cut. Only trees close to shore were cut, so they could be floated right to the mill. The impact of this logging was minimal. With the entry of the United States into World War I and the discovery that spruce was excellent for airplane construction, a specialized market did emerge for Sitka spruce. But this logging also focused on small pockets of trees, with little impact on the larger forest.

Fernow saw the poor quality of Alaska's timber and how difficult access was and concluded that it would be impossible to make a profit. His observations regarding the relatively spotty nature of Alaskan timber were correct. In the Pacific Northwest, rich soils and moderate climate lead to the development of dense, productive forests, but in Alaska this is rarely the case. From the deck of the *Clipper Odyssey*, we were seeing a nearly continuous parade of green onshore, but this sight was quite misleading. In fact, over a third of the Southeast Alaska landscape is peat bog or wetland, and half is alpine, snowfield, or glacier. Only a relatively small fraction of the land is forested, and less than a quarter of that area has timber of a quality sufficient to yield a profit with clear-cut logging—let alone selective cutting. In the 1980s, research by state and Forest Service biologists revealed that all logging that had been done in Southeast Alaska had targeted only the top 1 percent of the region's forests, the most dense forests with the tallest trees. Only the best timber could yield a profit at all; no wonder that such timber ran out quickly. Like many other industries in the state—gold, salmon, crab, fur— Alaska's timber industry followed a pattern of boom and bust.

In 1899 the story seemed to be over, and with it most of the logging of the Tongass. But then the story took a turn that Fernow could never have foreseen, a turn produced by a combination of government subsidies and global politics. The forests that Fernow saw as unprofitable began to be felled—precisely because they no longer had to yield a profit. In the 1920s, the Forest Service began to push the concept of a pulp industry for coastal Alaska. One of the first major sales was on Admiralty Island, to the newly formed Alaska Pulp & Paper Company. After two years, the operation failed. Subsequently, at least nine more attempts were made to establish pulp mills, but none proved successful. These attempts continued right into the 1940s. Fernow's assessment still seemed right on the money, but by the end of that decade everything would change for the Tongass.

The Forest Service found itself in a quandary: it owned millions of trees, but had no way to sell them. If the Alaskan pulp industry was to succeed, the Forest Service concluded, timber companies would have to be offered large amounts of timber at low cost. This approach would allow timber companies to invest with low risk in the construction of a pulp mill.

At about the same time, the Iron Curtain descended. The Soviet Union, so close to Alaska, became the cold war adversary of the United States. To the Department of State, it was now clearly in the national interest to promote the permanent settlement of the Alaska coastline. And the Alaska timber market could help with another post-war need: the reconstruction of Japan. By guaranteeing Japan a supply of (Alaskan) lumber at low prices, the government could kill two foreign-policy birds with one stone. Lumber from the Tongass would aid Japan, and the jobs thus created would help build up Alaska—the western front in the cold war against the Soviet Union.

The key leader in this forestry-as-foreign-policy effort was Frank Heintzleman. As a regional forester for the Forest Service in the 1940s, he estimated that with fifty-year contracts and proper management, Southeast Alaska could provide enough pulpwood for newsprint to provide jobs for fifty thousand people in perpetuity. (Significantly, a stable, year-round population would be critical in convincing Congress to allow Alaska to become the forty-ninth state.) Within a decade, Heintzleman had pulled it off. In 1947, the Forest Service awarded the first fifty-year contract, with others following in 1954, 1955, and 1957. Heintzleman himself was appointed territorial governor in 1953, and Alaska became a state in 1959. His plan seemed to be working out for everyone, including himself.

In 1955, the largest of the fifty-year timber contracts was awarded to the Georgia-Pacific Company. The contract included Admiralty Island and other areas around Juneau, the capital. Georgia-Pacific confidently planned to harvest 97 percent of the timber on the million-acre island. Its logging plan stated that no negative environmental effect was expected; it was widely assumed, after all, that logging created good wildlife habitat (especially for deer) and increased both water availability and forest growth. Even in 1964, the U.S. Forest Service saw clear-cutting as a desirable philosophy for "multiple-use" timber management: "About ninety-five percent of the commercial forest land of southeastern Alaska is occupied by overmature stands of hemlock, spruce and cedar. Silviculturally, these decadent stands should be removed by clear-cutting methods as soon as possible to make way for new stands of fast-growing second-growth timber."

But by 1964 the environmental movement had already begun to gain momentum in the Lower Forty-Eight. There were now two rival philosophies about the best use of a forest: logging and preservation. And they were already on a collision course: logging, even in the "infinite" resource called Alaska, was about to become a volatile national issue. Studies now showed that Admiralty Island had among the highest densities of bald eagles, grizzly bears, and other species that were rare or extinct in much of the Lower Forty-Eight; Admiralty also contained superlative examples of old-growth forest. Yet the Forest Service proposed to log most of the island. And the timber, which would have such a critical cost in environmental impact, would then be sold—at a fraction of the price of comparable timber in British Columbia and the Pacific Northwest. In effect, the Forest Service was giving the timber away. The Sierra Club under David Brower had been growing in prominence and power throughout the 1960s. From this position, it legally challenged the Forest Service's environmental assessment of the Admiralty Island pulp contract. Forest Service contracts had always been created in near privacy. That obscurity now melted away with the advent of polit-ical and environmental scrutiny. Legal challenges mounted until, in 1976, after nearly ten years of litigation, the contract was withdrawn. This was a vital victory for the envi-ronmental movement.

In 1978, only two years after the Forest Service dropped plans to log most of the island, President Jimmy Carter declared Admiralty Island a national monument. His action meant that timber could be felled on only a small fraction of the island, which now became an International Biosphere Reserve. As a result, scientists on the 2001 expedition could experience an environment widely recognized as the crown jewel of Alaska's coastal wilderness system.

LIKE THE AMERICAN WEST in the late nineteenth century, the Alaskan frontier is being integrated into a larger national and international society. I began my career in Alaska thirty years ago. At that time coastal Alaska was a kind of paradise for rugged individualists. People there had a deep-seated mistrust of the federal government, although Alaska was a huge beneficiary of federal dollars, and they paid no state income taxes because of revenue from the oil pipeline. Many people came to the region to live out a dream of working hard, making a lot of money—and moving on afterward. The phrase on our license plates, "North to the Future," captured the feel-ing. Alaska was a place of young people full of energy, filled with dreams for the future. A person who was willing to work hard and put up with a few inconveniences (like living in remote camps and getting to town only intermittently) could put away a sizeable amount of money.

These were also the boom years for logging in the Tongass National Forest. In some years, over twenty thousand acres were harvested. Thorne Bay, on Prince of Wales Island, was the largest logging camp in the country. It was a highly moveable feast: logging camps were constructed on logs floating in protected bays. After the clear-cuts were finished in one area, the camp was towed to another anchorage, and a new set of roads was constructed in another coastal watershed.

The timber industry dominated decision making related to the Alaskan forests through the 1970s. The industry authorities were the "experts" about forests, and most Alaskans felt they should trust the experts. Professional foresters lobbied Con-gress for the legislation that led to pulp-mill contracts. These highly trained profes-sionals were able to use their technical skills to create logging plans in the most economically efficient manner because there were no well-documented environmen-tal problems with logging.

In any evolving community, the people and opinions become more diverse with time. So it was with Southeast Alaska. Initially, many Alaskans considered *conservation* and *environmentalism* dirty words. People who tried to restrict logging were quickly ostracized in their communities. In some cases, businesses were boycotted and environmentalists themselves were harassed.

Nevertheless, a small, devoted, and vocal environmental movement was emerging. In Alaska, after all, independence and nonconformity were basic values. Eastern sophistication and upper-class standing and influence were virtues not universally admired. And a new group of people who began moving to the area were not interested primarily in making lots of money but sought instead an independent and unique lifestyle. As with many long-time residents, this dream closely connected them to the land. They gathered much of their own food through hunting and fishing, and many of them enjoyed hiking, boating, sea kayaking, wildlife watching, or photography. Although Alaska lagged a decade or more behind the strong social and economic shifts occurring around Puget Sound, it was nonetheless headed for significant social change.

Eventually the movement to restrict logging took on a paradoxical quality, making political bedfellows of people with ideologies at each end of the spectrum: ecology and conservative economics. Many saw that the logging in the Tongass forest was the result of an artificial economy; it could exist only with the aid of heavy government subsidies. Alaska's powerful congressional delegation worked vigorously for these guarantees, and those who directly benefited from the subsidies obviously endorsed them, but many conservatives did not. The debate over subsidies became increasingly intense in the 1980s, when pulp prices plummeted. Taxpayers were now paying an estimated $36,000 a year to support each logging job, even as timber sales lagged. Subsidies were still available for road building even if there was no timber to sell in the places where new roads ran. The antisubsidy slogan "Roads to Nowhere" began to attract national attention. The growing national visibility of the controversy eroded support for Tongass logging from conservative proponents of a free-trade system. Fernow was about to have his day. Despite decades of concerted Forest Service effort, the area's timber industry was clearly not profitable without subsidies. And economic woes were not the only problems for the loggers: the area's timber industry was a magnet for constant environmental protest.

The national debate also began to attract the attention of the scientific community. Up to this point, few studies addressed the impact of clear-cutting in Southeast Alaska. Research suggested that clear-cutting a square mile of forest, for example, created no significant problems for forest regrowth. Similarly, studies of fisheries had showed no clear negative impact of logging on salmon. Old growth was often considered a "biological desert" by logging industry scientists, whose research unsurprisingly endorsed logging in the Tongass. But when independent government and academic scientists started taking a closer look, large gaps in our understanding became clear.

When I began to study the ecology of the Tongass rainforests in 1976, little was known about temperate rainforests in general, and we had only scattered, incomplete pieces of information on the Tongass ecosystem itself. Just a year earlier, the Forest

Service had hired its first research wildlife biologist. Clearly, increased scientific effort was needed to offer a comprehensive view of the value of old-growth forests, so we could understand the Tongass as an ecosystem.

Ironically, it was a last minute pro-industry amendment to a bill in Congress that provided the opportunity we were looking for. The 1980 Alaska National Interest Lands Conservation Act (ANILCA) was a landmark in conservation. Its primary purpose was to establish one hundred million acres of new national parks, national wildlife refuges, scenic rivers, and wilderness areas. But the Alaska delegation, to ease the passage of ANILCA, introduced an amendment designed to make up for the "significant economic harm" resulting from wilderness-area designations. The amendment provided the Forest Service annually with $40 million—exempt from normal congressional budgetary review—to accelerate timber harvests within the Tongass National Forest. The Forest Service, in turn, allocated 1 percent of this money to study ways to accelerate timber harvests and to assess their impacts. We now had the funding to carry out broad-based ecological studies of the Tongass. Little did we realize that our studies would play a prominent role in redefining conservation strategies for the Tongass.

Our research team found that the Tongass, with its unique geography and climate, functions differently from most other forests. Fernow's writings of 1899 echoed in our findings, for logging practices that are relatively benign in coastal Washington can have a profoundly negative affect on many wildlife species within old-growth forests of the Tongass. We found that a host of species—including deer, grizzly bears, bald eagles, pine martens, flying squirrels, and wolves—were all harmed by clear-cutting and road building in Alaska's coastal forests. Prior studies, and some forest managers, essentially viewed the trees in the Tongass as separate from the unique surrounding environment. We established that the trees were a central element in this ecosystem, connected with other plants and wildlife in complex ways on many levels.

Although the media often used the word *rainforest*, we had to define what this term meant in the ecology of Alaska's coastal forests. A temperate Alaskan rainforest is the result of a unique climate: wet and consistently cold. Fire is not a significant factor in this forest, as is the case in many forests in the Lower Forty-Eight. Deep, thick soils develop in the Tongass, and, more important, little sunlight is available to food plants on the forest floor. For us, the critical questions were, How does this forest actually work? What are the impacts of clear-cutting? The results of our research were startling. To take one example, deer in Alaska, unlike those in most other forest regions, appear to depend on old-growth forest.

We also came to a striking general conclusion. Up to this point, it was always assumed that the Tongass forests, like others in the western states, were generally subject to large, catastrophic disturbances such as fire, avalanche, windstorm, and flooding. When forests grow back after such catastrophes, the trees are almost all the same age and size; the resulting forest structure looks like a cornfield, which is all planted at once. A clear-cut, for such a forest, is just another large-scale disturbance—an environmental event something like an artificially created forest fire. We discovered, however, that the Tongass seldom suffered from such large-scale disturbances. In some ways, the rainforests of Southeast Alaska were ecologically more like rainforests in the Amazon. In a tropical rainforest, large areas of trees rarely fall over all at once. Instead, individual trees frequently blow over or fall under their own weight, leaving a patchwork quilt of disturbance. Old-growth rainforests are a complex mixture of different-size trees, each originating from a different disturbance. It takes centuries to develop their biological complexity. Because catastrophic windthrow events are the exception rather than the rule for the Tongass, clear-cutting was a unique disturbance that led to a distinctive forest, a dramatic contrast with both wind-thrown and old-growth forests.

As the *Clipper Odyssey* made its way through Wrangell Narrows, we saw more and more of those strange, bright green rectangles: the clear-cut blocks scattered across the old-growth landscape. More than twenty years of hindsight made the new conclusions of the 1980s seem obvious. These geometric forms seemed to sit so uncomfortably on the rainforest-covered mountainsides for a fundamental reason: clear-cut logging was indeed a novel disturbance for this forest, quite unlike natural forces involved in the development of an old-growth ecosystem.

The choice between management strategies in the 1980s became starkly clear: one strategy favored ecological values; the other focused primarily on commercial timber production. The ecological strategy produces an old-growth, patchy environment, with fewer trees, a high degree of rot and decay, and less timber. In this model, however, ecosystem integrity and wildlife values are relatively high. The alternative strategy of clear-cuts produces more timber, but it places little value on sustaining biodiversity and wildlife. Although young clear-cuts provide abundant food for wildlife, especially during mild winters, they soon become dense, homogeneous second-growth forests—with little food for wildlife over eighty years or more of the standard one-hundred-year cutting cycle.

As if this weren't enough fuel for the controversy, our studies also showed that the most economically valuable old-growth forests—the "high-volume" stands—also provided essential wildlife habitat. In other words, the forests that offered the best profits were also the most important to wildlife. These forests occur on no more than 16 percent of the land in Southeast Alaska, but they were a primary focus of logging efforts in the twentieth century. Over half of them have been cut since the first Harriman expedition. The scientific consensus soon emerged that logging in these biologically rich old-growth forests as planned by the Forest Service would soon result in declines of many key wildlife species—and possibly their extinction on the local level.

Our initial research findings in the early 1980s drew harsh criticism, even straightforward attacks on the scientists themselves. Scientists and managers who valued these studies received personal threats. For some, transfer to another region or resignation was the ultimate price. Had the ecological studies stood alone, it's hard to say what the Tongass National Forest might have become. But the reports came out when Alaskan demographics were changing, and supports for subsidies were slipping away. Local and national political coalitions, deeply opposed to unchecked clear-cutting, became stronger. A national consensus eventually emerged that the Tongass rainforests are an ecologically unique natural treasure. It became generally accepted that inappropriate logging practices did significant harm to wildlife and fisheries habitat. The final straw, perhaps, was the simple fact that no apparent economic benefit to the nation accrued from federally subsidized logging.

In 1990, the U.S. government designated another million acres of forest as wilderness; at the same time, it eliminated both the $40 million annual subsidy to the logging industry and the timber harvest mandated by Congress. Left open to market forces and increasing political pressure, Alaskan pulp mills started to close down in 1996. The Forest Service's latest land-use plan was put into effect only after ten years of bitter controversy, but it calls for a fundamental redirection of activities. The government that once paid companies to log Alaskan forests and gave away the lumber now also works to preserve old-growth forests and has put in place extensive regulations to minimize the environmental impacts of logging. Fernow could not have dreamed in 1899 that his relatively simple assessment of Alaska's coastal forests and the economics of logging would be put to such an epic test. His observations then were based on another aesthetic, but he came to the same conclusion that almost a full century of history has produced: at least some of this forest is better left alone.

By late afternoon we were leaving Wrangell Narrows behind. A number of shipmates asked me the same question: "So that's the end of the story, right?" Well, no. Southeast Alaska now has one of the world's best-preserved temperate rainforests. Although clear-cut logging is usually the most economical technique in the marginally profitable lands of the Tongass, it has unacceptable costs for many wildlife species. The easy solution would be simply to take Fernow's advice and dismiss the notion of commercial logging within the Tongass altogether. Yet walking away from the millions of acres of timber on U.S. soil has important global consequences as well. The United States is one of the dominant users of wood products in the world. It is unable to—or thus far has been unwilling to—decrease use of wood in proportion to the decrease in domestic timber production. As a result the United States has drastically increased its imports of timber during the past decade. When the United States curtailed logging in the Pacific Northwest to protect spotted-owl habitat and old-growth Douglas fir forests, it experienced no lumber shortage. It simply increased imports from Canada and developing countries.

Although the Forest Service, under considerable public pressure, has successfully reduced the environmental costs of logging in the Tongass and many other national forests, the result is not necessarily a total environmental gain. Instead, U.S. consumers buy more timber from countries with much lower environmental standards.

When we import timber from the southern hemisphere, we create or at least abet a more profound environmental impact. We cannot ignore Southeast Alaska's timber resources. The ideal solution, it would seem, is to develop logging practices in Alaska that would provide high levels of local employment and have acceptable environmental costs. A pipe dream? Perhaps, but interest in a new, more scientifically sound vision for a sustainable timber industry in Southeast Alaska is growing. Our research shows that it may be possible to mimic natural disturbances through logging techniques that are compatible with old-growth ecology and thereby contribute to a diverse and stable Alaskan economy.

Much innovation and risk are clearly necessary to develop economically viable timber harvesting without unacceptable environmental costs in this remote region. But amazing transformations in our technology and ecological understanding have characterized the past century. It is well within our capabilities to imagine solutions for both ecological and societal challenges. I would love the opportunity to take the debate into an otherworldly dimension and to convince Fernow himself that we can both protect these awe-inspiring rainforests and create a sustainable timber industry in Alaska.

Marbled Murrelet in Nest

© PATRICIA SAVAGE

Navigating the Islands and into the Cities—
Juneau, Skagway, Sitka

25 July 2001

There is comfort in following the route of a historic voyage, but change has reshaped old ideas and moved us into the present. Sooner than imagined, contrasts with 1899 began to accumulate and set us on divergent paths. Just yesterday, as we entered Frederick Sound from Wrangell Narrows, our base in Seattle radioed to report that the *Odyssey* did not have permission to enter Taku. In that former Tlingit village, now a historical site, C. Hart Merriam and Albert Fisher had begun their coastal survey of small mammals, while others observed the remains of a Native community decimated by foreign diseases. With the entangled history of our Tlingit friends and the 1899 expedition fresh in mind, the expedition team huddled around the chart table to consider other possibilities. At the end of a conversation that touched on geology, esthetics, tourism, logging, and jurisdiction, a consensus emerged: Tracy Arm would be a new part of an old story. Before dawn this morning, the *Odyssey* steered northeast off Stephens Passage into Holkham Bay, Harbor Island to starboard. Before us was a twenty-five-mile sail up Tracy Arm to the tidewater of South Sawyer Glacier. Our first view of this narrow fjord and its steep three-thousand-foot-high granite walls rising abruptly from the water had to wait—sunrise illuminated only the thick silvery fog enveloping the ship.

With the long view shrouded, the activity on the ship's bridge and the monotone conversation between the pilot and helmsman came into focus. Unlike the helmsman, who is responsible for steering the ship, the pilot is not a member of the crew. Within Alaska's "compulsory pilotage waters," licensed pilots are required in order to steer the vessels through seas, bays, and fjords they know intimately. It is a serious matter for a captain to challenge a pilot's navigational instructions; the captain had better have an excellent reason for doing so. Long gone are the days when an E. H. Harriman could wave off both the captain and the pilot and take the helm to explore an uncharted fjord.

Even without darkness and fog, these are tricky waters to sail. The face of South Sawyer Glacier frequently calves large blocks of ice, creating a parade of "hazards to navigation." Particularly in the narrower sections of Tracy Arm, which in some places is less than half a mile wide, eddies forming around icebergs can push or pull a ship into the unforgiving walls of stone.

As the fog swirled around the deck, I quickly grasped the reasons for the intensity of the dialogue between the pilot and quartermaster, a dialogue composed simply, entirely of compass bearings. The two constantly were checking the compasses before them and the radar screens glowing with an otherworldly, iridescent green light. The ship awakened and activity on the bridge increased, but the exchange between the pilot and quartermaster was intensely focused.

> PILOT: Two hundred twenty-eight degrees.
>
> HELMSMAN: Two hundred twenty-eight degrees.
>
> PILOT: Two hundred thirty degrees.
>
> HELMSMAN: Two hundred thirty degrees.
>
> PILOT: Starboard five degrees.
>
> HELMSMAN: Starboard five degrees.
>
> PILOT: Two hundred thirty-five degrees.
>
> HELMSMAN: Two hundred thirty-five degrees.

So it goes as we sail up the Alaska coast. The discipline of this maritime practice and countless others transcends any mood on the ship, political issue discussed, or natural wonder observed. Out of necessity the crew's seamanship creates a world apart from the passengers—an island of order in a watery environment that can be simultaneously magnificent and hostile.

As the fog broke up, scattered, and drifted away, views of Tracy Arm opened all around us. The *Odyssey*'s decks became animated with awestruck naturalists and artists. Long wispy banners of fog draped branches of the spruce and hemlock trees that covered the looming fjord walls. The intermittent sound of rushing water had been with us all along, but its source was now revealed—waterfalls. We were passing dozens of them cascading down escarpments, becoming airborne streams before crashing and splaying over the next tier hundreds of feet below.

Arctic terns and cliff swallows traversed the space above the ship. The amount of floating ice increased with each mile, until it grew so thick and crowded we knew the fjord's terminus and glacier must be close. As we rounded the final bend, a thunderous crack instantly seized everyone's attention. A massive four-story-high piece of ice sheared off South Sawyer's face, sliding, then tumbling into the sea, sending a great plume of water and shards of ice into the air. The *Odyssey* maneuvered its bow to intercept the ice-littered waves that rolled directly toward us. In this isolated embayment filled with acres of vibrant aquamarine ice, we idled, entranced by Alaskan wilderness, until commitments pulled us away.

By noon, we had emerged from Holkham Bay into Stephens Passage and were steering north for Juneau. With the passengers still under the spell of Tracy Arm, Pamela Wight had the delicate task of steering us into the cultural crosscurrents that would confront us at ports of call in Juneau, Skagway, and Sitka.

The seemingly private wilderness we had just enjoyed, she explained to us, is in fact shared by thousands of people a year traveling on dozens of tour ships that routinely sail Tracy Arm. In 1899, Wight's discipline—tourism and economic development—did not exist. Today, tourism in Alaska is big business and an economic force.

In the evening, after we reached Juneau, Alaska governor Tony Knowles came aboard. His words built on Wight's and outlined a debate that would be with us for the remainder of the voyage:

> Alaska encompasses more park and refuge land than the rest of the nation combined. About 40 percent of the state, an area roughly equal to Texas, is reserved as parks and refuges, something that would please

Henry Gannett, who observed: "The Alaska coast is to become the showplace of the earth, and pilgrims will throng in endless procession to see it. Its grandeur is more valuable than the gold or fish or timber."

But even in 1899, "throngs" of pilgrims brought challenges of their own. Today, the tourism industry that Gannett envisioned has also brought concerns about waste-water discharges and smokestack emissions, overcrowding and noise pollution. One hundred years ago, Harriman Expedition members debated the relationship between development and conservation of Alaska's resources, and that debate continues today. Although some frame it as an "either/or" debate, I don't accept that paradigm. I think development and environmental protection go hand in hand.

The Clipper Odyssey *with* Zodiak

CHAPTER FIVE

ALL THAT GLITTERS:

Tourism on the Alaska Coast

PAMELA A. WIGHT

WHO DOESN'T DREAM of the ideal vacation? I do, and so do millions like me. Sometimes my dreams involve nothing more than rest and relaxation, maybe on a hot and sunny beach. But much more often I want to have special experiences—to do something different. This fantasy often includes action, excitement, and even inspiration in exotic places.

The North has always been a frontier land, and going north to Alaska is a lifetime dream for many of us. Alaska is definitely an exotic place, a distant land of extremes of temperature and landscape, where adventure and opportunity abound and where the scenery is spectacular.

Even in 1899, Alaska attracted many tourists. Harriman Expedition members saw significant numbers of tourists, including elite travelers, professional scientists, sightseers, and those seeking a fashionable vacation spot. Tourists came to Alaska by the boatload, stopping at ports on the steamship routes. While in a port of call, they reportedly swarmed around the town, visiting stores and curiosity shops for souvenirs and cultural artifacts, buying trinkets and furs directly from the Natives, and snapping photos.

Alaska's attraction for tourists continued to increase over the past century, and little wonder. Alaska's natural and heritage resources are enormously rich and varied. There are more than 130 million acres of parks and wildlife refuges—that's one-and-a-half times the size of California! The number of visitors to Alaska has been growing steadily, now reaching 1.2 million a year, or about twice the state's population. During their visits, these visitors spend almost $1 billion each year; the tourism industry is responsible for one in ten jobs. In providing employment, tourism is in the same league as commercial fishing.

Tourism opportunities exist throughout Alaska, from the smallest region to the rich coastal towns: tourism can occur almost any place a group wants to visit or can be encouraged to visit. The 1899 expedition had no intention of going beyond the Pribilofs, much to the ever-seasick John Burroughs's relief. But Mrs. Harriman wanted to go beyond in order to gather stories to tell back in New York society. The Harrimans had the means to do it: a well-outfitted ship and a spirit of adventure. As Edward Harriman put it, "The long voyage, made often in the midst of fog, through imperfectly charted waters, and along a treacherous coast unguarded by lighthouses or danger signals, was accomplished in safety and without serious accident." The determination of an adventure tourist prevailed, and the Harrimans and the rest of the expedition party sailed the entire Alaska coast.

Tourism has become a power social and economic force—it is now the world's largest industry. During the last century, with rapid expansion in the last two decades, the global tourism industry has grown and diversified. In many ways, this is a direct result of changing lifestyles around the globe. Urbanization is growing, and many people's lives are more intensely work-focused; they need a break. As the middle class has grown in both size and wealth, tourist trips that were once available only to the wealthy are being repackaged to tap this vast, eager market. Leisure patterns are changing, and travel options proliferate.

The Harriman family planned a voyage of two months' duration. Today, people still plan exotic trips, but most do not have the wealth to support such a grand vacation. And although our expectations may be as great as the Harrimans', the amount of time we can devote, or want to devote, to a trip has changed dramatically. We now expect to experience new places, new activities, and new people in a short period—we want it all, and we want it in a week or two.

Space as well as time has shrunk for travelers. Larger numbers of experienced travelers are circling the globe in search of ever more exotic or remote and pristine destinations, and tour companies are developing packages that make it possible. This dramatic shift has an ironic cost. Remote areas are opened to tourism-based development, and these locations become platforms to explore even more remote regions. As the number of natural and wild places are reduced by the incremental incursions of humans, people seek out the next "special" experience, often by finding places that have not yet been discovered. As the process advances in uneven waves around the globe, environmental and cultural changes are becoming apparent and are of concern throughout the world.

As a tourism planner, I know that ultimately the number of special places on the globe is finite. Although Alaska is vast and wild, a competent tour operator can get a group of willing travelers almost everywhere. A little more than a hundred years ago, the "remote" Harriman Fjord and Harriman Glacier were first charted and named by Euro-Americans. Today they are a regular stop on Prince William Sound glacier tours.

In addition, a completely different type of traveler exists from those found in Harriman's day. Mass tourism still proliferates; and many travelers still join the elite in looking for a collectible new vacation. A new breed of experiential travelers, however, are more likely to be motivated by a desire to learn about the environment, understand local cultures, and have hands-on experiences. Often, they are interested in the natural environment and in adventurous and physically challenging activities in spectacular landscapes. The broader environment is, in part, a backdrop to visitors' increased connection with a place's people, plants, and wildlife.

Experiential travel appeals to all ages and equally to women and men. This large, important market is significantly influencing mainstream tourism—and Alaska. Like some of the members of the 1899 expedition who voiced concerns about the future of Alaska's natural resources, today's education-oriented ecotourists are asking hard questions. The ecotourist is as likely to ask, "What is the impact of this activity on the environment?" or "Who benefits—locals or outside developers—from this development?" as they are to ask, "What bird is that?" This new ethically minded traveler is being heard within the tourism industry.

These important questions start to tease apart the many complicated, interacting factors that underlie Alaska's tourism industry. Like salmon, gold, or timber, tourism is an Alaskan resource that economically benefits, to different degrees, local communities and non-Alaskan corporations. Like issues relating to Alaska's natural resources, economic issues will continue to play an important and powerful role in directing the future of Alaskan tourism. As other industries decline, tourism emerges as an engine that can boost a flagging local economy or stimulate economic development in new regions. In fact, tourism is often seen as a panacea for economic problems, with little recognition of the nature of the changes that it may bring about.

Exploration of tourism as an option for economic development can be motivated by a number of factors, ranging from entrepreneurial ingenuity to economic survival to a desire for nature or culture conservation. A healthy community serves as a solid starting point for additional economic development. If tourists want to fish or observe wildlife, and you can get them from the airport to the activity while making a profit, you have begun to create a successful business. If they stay at the local bed and breakfast or hotel and buy locally made gifts, all the better. Or, when a traditional way of life or industry that economically supported the community declines—and people lose jobs, tax revenues decrease, and community services need funds—tourism can also be a promising alternative. How tourism development moves forward in such a case is critical to the future well-being of the community.

Many times tourism is condemned when its impact is too great or when it overwhelms the local population. Like Alaska's fishing and timber industries, tourism may be developed by outsiders without consultation with and the involvement of local community members. A sense of place may be ignored, as well as the need for environmental or cultural protection. Much of the revenue may bypass the local community, flowing to corporations in the Lower Forty-Eight and beyond. A local population that does not directly benefit from the influx of tourists can quickly become disenchanted, resenting the visitors who are clogging its streets and changing its way of life. The very environment that originally attracted tourism declines, and visitor satisfaction suffers, as does economic viability. Just another Alaskan boom-and-bust story? In this case, Alaska is not unique—this paradoxical problem exists in most countries around the world.

Although the 1899 expedition had a distinguished group of scholars onboard, there was no "tourism planner" among them. Even during our retracing of that voyage, I found myself in a curious position in relation to my shipmate scholars. They looked at the seals, birds, trees, and fish to pursue their studies and comparisons. For my focus of study, I looked to us—visitors from "away," on a ship of foreign registry owned by a midwestern company, heading to places both on and off the well-traveled Alaskan tourist trail. For me, we were simultaneously the researchers and the subject. Yes, several of our party were Alaskans, but on this long coastal voyage, even the Alaska residents were visiting many of our destinations for the first time. Like the rest of us, they wanted to experience the adventure of yet unknown places.

As each day unfolded on this personal and collective voyage through Alaska, I was curious to see what approaches communities were taking toward tourism. Did they feel in control of their own development and future? Often those who take an active hand in managing their future—making the hard decisions, evaluating options and development plans—are most satisfied with the results and their quality of life. Too often, communities feel that growth per se is a desirable goal, and more of a good thing must be better. This perspective can have a sweeping impact, as Alaska's resource-extraction industries—fishing, mining, and timber—decline and more Alaskan communities turn to tourism to stabilize their economies. Even state of Alaska officials acknowledge that in the past they just wanted more visitors. In recent years, though, the option of sustainable development has received increased attention, as many communities come to understand that unabated growth may create as many problems as it solves. I was eager to see how tourism was faring in this resource-rich state, which has experienced many boom-and-bust cycles, in the face of powerful global trends. We were just three days underway when I had the opportunity to observe Alaskan tourism unfolding in two different ways, first in Skagway, then in Sitka.

On July 26, we visited Skagway. Skagway has long been associated with the gold-rush days and a burst of wealth that ended almost a century ago. Nearly twenty thousand gold miners came through Skagway on their way to the Klondike gold fields. As the *Clipper Odyssey* slowly sailed up the Lynn Canal in the brightening early-morning light, I had a sense of expectancy. I was curious to see how this town had adapted tourism to its situation. Once a small Tlingit village, in 1899 Skagway, John Muir said, was like "a nest of ants . . . stirred up by a stick" (quoted by S. Hall Young). Skagway, in its incarnation as a mining town, was just two years old when Muir saw it and very different from any other place the expedition visited during its two-month voyage. "The pier is swarming with people," wrote John Burroughs. "Such a gathering and such curiosity and alertness we had not seen. Hotel runners flourished their cards and called out the names of their various hostelries. . . . Boys greeted us with shouts[;] . . . women and girls . . . pushed to the front and gazed intently at the strangers. Born of the gold fever [Skagway] is still feverish and excitable."

The gold rush and the fledgling tourist industry were good partners—until the gold rush moved to Nome, taking Skagway's attraction with it. Within a few years after the 1899 expedition's visit, Skagway was in danger of becoming a ghost town. Foreshadowing the future, the White Pass Railroad became its saving grace. Originally constructed to move miners and supplies to and from the gold fields, the railroad, which made a dramatic twenty-nine-thousand-foot ascent up to Dead Horse Trail, also proved attractive to tourists. With this resourceful re-adaptation, packaged with the romance of the gold-rush legacy, Skagway has emerged during the last century as a significant seasonal tourist destination. The miners are a distant memory, but the streets are still bustling—with tourists.

As we approached Skagway's docks in 2001, we felt no less a sense of awe at the sights before us. Today, Skagway is the seventeenth most-visited port in the world and the primary destination of the Inland Passage cruise industry, attracting half of all Alaska cruise visitors. Having just left the rainforest wilderness, we found that the feeling of being dwarfed by the towering mountains was quickly replaced by the sense of being dwarfed by the massive liners at the dock. Staring up in wonder as we lined up along the *Odyssey*'s rails, we craned our necks to see their topmost decks.

As we prepared to leave the ship, the order of the day clearly was people management. Like the Harriman Expedition members, we all turned our nametags on the pegboard by the gangway to the "out" position. This system, widely used today, was developed by the 1899 Harriman Expedition after some of its members missed the boat on several occasions. With increasingly large numbers of tourists to handle, developing people-management systems has become a top priority in the industry. Our group was divided into those taking the train and those taking the bus to the White Pass summit. At the top, the groups switched—bus group down by train, train group down by bus—an ideal way to manage large numbers of visitors while decreasing pressure on an individual site. The young, scripted seasonal tour guide left me feeling curiously dissociated from the town's history, but oh, what a view from the summit: the entire town, the docks, and the quiet mountains, forests, and ocean beyond. From this vantage, I could see that the number of large cruise ships had multiplied since our arrival. Five of these large vessels were at the dock; with crew, that was a potential influx of ten thousand people into Skagway in one day. These ships created a canyon surrounding the *Clipper Odyssey*.

Although the gold rush may be Skagway's theme, the town is also an impressive, incredibly efficient hub of transportation. Arriving by modern cruise liners, visitors may choose to take the White Pass & Yukon Railroad or drive to Whitehorse, go on helicopter and airplane "flightseeing" trips, or ride one of the historic buses originally used in Yellowstone National Park. All these options expose thousands to Skagway and Alaska history, while putting the beauty of the area on display. This formula— combining history and scenery—makes Skagway a very, very busy place.

I was not fully able to appreciate how busy, focused, and efficient the Skagway tourist industry is until our train delivered us to the town center. In a sense, Skagway, a Victorian city of pretty pastel paint, interesting false fronts, and boardwalks, is a museum piece. The downtown is a seven-block-long historic district known as the Klondike Gold Rush National Historical Park. Although turn-of-the-century shops, hotels, and saloons are still open for business, mostly we found shops. Some offered wonderful arts and crafts and items representative of Alaska today. There were also the T-shirt and kitsch shops catering to mass tourism. Significantly, the match between the types and expectations of the people who visit and what the town offers is a good one. Skagway merchants know who their customers are and serve their needs.

As a colleague and I wandered along the streets of Skagway, he asked many questions: "What do you think of this Hollywood–Disney World version of a town?" "Does Skagway represent a *real* town?" "Is it authentic?" "Where are the townsfolk going about their normal activities, visiting the library or dentist's office, shopping for groceries, going to school?" In fact, for Skagway in summer, tourists are the normal life of the town. Most citizens have chosen this seasonal feast-or-famine lifestyle, and, according to residents we spoke to, they relish both the busy, "working and earning" tourist season and the quiet off-season. In winter the resident population shrinks from its tourist-season peak of almost 900 to about 250. Many residents go on extended winter vacations. Having essentially made their money for the year, others enjoy this quiet time, when only about six businesses are open, and the peaceful life of a tight-knit community. Skagway's tourist industry has been purposefully designed—tourists are understood, managed, and even welcomed by the town's residents. Tourism has helped Skagway reinvent itself, and Skagway has found a profitable niche within the tourism industry.

Back onboard the *Clipper Odyssey* for our return sail down the Lynn Canal, our debate ranged—and raged—in many directions. Most could agree that Skagway had fostered a profitable industry. Clearly an economic benefit results from the sheer volume of visitors. But how does this influx affect environmental and social concerns? When other communities look to Skagway's success, do they understand the far-ranging implications? What about negative impacts, such as noise, air, and water pollution? How do large numbers of people, wear and tear on community resources, high prices, and some loss of authenticity influence the quality of life for residents?

FIGURE 10. *Tlingit women selling goods to tourists on the sidewalk, Sitka, circa 1900.*
Credit: Fred W. Carylon. Source: Manuscripts Special Collections, University Archives,
University of Washington Libraries, NA 2577.

What are the sacrifices? Sometimes the appearance a community reveals to its visitors masks the community's real identity.

Our debate surrounding the role of tourism on the Alaska coast did not subside when we left Skagway but in fact was reenergized as we tied up to Sitka's dock the next morning. Like Skagway, Sitka is no stranger to tourism, having benefited from being the last stop on the early steamship tours up the Alaska coast. It too has an interesting history that attracts the adventurous tourist.

Sitka has been a Tlingit community for more than nine thousand years, and that rich cultural heritage is evident. The Russians had a profound influence on the area through their fur-trade empire. The remains of the original Russian settlement are also still evident, including the spire of the wooden, onion-domed St. Michael's Cathedral rising elegantly above the town. Sitka's tourist appeal is further enhanced by the fact that, with Seward's Folly, the purchase of Alaska in 1867, Sitka became Alaska's territorial capital.

Sitka's cultural activities did not escape the Harriman party's attention. John Burroughs wrote: "People actually live in Sitka from choice, and seem to find life sweet. There are homes of culture and refinement. . . . We spent the time there after the usual manner of tourists: walking about the town, visiting the Indian village, the museum, the Greek Church[,] . . . making a trip to some nearby mines, and climbing the mountains." Burroughs's description of Sitka presents quite a contrast to his description of "feverish and excitable" Skagway.

Sitka has a natural advantage that has contributed to its historic and economic wealth and centuries-old sense of place—its relationship with the ocean and surrounding rainforest. On our approach to Sitka, we saw shores carpeted with forest; the harbor was filled with a massive fleet of boats. The ocean has a pervasive influence on Sitka, which is known for the quality and quantity of fish harvested in nearby waters. The fishing industry contributes more than $20 million a year to the economy.

Since the end of World War II, when the Alaska Pulp Corporation's mill opened, the forests have also played an important role in Sitka's economy. At its peak, the pulp mill employed eight hundred people, and many other townspeople supported themselves by providing products and services to the mill. In a community of eighty-eight hundred, a significant percentage of the workforce depended on the mill for their livelihood. A tremor went through Sitka in 1993, when the mill's closing was announced, with many predicting a disastrous economic decline. And hundreds did lose their jobs.

Community leaders quickly turned to studying the options. Before long, in some quarters, tourism was seen as the panacea. A proposal emerged to expand Sitka's docking facilities to accommodate large passenger ships. Up to this point, large ships had to ferry passengers into Sitka in small boats. From the people-management perspective, the ferrying was considered inconvenient, inefficient for short visits, and a deterrent to easy access for larger numbers of tourists. Supporters of the dock saw it as a boon to the economy and considered crowding a reasonable price to pay for the benefit. Those opposed to the dock felt that for the size of the community the current level of tourism was right; it didn't threaten the quality of life Sitka enjoyed. They pointed to Juneau, where large ships and their passengers now dominate the waterfront. The closing of Juneau's Main Street hardware store to make room for another tourist service had made headlines. Dock opponents argued that a diversified economy would, in the long run, be more stable than one that was dependent on any one sector. Because the expanded dock would be built on land leased from the municipality, a referendum was called. In effect, the referendum was about the appropriate scale of tourism for the life of the community. The community examined the issues on both sides and was actively involved in the debate.

Diversification seems to be the route that Sitka is taking. In 1998, Sitka residents voted two to one against expanding cruise-ship docking facilities. At least for the time being, the economic mix will include fishing, tourism, reorientation of the wood-products industry, marine fabrication, and service-industry initiatives. Remarkably, the Southeast Regional Health Corporation is now Sitka's largest employer. Many argue that Sitka weathered the closing of the pulp mill because of its diversified economy. Had the community been more dependent on the pulp mill, the impact on the community might have been very different. Although Sitka is ten times larger than Skagway, its cruise industry represents just 20 percent, or $11 million, of its economy compared with Skagway's $60 million tourist industry. In Sitka, tourism is part of the economy, not *the* economy.

For Sitka, Skagway, and Juneau, or any other community exploring the role of tourism in the local economy, there are complicated issues and no simple answers. But what a community does decide may irreversibly change its environment, quality of life, and future. What are the major areas of debate within a community considering expanding into tourism? If Sitka is any indication, the impact of the cruise-ship industry is high on the list for coastal towns; this global industry has a huge potential for reshaping Alaskan communities. Today, twenty-two large ships, belonging to nine major companies, cruise Alaska waters. They carry approximately 680,000 passengers to Alaska each year, and almost as many more crew. About half of all summer visitors to Alaska arrive by cruise ship. The number of passengers arriving on cruise ships has almost tripled since 1990, and the number of ships plying the Inside Passage has more than doubled.

In response to this rapid growth, citizens in various Alaskan ports of call are increasingly expressing concern. A century ago, no one worried much about pollution or the role that a steamship played as a polluter. Today, pollution is a significant issue given that cruise ships are basically small floating cities. These seagoing resorts must dispose of many products, including chemicals used for photo processing, dry cleaning, and printing; they produce thousands of gallons of bilge water, oily residues, and sewage. The volume of gray wastewater is huge in a ship that has sinks, showers, laundry service, and galleys to support two thousand passengers. Millions of gallons of various wastes are dumped at sea in the Inside Passage every summer.

In addition to these offshore issues, dockside concerns include smokestack pollution and the aircraft noise of flightseeing excursions that visiting ships generate. And a new phrase, people pollution, is being used in many communities to describe massive crowds of tourists arriving by ship in a short period of time, congesting streets, and spilling into residential areas. Docks and facilities must be built and maintained to accommodate large numbers of people.

In looking at these issues, a 2001 Alaska Department of Environmental Conservation study found that all the major cruise lines operating in Alaska violated air-pollution laws. In the same period, the state of Alaska began to monitor the industry by means that included a program of voluntary effluents testing. Residents were astounded to learn that in 2000, seventy-nine of eighty ships tested had effluent with fecal coliform or total suspended solid levels that would be illegal on land—up to fifty thousand times higher than acceptable federal standards! The following year, most cruise-ship companies chose not to participate in the voluntary testing program. The one ship that passed in 2000? The *Clipper Odyssey*!

FIGURE *11. Mary Harriman with her Kodak. Source: Fuertes Collection, Cornell University.*

In Juneau, citizens organized protests against cruise-ship pollution and created a watchdog organization called Cruise Control. They are concerned about all the benefits that make a place livable: clean air, clean water, peace and quiet. Robert Reges, a Juneau attorney and Cruise Control organizer, has explained that although Cruise Control understands the economic benefits of the cruise industry, it also recognizes the economic and social burdens this industry imposes, and it is trying to ensure that those burdens are either mitigated or are internalized and paid for by the cruise operators. However, when Juneau proposed a $50 per passenger tax to help cover the cost of visiting ships, many shipowners decided to exclude Juneau from their itineraries. For Juneau businesses that were dependent on tourism, the message was clear. In a sense, the cruise industry is not often prepared to pay the real cost of visits to host communities.

As concerns mounted along the coast, the state of Alaska chose to get involved. At the very time Harriman Retraced was sailing the Inside Passage in July 2001, Alaska began to regulate the cruise-tourism industry. Alaska was the first state to develop ship-discharge guidelines that exceeded federal standards, with the cost of the monitoring program subsidized by a fee of $1 per passenger. At the same time, the International Council of Cruise Lines developed standards that matched those of

Alaska and indicated that all cruise lines, globally, must meet or exceed the guidelines or face losing their membership in the influential council. Thus the actions of Alaskan coastal communities, in conjunction with the state government, resulted in positive impacts far beyond their shores.

Although the role of cruise ships is often highly visible within a coastal community, another, more subtle issue is in play. Whether we are talking about tourism in Skagway, Sitka, or Juneau, we evoke the image of Main Street: shops, museums, restaurants, churches, community centers. But more and more, these communities are serving as staging areas for tourists to venture far from Main Street. About half of all cruise passengers take some form of land tour in addition to their ship's voyage. Here we encounter an expanding segment of the market: those visitors less interested in Main Street and more interested in seeking a connection with nature, physical challenges, and adventure. "Soft adventure" is booming, as rising incomes for larger numbers of people expand the audience. That people come to Alaska seeking a wilderness experience is no accident. This is, after all, one of the great images that Alaska presents to the world: open spaces, massive natural resources, and pristine wilderness. The community becomes a logistical hub for an activity that provides an economic boost to the broader region and dozens of businesses. And because the hubs make it convenient, wilderness areas that once saw few visitors are becoming regular stops on tours. Like salmon or timber, is Alaskan wilderness the next resource to be overexploited?

OUR DEBATE ABOUT the role of tourism in Alaska coastal communities was far from over as we reboarded the *Clipper Odyssey* in Sitka and headed for Glacier Bay. We were a bit sheepish, though. As we came to understand the complexities of tourism, we found, like tourists all over the world, we could enjoy the best and leave the troubles behind. That evening, many of my shipmates who were experienced travelers told me they hadn't thought much about the economic, environmental, and social impacts of the cruise industry. (If tour operators are doing their job, they protect their customers from the "behind-the-scenes" issues.) Some of us felt torn, enjoying the experience of Harriman Retraced aboard our well-appointed ship but also wanting to be a positive force in tourism.

Often in these situations it is human nature to see the problem as someone else's fault. In this respect, not much has changed since 1899. Muir was often hostile toward those who entered his cherished wilderness, and he grumbled about the streams of sightseers he encountered: "What a show they made with their ribbons and Kodaks! All seemed happy and enthusiastic, though it was curious to see how promptly all of them ceased gazing when the dinner bell rang." All along the shore of Glacier Bay, his party found plank walkways placed by steamboat companies to accommodate shore visits and sightseers. Muir decried these signs of tourism. Yet the 1899 expedition participated in the same pleasures. Years earlier, Muir himself had built a cabin at the head of Glacier Bay, eroding the sense of wilderness. Ironically, Muir's cabin itself was a tourist attraction, judging by the evidence other campers and day visitors left strewn about nearby. Whether he liked tourists or not, Muir, too, was one of them. During the course of our voyage I sometimes heard similar, slightly disparaging comments about larger cruise ships: "We have only 120 passengers; they have 1,500." When I heard such statements, I couldn't help but wonder, "What do the kayakers think of us?"

As we stood along the rail of our ship, soaking in the beauty of Glacier Bay and struggling to understand the relationship between global warming and glaciers, I knew that this ship full of scholars was on a voyage of learning. I also knew that it was a personal quest for understanding. In this respect, we resembled both the original Harriman Expedition, whose members sought to expand scientific knowledge, and the new breed of exploratory travelers, who are evaluating their own impact on the world they seek to study and understand. Many questions concerning the impact of tourism on the world around us will not be answered quickly.

Significantly, two trends we observed during our voyage may speed up the process. At many ports of call, we noted that a successful marriage between tourism and a community required a deep involvement by the whole community in planning and decision making. Local knowledge is the key to preventing exploitation and supporting sustainability. Inviting tourists into a community does not have to be a take-it-or-leave-it decision; rather the choice should grow out of a discussion that seeks to harmonize development, economic diversity, quality of life, the environment, and social stability. Although the tourist industry wields considerable power, including the power to abandon communities, citizens can make a critical difference when they act in concert and with determination.

The second important trend is a growing mindfulness by travelers that their individual actions matter. More travelers are asking harder questions about the social, economic, and environmental impacts of their involvement in the tourism industry. No one makes a person go on a cruise or take any vacation. Tourism is a service industry that aims to please; it provides what its clients are willing to pay for. If enough clients demand an environmentally and socially responsible travel experience, the industry will provide it. This, too, is a matter of choice.

A Wilderness Debate in Glacier Bay

28 July 2001

Late afternoon yesterday, we made our way back to the Sitka dock and the waiting ship. It had been a fast-paced three days as the *Odyssey* made port calls in Juneau, Skagway, and now Sitka. Our floating university was now fully engaged, with onboard lectures preparing us for each visit. As we sailed up the Lynn Canal for Skagway, environmental historian William Cronon spoke of the Klondike gold rush and its impact on Southeast Alaska's culture and economy. On our way southbound for Sitka, writer Richard Nelson explained how our upcoming destination, his hometown, was working to balance community values and economic development.

Starting with Wrangell, we had found communities proud of their histories and accomplishments and deeply engaged in debating their futures. Perspectives on Sitka's future had come into focus at a community meeting where school-committee members and representatives of the fishing and tourism industries and the medical professions discussed successes and the challenges they foresaw. The location of our meeting, with Mount Edgecumbe and Sitka Sound beyond the windows, provided a distinctive, spectacular setting. But the conversation could have been happening in any town hall in the United States, as Sitka residents described the excitement and fears they had about what might lie ahead.

The *Odyssey* left Sitka dock minutes after the last stragglers cleared the gangway, backtracking along the serpentine route that brought us from Skagway. Winding through straits and narrows that separated Baranof Island from Kruzof and Chichagof islands, we watched the wildlife living within the Alexander Archipelago ecosystem—a foraging sow brown bear with cub, many bald eagles, Sitka black-tailed deer, harbor seals, and flocks of marbled murrelets. With the ship often passing close between two shores, the smells of saltwater and old, wet forest combined into a wild fragrance of its own. At midnight, we left

Peril Strait for the larger waters of Chatham Strait, steering north for Glacier Bay.

The new day began at 5:30 A.M. in Icy Strait, off Point Adolphus. These waters, well known as whale feeding grounds, did not disappoint us. A pod of twelve humpback whales surrounded the ship, feeding in the gray morning light. Reaction from the deck ranged from silent admiration to involuntary expressions of joy as a whale exploded from the surface, seeming to balance on the tip of its tail. We were astonished at the strength and agility these thirty-five-ton creatures use to launch their fifty-foot bodies out the water. It was a quiet yet exhilarating beginning to a day that would become increasingly complex and, at times, emotional.

The *Clipper Odyssey* sailed into Glacier Bay National Park at 7:30 A.M. and entered a world that spread in all directions. On our last day before leaving the Inside Passage for the Gulf of Alaska, it was uncanny to find ourselves at such a confluence of both social issues and awe-inspiring beauty. Glacier Bay was a surprise grand finale, a single place that summarized all the complicated history and issues we had encountered during our voyage through Southeast Alaska.

For nine thousand years the Hoonah Tlingit hunted and fished Glacier Bay as part of their homeland. The Russians came, followed by the British and Americans. British Captain George Vancouver explored Icy Strait in 1794, noting the visible impact the Russians were having on the region's marine mammals and forests. His ship could not sail into Glacier Bay because of the ice sheet that extended all the way to the strait. When John Muir first explored and mapped Glacier Bay in 1879, the glaciers had retreated twenty miles up the bay. Muir returned in 1899 with the

Harriman Expedition to stand triumphantly before his namesake, Muir Glacier. Already a tourist destination, Glacier Bay was one of the 1899 expedition's longest stops; members spent five days there exploring, collecting, and measuring. Burroughs captured their impressions of the glaciers: "We saw the world-shaping forces at work. . . . We saw them transport enormous rocks, and tons on tons of soil and debris from distant mountains; we saw the remains of extensive forests they had engulfed within the century, and were now uncovering again. . . . We were really in one of the workshops and laboratories of the elder gods."

We sailed sixty miles into the narrowing upper reaches of the bay—forty miles farther than the *Elder* could sail a hundred years ago—to find Grand Pacific and Margerie glaciers. Our journey began at 8:00 A.M., when the Glacier Bay National Park patrol boat, *Serac*, met the *Odyssey* off Gustavus to transfer our day travelers. Joining us were Park Superintendent Tommie Lee and Park Ranger Rosemarie Salazar, Alaska Board of Game Chair Greg Streveler, Johanna Dybdahl of the Hoonah Indian Association, retired National Park Service historian Bill Brown, conservationist Jim Mackjovak, and Friends of Glacier Bay president Hank Lentfer.

Throughout the day, our guests shared their love of Glacier Bay and its natural history. At the end of the day, they shared their concerns. Harriman Retraced expedition photographer Kim Heacox, a twenty-year resident of Glacier Bay, convened the discussion, then stood off to the side listening intently. Various people spoke of the commercialization of Glacier Bay, the impact of cruise ships, and the lawsuits regulating their activity—lawsuits and jurisdictions were recurring themes. They pointed to the loss of traditional fishing grounds and, as one person put it, the "raw, open wounds" that still exist.

The discussion moved on to the Glacier Bay version of now familiar topics: commercial fishing, logging, and tourism. Every one of our guests was worried that Glacier Bay, the wilderness, would be lost, but they also saw an opportunity not to make the mistakes made in the Lower Forty-Eight's national parks—mistakes that had resulted in crowds, pollution, noise, declining biodiversity, and problems created by the introduction of exotic species. Lentfer gave a glimpse of the struggles ahead for these Alaskans: "I have lived in Alaska my whole life, and I find regulations pretty damn distasteful. The only thing I find more distasteful is how badly we need them. . . . Glacier Bay was listed in *Consumer Reports* as the number-one national park. It is not the ranking I mind, but the fact that it was listed in *Consumer Reports* in the first place—Glacier Bay as a commodity."

Killer Whales

© PATRICIA SAVAGE

CHAPTER SIX

THE POLITICS OF BEAUTY

◦

KIM HEACOX

As dawn leaked through the bruised clouds of Southeast Alaska, the M/V *Clipper Odyssey* drifted off Point Adolphus, the northernmost reach of Chichagof Island. We stood on deck, bundled against the chill, and watched a dozen humpback whales spout and roll in the slate-gray morning sea. First three whales appeared off starboard, then two to port, then one directly off the bow. They were far enough off so that their tail lobbing and flipper flapping did not elicit the spontaneous roar of approval that closer sightings ignite. Instead, a reverent stillness settled over us. This was not a sporting performance but rather a sanctified and ancient reminder of how we as a people have changed in our attitudes about whales. Looking into the waters below, we could see eddies created by strong tides and upwellings, a process that makes this one of the most productive summer whale-feeding areas in the entire North Pacific. Not long ago the whales had this place to themselves. Now tour boats and cruise ships visit daily and sometimes encircle the whales like Land Rovers around lions on the Serengeti. By arriving at dawn, we had avoided the crowds and soon found ourselves steaming north across Icy Strait.

An hour later, as we slipped into Glacier Bay National Park, I surveyed the shore with binoculars and found what I was looking for: a dead humpback whale on shore at Point Gustavus. It made a sobering counterpoint to our experience of an hour before, and it underscored the mounting pressure of tourism and other industries on wild Alaska. As we watched from the ship's rail, I told those around me that the whale had been there for one week and had been on the front page of the *Anchorage Daily News* and the *Juneau Empire*. National Park Service biologists were conducting a necropsy. From the crushed skull and nearly severed head they had a strong idea that the whale—a pregnant, thirty-seven-year-old female—had been struck by a cruise ship. In the parlance of science they called her "Whale Number 68." They had first recorded her in Glacier Bay twenty-two years before, in 1979, which had special significance for me. That was my first year in Glacier Bay as well.

When the Harriman party entered here in 1899, whales were scarce and icebergs abundant. Now the opposite is true. The two great glaciers that filled the upper bay then, Grand Pacific and Muir, have since retreated ten and thirty miles respectively. Their retreats have unveiled entire new geographies filled with emerging communities of plants, habitats, and wildlife. Muir Glacier itself is off tidewater, having retreated deep into its rock-ribbed inlet, perhaps to wait for global warming to cease, and then to advance again. About a dozen tidewater glaciers still occupy the upper inlets of the bay. Although impressive, with their minaret-like seracs—towers of ice—that calve into the sea, these glaciers are mere vestiges of what once filled the bay. Most continue to retreat, a few have stabilized, and fewer still threaten to advance. Imagine their breathtaking return, the headlines proclaiming "Glaciers Retake Glacier Bay."

It's happened before. The native Hoonah Tlingit have a rich oral history, carefully preserved from mother to daughter for many generations; they tell of a glacier that marched down Glacier Bay and pushed them from their villages. The Tlingit moved across Icy Strait to Hoonah, on Chichagof Island, not far from Point Adolphus, where they live today. They still consider Glacier Bay their homeland. Geological evidence confirms that glaciers advanced in many parts of the world in the 1300s and 1400s, during a cooling period known as the Little Ice Age. During my more than twenty years in Glacier Bay, I have found this history both peaceful and awesome. The peace comes from knowing there is much wild, roadless country still out there, so many places that have never felt the tread of human feet. But increasingly I—and others like me—worry about wild Alaska's future. No place is getting wilder.

A century ago, the United States had only ten miles of paved roads. Today, 5 percent is under concrete and asphalt—and that percentage continues to grow. Statistics like these tell me that commerce and industry will chew away at Alaska just as they have destroyed most of the wild Lower Forty-Eight, leaving us with only remnants of where we came from and what we once were. As John Muir said, "Nothing dollarable is safe." If we lose sight of the land and the silence that nurtured our legs and lungs, then what—or who—will tell us where we should go? The smoothest politician? He or she will certainly try. The cleverest advertiser? The business of the United States is business, and advertisers everywhere are out to convince us of one thing: whatever possessions we have, they're not enough; we need more. So I like the metronome and morality of glaciers, the give-and-take of ice, the hardness of water. I want the glaciers to march back down at least one inlet in Glacier Bay to erode and reshape the land. I want a silence, as Barry Lopez described in *Arctic Dreams,* "stretching all the way to Asia."

The members of the 1899 expedition, although intelligent and farsighted, could hardly have imagined the pressures that would be brought to bear on the national

FIGURE 12. *"The two Johnnies": John Muir and John Burroughs.*
Credit: Edward S. Curtis. Source: Harriman family collection.

park system some of them helped create. Both C. Hart Merriam and Henry Gannett were members of the 1871 Hayden Expedition to Yellowstone, which figured prominently in the creation of Yellowstone as the first national park in 1872. Colleagues Merriam and George Bird Grinnell were conservation advocates for Mount Rainier National Park. Muir worked doggedly for the creation of national parks; he camped with Teddy Roosevelt in Yosemite so the president could see the grandeur with his own eyes. With the support of Roosevelt and Edward Harriman, Muir successfully argued for the expansion of Yosemite National Park in 1906. The U.S. Army was posted in these places to help protect them, for not until 1916 was the National Park Service born.

Muir's early exploration of both Alaska and the yet-unnamed Glacier Bay, starting in 1879, laid the foundation for the establishment of Glacier Bay National Park. In 1916, an ecologist from Minnesota, William Cooper, arrived in the bay to establish several vegetation plots in order to study the process of primary plant succession in the aftermath of glacial recession. Cooper was so impressed by the wild country and so excited by the opportunities for scientific research that he proposed the entire bay and surrounding mountains be established as a national monument.

A hot debate ensued. In 1924, a quarter century after the Harriman expedition had come and gone, the *Juneau Daily Empire* denounced the idea of a Glacier Bay national monument as a "monstrous proposition." The paper editorialized (quoted by Bohn): "It tempts patience to try to discuss such nonsensical performances. The suggestion that a reserve be established to protect a glacier that none could disturb if he wanted . . . is the quintessence of silliness." It was, the paper concluded, "a monstrous crime against development and advancement. It leads one to wonder if Washington has gone crazy through catering to conservation faddists."

The following year, President Calvin Coolidge signed the proclamation making Glacier Bay a national monument. With passage of the Alaska National Interest Lands Conservation Act in 1980, Glacier Bay became a national park. This same act also expanded Mount McKinley National Park from two million acres to six million acres and renamed it Denali National Park and Preserve. Katmai, until then a national monument, became a national park. Five new national parks were established: Wrangell–St. Elias, Kenai Fjords, Lake Clark, Gates of the Arctic, and Kobuk Valley. Although hailed as the Louisiana Purchase of the conservation movement, this act infuriated many Alaskans. President Jimmy Carter, who worked tirelessly to bring the act to completion, signed the legislation in the final days of his presidency. Protestors in Anchorage and Fairbanks burned him in effigy.

Many political and economic leaders in Alaska today support national parks only insofar as the parks provide jobs and industry. In this regard, things have not changed much in a hundred years. Edward Harriman's support of national parks did not stop with Muir's conservation goals. Harriman's logic was straightforward: parks would become tourist attractions; tourists would need transportation; and he would build the railroads to get them there. Parks would be good for business. Not until Alaska's Kenai Fjords National Park turned into a tourism magnet did residents in the nearby town of Seward support it. Before then, they marched in protest against its creation.

Had it been left to a majority vote of Alaskans in 1980 and before, few if any national parks of significant size or ecological importance would exist in Alaska. More troubling still, Alaskans are not alone in their opposition to sweeping public lands conservation near their homes. The people of Montana did not fight to create Yellowstone or later to protect it from incursions by railroads. Nor did the people of California, except for Muir and a few others, fight for the creation of Yosemite. Rather, it was the United States at large that established and later protected these places. When it comes to public lands conservation at the local or regional level, Americans seem incapable of accepting strict limits and forgoing profits in order to promote conservation, which will serve generations into the future. Civil libertarians decry this long arm of preservation as a "lockup." But it is their settling and taming of a place that locks it up and makes it impossible for every generation in the future to find it as wild and pristine as they did. Historians call this the "pioneer's paradox," the process of destroying that which we love.

Large-scale conservation is a powerful tool; it slows development and gives our grandchildren a hand in deciding their own futures. Preservation expands the discussion from "what about me?" to "what about them?" Because the allure of short-term profits is equally powerful, it often takes a removed, national perspective to apply the brakes. Outsiders who set aside home rule invariably incense the local population and may even be burned in effigy. But they test our collective commitment to a national vision.

In *Democracy in America,* Alexis de Tocqueville wrote, "Democratic nations . . . will habitually prefer the useful to the beautiful, and they will insist that the beautiful should be useful." This is the politics of beauty. Americans make commodities of everything. We establish national parks, put them on T-shirts, and love them to death. These problems have not yet appeared in some parts in Alaska, where visitation is relatively low, although they plague the Lower Forty-Eight. Yet even in Alaska the early signs of overuse are undeniable. For Glacier Bay and Denali, the old Chinese conundrum fits: discover a beautiful place, announce it to the world, the world arrives, and it is beautiful no more. When *Consumer Reports* ranked Glacier Bay the number one national park in the United States in 1997, sandwiching it between rankings of toasters and riding lawn mowers, it did not comment on the irony of those parks that had been ranked number one in the past and were now listed as "overcrowded."

National parks are paradoxical places. They belong to everyone and to no one. They are islands of socialism in a sea of capitalism. As a result they come under constant attack. The federal government owns 60 percent of Alaska's acreage. Two-thirds of the land in the U.S. national park system is in Alaska, as well as nearly 90 percent of the acreage in the national wildlife refuge system. Although some Alaskans find this situation gratifying; others chafe at the limits, rules, and restrictions that come with wilderness and wildlife protection.

Compared with the federal government's current emphasis on conservation and preservation, the Alaska state constitution encourages the management and harvesting of virtually all natural resources—plant, animal, and mineral. Many of the state's political and business leaders are beholden constitutionally and politically to the consumption of these resources and the special interests that profit from their harvest. The goal among national environmentalist groups, in contrast, is to save Alaska from Alaskans, and without apologies, in an attempt to keep history from repeating itself. The tension between the harvest-it camp and the leave-it-alone camp is often rancorous. As Edward Abbey wrote: "Alaska is not, as the license plates assert, the 'Last Frontier.' Alaska is the final big bite on the American table, where there is never quite enough to go around. . . . For Americans, Alaska is the last pork chop."

Thirty years ago in the United States, two universities offered degrees in environmental sciences; today, two hundred universities offer those degrees. A new youth is arriving in Alaska, one versed in Henry David Thoreau, Aldo Leopold, Rachel Carson, Abbey, and Muir. These young people understand the consequences of over-consumption and are ready to help carry the banner of restraint in order to reinforce those Alaskans—a small but dedicated and growing minority—who have fought for decades to keep Alaska off the chopping block. A few of those bright, young people sailed with us on the *Clipper Odyssey,* and they were a constant delight.

From the ship's bridge, Glacier Bay appeared as wild as one could imagine. We traveled north past islands rich with nesting seabirds and jousting Steller sea lions. Mysterious coves came into view and disappeared. We entered secluded inlets and looked for coastal brown bears. We learned that the story of Glacier Bay is one of glacial recession, plant succession, and wildlife immigration. Rivers of ice have retreated, and in their wake communities of plants have arrived to pioneer barren ground, with each community displacing the one before it. On this shifting ecological stage, wildlife populations have ebbed and flowed as one habitat turns into another. All around us, without notice or acclaim, these millennia-old patterns unfolded and continued to unfold. I have often considered Glacier Bay a renaissance place, a land of beginnings where those who give it time will awaken and see the world as both ancient and new.

The 1899 expedition had five days in Glacier Bay; we had only one and did not get ashore. Like those on the previous voyage, we were both researchers and tourists. Eighty percent of the visitors to Glacier Bay never set foot on the land. They arrive by cruise ship and tour boat, spend only a day, and leave. Glacier Bay for them is a scenery experience, not a wilderness experience—the distinction is important. In scenery you see more than you can absorb; in wilderness you absorb more than you can see. In wilderness you sleep on the ground and become acutely aware of the small yet profound things. You cope with discomfort and inconveniences, perhaps even with trepidation and fear. All your wits come into play. You hear a seal breathe across a cove in the prism of a windless morning. You fall asleep to spouting whales that swim into your dreams. You understand that Glacier Bay is a land of rebirth and that you too, in your own way, can be reborn here. You discover a laugh and a sincerity you haven't heard in your voice in years, deeper than anything you'll find on Wall Street or on television. Every gift and sense come into play, and so too every infraction.

This is not to say that stockbrokers from New York City who visit for a day on a cruise ship cannot be deeply moved by the scenery. They can, and they are, every day of summer. Their claim to Glacier Bay is no less valid than that of the solo kayaker, who, in fact, although having a more intimate experience low to the water, can disrupt bird life and plant life (while camping) in a way that two thousand passengers on a cruise ship cannot. The value of Glacier Bay and of all carefully protected public lands is how visitors on many levels find the memory in their blood, a place unlike anything they've experienced before in their lives. They go back to New York or Chicago or California with a new clarity, knowing in some small but significant way that perhaps this wild earth is where they came from. It is their ancient home: the unpaved, uncrowded land.

FIGURE 13. *Henry Gannett surveying in Glacier Bay.*
Credit: Edward S. Curtis. Source: Harriman family collection.

Limits are important. The amount of airplane traffic and vessel traffic (of all kinds, from kayaks to tour boats to cruise ships) in Glacier Bay has increased dramatically in the last twenty years. Pressure from regional businesses in partnership with Alaska's congressional delegation has been relentless on the National Park Service to "open" Glacier Bay to more and more economic opportunities. Many politicians and business people don't see the bay as full but as "underutilized." To that end, the ships have gotten bigger and the cruise industry stronger, and the politicians the industry finances have called for a new vessel-management plan that would increase the number of cruise-ship visits per summer from 107 to 184. In 1979, the year Whale Number 68 first appeared in Glacier Bay, total visitation was 122,000. Twenty-two years later, when the whale was struck by a ship (which didn't report the incident), total visitation in Glacier Bay was 382,000—a 313 percent increase.

The debate over the future of Glacier Bay also erupted in 1996, when the National Park Service proposed closing the bay to commercial fishing. For environmentalists, this was a bold step toward creating the first national marine preserve in Alaska. In response, the Alaska governor, state legislature, and congressional delegation threatened the National Park Service with legal action. Native corporations accused the National Park Service of undermining their heritage. As the rhetoric heated up, the distinction between subsistence and commercial fishing blurred. Editorialists across the state rose to the fishermen's defense and portrayed the fish stocks as a well-managed, never-ending resource that provided jobs and helped to feed the world. Environmentalists replied that it was not Glacier Bay's responsibility to improve the restaurant menus of Seattle and Los Angeles or to provide jobs. Was it asking too much that there be one place in Alaska's thirty-four thousand miles of coastline that was not commercially fished? Apparently it was. The state of Alaska filed a lawsuit to gain control of the bay's submerged lands from the federal government (a lawsuit that, as I write, is headed for the Supreme Court). Remarkably, that was just one of about a dozen major issues facing Glacier Bay at the time. When I asked a park employee how things were going in the office, she told me it was "raining hand grenades."

In the midst of the debate, an important question arose: Would the closing of commercial fishing in Glacier Bay damage the economy of Southeast Alaska to such an extent that it would outweigh the value of having both a nursery ground for fish and an internationally recognized marine sanctuary? No other coastal national park in Alaska—Wrangell–St. Elias, Kenai Fjords, Lake Clark, Katmai—has jurisdiction over its marine waters. In all of Southeast Alaska, which includes roughly ten thousand miles of coastline and one thousand islands punctuating the famous Inside Passage, nothing restricts the numbers or types of vessels anywhere except the National Park Service in Glacier Bay. In the final analysis, the questions are: How will the economics of closing this single fishery be measured against what can be learned from the "nursery effect"? What will be the benefits of leaving just one place alone, just one place where the fish, crabs, and shrimp are not harvested, where the ecosystem is allowed to oscillate to the free rhythms of nature?

From an ecological and aesthetic point of view, Glacier Bay stands as a benchmark and a beacon of hope for Muir-minded preservationists. If nothing else, this place, this debate, forces us to ask whether our claims have no boundaries. For many, Alaska seems so big and devoid of human activity that these questions are irrelevant; but then we realize that the same could have been said two hundred years ago for all of the United States. How many millions of acres of wilderness went unprotected because of a blind belief in the myth of superabundance? Now the fish and wildlife are gone, and we are left with only remnants.

From the deck of the *Clipper Odyssey*, I saw a landscape that has been slowly shaped by immeasurable tons of ice over thousands of years. In the short period of the last century, change has come faster, with the promise of larger economic gains. Old industries have expanded, and new industries have been born to fill any available void, all while the wilderness, the original land, shrinks or gets in the way. The cruise ship that hit Whale Number 68 at the entrance of Glacier Bay may have been traveling at the proper speed and in the middle of the channel, as required. Whales can get confused in a sound hole off the bow of an approaching ship. They can misjudge the size and speed of the people-made world today and get hurt. So can we all. Change is occurring faster all the time. Some things are unable to adapt. New stresses occur. Lives are lost and are gone.

Not until we as a culture and a nation practice a restraint uncommon in our history and not until we bestow on some still-wild places the sanctity they require and deserve will Glacier Bay be safe. Alaska is our second chance. It fills many of us with a burning hope that this time around we can do things right; we can save more than just remnants of the country we came from. I detected this hope on the *Clipper Odyssey.* It was the reason many of us joined the voyage. Shipmates—Alaskans and non-Alaskans alike—greeted my concerns with calls for solutions and new resolve. The gnawing in my stomach faded but did not go away. As I watched the bay disappear off the stern that night, Whale Number 68 was not far from my thoughts. Deep inside, I wanted one tidewater glacier, just one, to re-advance back down its inlet and make us think about the long history of ice and our place in time.

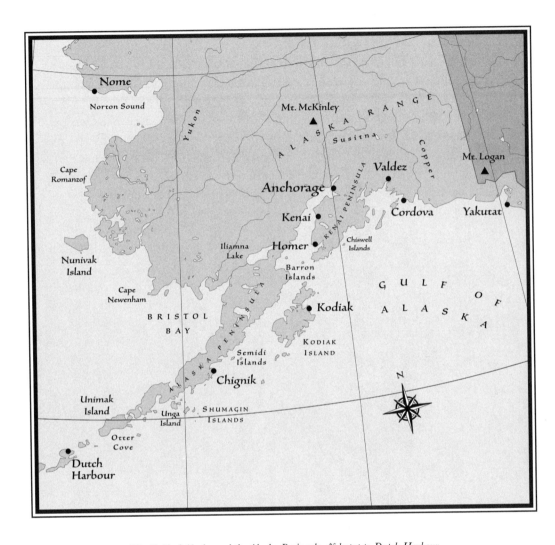

The Gulf of Alaska and the Alaska Peninsula, Yakutat to Dutch Harbour

PART THREE

GULF OF ALASKA AND ALASKA PENINSULA

❦

{Prince William Sound}

EXPLORING LATOUCHE ISLAND

I remember walking the trail
with you at Latouche. You found pieces
of lavender glass: a bottle, you said, 1890s.
First we are story, you said, then history.
Later, at the rusty stream, I discovered shards
of a cream-colored cup with stripes of red and blue:
Archaeology, I added, and then geology.
We become the land.
It was a perfect summer's day—
bright sky, old mine, black bear in the berries—
an image now broken in pieces along our path.

— SHEILA NICKERSON

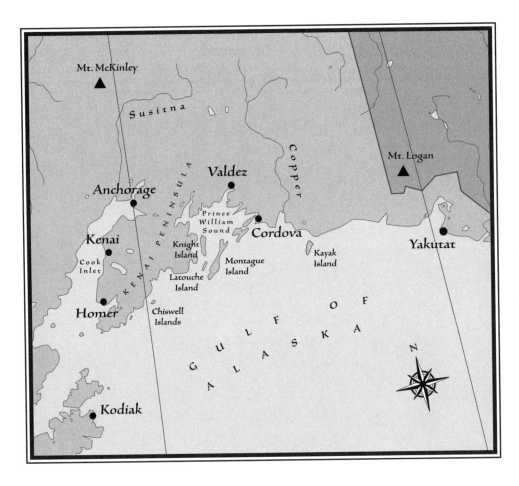

The Gulf of Alaska, Yakutat to Kodiak

Sailing into Open Waters— Yakutat to Cordova

29 July 2001

With the passage of a week, the deck plan of the *Clipper Odyssey* is now familiar to me, at least enough so as to reduce circuitous adventures around the ship. The creation of small routines and the fact that I can make my way directly from almost any place on the ship to my cabin hint that the ship is becoming home. At the end of each day, dinner conversations and evening lectures wind down, and shipmates slip off for their night's rest. Like an exhausted child needing to stay up "just one more minute," I drift off for a last visit to the bridge. In good weather, the night watch is usually quiet and the bridge dark, settled in for a predetermined run over some distance to get us to a new location by morning. Staring out over the water at night brings a calm that lets the disjointed pieces of the day find a place in the larger unfolding story.

Once in my bunk, I have one last routine to complete the day—I read the passages from the *Harriman Alaska Expedition* series cor-responding to the place we will awake to the next morning. In last evening's passage, my historical colleague John Burroughs was again prophetic: "We turned our faces for the first time toward the open ocean, our objective point being Yakutat Bay, a day's run further north. The usual Alaska excursion ends at Sitka, but ours was now only fairly begun. The Pacific was very good to us and used us as gently as an inland lake, there being only a low sleepy swell that did not disturb the most sensitive."

For now at least, it seems the North Pacific is going to be good to Harriman Retraced as well. While all but a few of the ship's crew slept, the *Odyssey* sailed out of Cross Sound and into the Gulf of Alaska. Behind us were the protected waters and passionate debates of the Inside Passage. The Cape Spencer Lighthouse off starboard and the long "sleepy" ocean-born swells that lifted the ship introduced the next leg of our journey. Unceremoniously, we had entered the planet's largest ocean, covering sixty-four million square miles—28 percent of the earth's surface and equal to the land area of all seven continents combined. The *Odyssey* was navigating on the northern edge of an ocean extending from Alaska to Antarctica and containing over half the world's water.

Within this ocean vast currents circulate between Japan and the west coast of North America. Flowing from Japan, the warm-water Kuroshio Current divides as it crosses the North Pacific, splitting south into the California Current and north into the Alaska Current. Coming off deep ocean waters, the Alaska Current forms an expansive counterclockwise swirl of flowing water following the Gulf of Alaska's arching coast. Out along the Alaska Peninsula the flow joins the Aleutian Current and the waters stream offshore away from the Aleutian Islands. At sea once again, the current continues on counterclockwise and eastward toward the relatively shallow continental shelf.

This invisible flow, spanning five thousand miles, has a magnificent and profound effect on the wildlife and the people living within the ecosystem it has helped create. Warm waters contribute to a climate that allows giant rainforest trees to grow. The offshore current brings upwellings of nutrient-rich deep waters to Alaska's continental shelf, bathing the ecosystem in a continuous supply of natural fertilizer and food. Plankton and seaweeds flourish among the submerged coastal mountains, providing food and habitat for all forms of marine life. Predatory carnivores eat the plant eaters; large carnivores eat the small carnivores. Populations of whales, seals, otters, sea lions, fish, and birds live interconnected lives within vibrant coastal ecological communities, all nurtured by the water and nutrients carried by North Pacific Ocean currents. Not surprisingly, the Gulf of Alaska is home to 25 marine mammal species, 26 seabird species, and an astounding 287 fish species. Around the world, these rich areas of upwelling represent a mere 1 percent of the ocean's surface—but account for half of all fishery catches.

Human communities living at the top of the Gulf of Alaska's food chain have prospered from this bounty for thousands of years. Gulf fishermen earn nearly a half billion dollars a year for catches dominated by salmon, halibut, and herring. Salmon and other fish, as well as marine mammals, contribute significantly to Native Alaskan subsistence harvests and play an important role in community life. This morning we sailed into the Tlingit community of Yakutat and found the legacy of favorable oceans currents: lush Sitka spruce and hemlock forests, fish, marine mammals, and human culture woven together.

With my first cup of coffee in hand, I eagerly awaited my meeting with the Yakutat Tlingit Tribe leaders and the schoolchildren who would sail with us through tribal lands to Hubbard Glacier. From our earliest conversations to plan this stop at Yakutat, I sensed concern among some community members about our visit but didn't know exactly what lay behind it. I knew that more and more cruise ships were making their way into Yakutat Bay, as Malaspina Glacier, Disenchantment Bay, Hubbard Glacier, and Russell Fjord became fixtures of tour itineraries. I also knew that the residents of Yakutat, a small community of seven hundred people, were becoming worried about air and wastewater pollution caused by cruise ships that had little contact with the village. Deepening their concern was a dramatic decline in the population of the harbor seal, an animal central to the subsis-

FIGURE 14. *A Yakutat Tlingit sealing camp at Disenchantment Bay.*
Credit: Edward Henry Harriman. Source: Harriman family collection.

tence culture and history of the Yakutat Tlin-git. Significant declines in the numbers of seal pups in Disenchantment Bay and Russell Fjord—dozens when there should have been hundreds—moved Yakutat to restrict visitor access to those places during the breeding season. Although these issues may have contributed to the reticence I felt from community members, I sensed something more.

At 7:45 A.M. the pilot boat met us at the mouth of Monti Bay and dropped off our guests. The Yakutat upper-school students and teachers joined the Harriman Retraced Young Explorers Team, composed of students and teachers from Alaska and Massachusetts, and they set off on a tour of the ship. Joining us for a week as a Harriman Scholar was Elaine Abraham in her capacity as secretary of the

Alaska Native Science Commission. Elaine, daughter of a Yakutat Tlingit chief, was accompanied by her own son and daughter, David and Judy Ramos.

As the crowd at the pilot-boat door dispersed, it was clear that Yakutat leaders George Ramos Sr., Bert Adams Sr., Victoria Demmert, Arlene Henry, and Ted Valle Sr. had something important on their minds that they wanted to talk about. We poured ourselves some coffee and found a quiet corner in the dining room to talk. As the conversation unfolded, the history of the 1899 expedition and the historical oppression of Native Alaskans once again intersected with Harriman Retraced. As with Native communities throughout the Alaska coast, the Yakutat Tlingits' contact with foreign governments, traders, and missionaries was devastating to themselves and their culture. The Tlingit leaders spoke solemnly of this history, the racism that has persisted, and the pain of explaining these attitudes to their children. Like all parents, they wanted their children to be proud of their heritage, to develop self-esteem, and to move into the future with opportunities. The courage these leaders showed, coming onto this ship full of strangers, with their children, suddenly became clear—as did the connection with the 1899 expedition.

When the 1899 expedition came to Disenchantment Bay, it visited the Yakutat Tlingit sealing camp at Point Latouche. Burroughs's official account of the visit describes the landscape in glorious terms, with a brief description of the sealing camp. It was not this account that pained the present-day Yakutat community but the journal accounts and letters of a few individual expedition members that were later published. The traditional Tlingit subsistence way of life, deeply rooted in their culture and religion, was described in condescending, derogatory terms. These specific dehumanizing insults became embedded in a broader history of cultural oppression and racism. Then one day, a hundred years later, a fellow calls from Massachusetts. He says he wants to visit Yakutat with a large ship that will be retracing the 1899 Harriman Alaska Expedition. When the community leaders reached this point in our conversation, I could understand the anxiety and even anger that my call had stirred up in Yakutat on the other end of the line.

By the time we finished our coffee that morning, a fragile mutual trust had been born. Our hosts seemed ready to believe that this ship of strangers came with goodwill and respect for the Yakutat Tlingits. As the day progressed and we all came to know each other better, the trust grew stronger. Approaching Hubbard Glacier, or Sit Tlien, as the Yakutat know it, we gathered on the bow for an offering of tobacco to Situ Qwani, the spirit of the glacier. Before us was the largest tidewater glacier in North America.

Later, all the ship's party came together in the lounge to hear each of the Yakutat teenagers give a report on the life and history of their community. The applause that they received was a recognition not only of the quality of their reports but also of the poise, confidence, and spirit they displayed.

At day's end the *Odyssey* tied up at the Sitka Sound Company's dock, next to the fish-processing and cold-storage plant. Yakutat's economy is heavily dependent on fishing, and the plant is one of the village's largest employers. The ship's party and Yakutat hosts passed the plant's large bay doors and the bins filled with tons of fish and climbed the hill to the Alaskan Native Brotherhood Hall for a community meeting. All the teenagers, their work for the day completed, set off to explore the village.

At the hall, the meeting began with prayer, followed by open, heartfelt discussion of the past and a new vision for the future. The room was quiet, the audience's attention fixed on Elder Lena Farkas as she told her story of growing up in the grip of prejudice and the impact it had on her life. With both anger and sadness, Elder Farkas insisted that this not be the fate of her children and grandchildren, some of whom now walked the village with children from the ship. Although Harriman Retraced's participants could not change history or erase the hurtful words spoken a century ago, we could recognize the ignorance of an earlier time and the harm it has caused. And we could appreciate, in the shadow of these sobering historical circumstances, that the Yakutat Tlingit Tribe still chose to extend hospitality and friendship to the "strangers from the ship."

The meeting ended with a performance by the Elias Dancers and the presentation of an eagle feather and a prayer. Both, George Ramos Sr. told the room, were intended to "bring peace between us." His prayer asked that Harriman Retraced be under the wing of the eagle and have fair weather and good sailing for the rest of its voyage. For us, the official record will also show that Yakutat was a place where our children came together as equals, became friends, laughed, and shared their stories and dreams.

Dinner onboard the *Odyssey* was winding down as the ship prepared for its 11:00 P.M. departure for Cordova. We said our good-byes to the community members who had joined us for the meal, and they filed down the gangway and off into the village. As we watched them go from the top of the gangway, fisheries biologist David Policansky and I agreed to stretch our legs and walk along the dock beside the packing plant. Standing just inside an open bay door was a small group of fishermen who sold to the plant. We asked what they fished for, and one fellow replied for all, "Mostly salmon." To the universal next question, "How's the fishing?" the same fellow replied, "Not so good." The others nodded in agreement.

Sockeye Salmon

© PATRICIA SAVAGE

CHAPTER SEVEN

SALMON AND STATEHOOD

DAVID POLICANSKY

If one inquires of an individual connected with the salmon industry in Alaska something about their numbers, he is at once told of the millions found there, and informed that the supply is inexhaustible. The same language will be used that was heard in past years with regard to the abundance of wild pigeons, or of the buffalo.

– *George Bird Grinnell, "The Salmon Industry," in vol. 2 of* Harriman Alaska Expedition

CORDOVA IS A FISHING VILLAGE. Sailing in from the Gulf of Alaska on July 31, we entered its harbor, filled with hundreds of fishing boats, most of which were tied up at the dock. The low clouds and drizzle softened the Chugach Mountains beyond the harbor, providing a gauzy, impressionistic background for all those tethered boats. For fishermen, this place was clearly a respite from the open sea where they earned their livelihood. Soon after I grasped the beauty and geography of this place, a seemingly simple question came into my mind, "Why aren't these boats out fishing?"

I had the same thought at the nearby Orca Cannery, now a tourist attraction but no longer an active salmon cannery. The cannery is situated on a quiet inlet, the calm waters of which were dimpled everywhere by the swirls of pink salmon. Off the dock, thousands of fish congregated, some jumping clear of the water, others milling around in tight schools as they prepared to enter freshwater rivers to spawn. Gulls and eagles were in the air, on the water, and in the trees, ready to profit from nature's bounty. With these sights before me, I had my own strong urge to drift off from my shipmates, fly rod in hand.

Still, the image of all those tethered boats kept coming back to me. Perhaps nothing was in season at that moment; perhaps the inlet was closed to fishing. Locals com-

FIGURE 15. *Orca Cannery, Town of Orca, Prince William Sound.*
Credit: Edward S. Curtis. Source: Harriman family collection.

plained about how hard it was to earn a living salmon fishing these days. I struggled to reconcile that complaint with the fish I saw everywhere we went. And what multitudes there were! Since the beginning of our journey, and much to my delight, we had watched salmon leaping in bays, passes, and inlets—a leaping salmon was as exciting for me as a breaching whale.

In the midst of all these fish and surrounded by all these boats and beauty, I couldn't help but see how intertwined the lives of Alaskans and the salmon have become. From the beginnings of Alaska's original Native cultures to contemporary society, salmon have been influencing human cultures and economies throughout this coastline. So important are these fish to Alaska that George Bird Grinnell devoted an entire chapter to them in the 1899 expedition report. Salmon images are ubiquitous in Southeast Alaska, in Tlingit and Haida art, on storefronts, and in galleries. Salmon are deeply ingrained in Alaska's economy and its state, regional, and global politics. In fact, salmon played a significant role in Alaska's achieving statehood. The legacy of these remarkable fish is a quilt of biology, politics, history, global and local interests, and luck. What would Grinnell and the other Harriman scholars have thought of the scene now at the Orca Cannery? Would Grinnell be surprised or simply say, "I told you so"? To make sense of all these pieces, you have to follow salmon migration and the money.

The first wild salmon I ever saw were swimming up a stream in California's Muir Woods, named for John Muir. The salmon that I watched so eagerly at Cordova, like those in Muir Woods, were visible because they were heading through clear, shallow waters on their way upstream toward their freshwater spawning sites. Anglers, naturalists, tourists, gulls, eagles, and bears all congregate to watch, and eat, salmon during their migration. Their special, anadromous life cycle profoundly influences how people relate to them. They grow to adulthood in the open ocean but deposit their eggs in rivers. The eggs hatch into fry, which spend a few weeks to a few years in the river before they migrate to the sea and adulthood.

The pink salmon, or humpbacks, we saw at the Orca Cannery are the smallest and most abundant of the five species of Pacific salmon that inhabit Alaska's waters. The other species, all found in the North Pacific from California to Russia and Japan, are the Chinook (or king), coho (or silver), chum (or dog), and red (or sockeye) salmon. Adults range in size from the hundred-pound Chinook to the pink, weighing five pounds or less. Each species plays a role in Alaska's coastal ecosystems and the human cultures that live within them.

After spawning, Pacific salmon always die, unlike their Atlantic cousins or steelhead trout, some of which survive spawning to breed again. Not only do all the Pacific salmon return to fresh water to spawn, but they almost all return to the exact stream where they hatched. Some migrate more than a thousand miles upriver to spawn—journeys that take them far up the Yukon River, to interior Fairbanks or Whitehorse in Canada.

These reliable and predictable runs, usually from May to October, have allowed other animals and people to weave them into their own ecological cycles. If you live on a river where the salmon spawn, quite conveniently they come to you. This situation is different from having to travel out to sea to catch fish like cod or halibut. When salmon spawn, they leave eggs and their own carcasses in the rivers for other species of fish, as well as birds and mammals, to feed on. The young salmon are also food for birds and other species of fish. Finally—and perhaps most important for this story— the predictable and rich runs of salmon allow stable human communities to develop along the coast and on rivers.

The sheer numbers of salmon migrating into many rivers are mind boggling. The Columbia River in the Pacific Northwest had between ten and sixteen million adult salmon running upriver each year during the early nineteenth century. Sadly, fishing, dams, and other changes to the landscape have greatly reduced those runs. Alaska's Kvichak River has runs of sockeye salmon with a five-year cycle of abundance; the peak runs have approached forty million fish in a season! Although few if any Alaskan rivers can match the average production of the Columbia at its height, the state has so many rivers and streams that its total potential production of wild salmon dwarfs that of other parts of the United States.

How can a fish that has been so abundant fail to provide a steady living for Alaska's fishermen? Ironically, part of the answer stood before me on the *Clipper Odyssey*'s bridge. High above the ocean's surface, the bridge is a fascinating place full of glowing screens and dials. Displays of radar and sonar, gyroscopic compasses, satellite navigation systems, and other modern marvels helped us navigate through fog, rain, and currents. These technological advances also help people find, catch, and distribute fish—and they have changed the face of the fishing industry. Over the decades, the fishing industry has swapped sails for engines and switched to more durable synthetic materials for nets and lines; it has brought onboard freezers and satellite information-gathering equipment. Significantly, these advances all contribute to a more efficient harvesting of greater numbers of these wild fish.

We don't currently think of canneries or railroads as advanced technologies, but they were in the middle of the nineteenth century, and they created new opportunities. Canneries preserve fish, allowing their distribution from place of capture in sparsely populated Alaska to consumer markets in the Lower Forty-Eight. Alaska's first two canneries were established in 1878, just under a decade after completion of the transcontinental railroad. Thus, the combination of canneries and railroads made Alaska's canned salmon widely available to consumers throughout the United States. Although cannery production grew slowly at first, averaging between 1890 and 1899 only about eight hundred thousand to one million forty-eight-pound cases, or about forty-three million total pounds of packed salmon, each year, the consequences of these new technologies for Alaska's salmon were profound. Production of canned salmon peaked in 1936, with 8.5 million cases produced, or four hundred million total pounds. By 1959, the year Alaska became a state, only 1.6 million cases were packed. Even as early as the 1899 expedition, when salmon production was still only about one-tenth that at its peak, Grinnell's observations of the salmon industry were somber and prophetic:

> The salmon of Alaska, numerous as they have been and in some places still are, are being destroyed at so wholesale a rate that before long the canning industry must cease to be profitable. . . . This destruction of salmon comes about through the competition between the various canneries. Their greed is so great that each strives to catch all the fish there are, and all at one time, in order that its rivals may secure as few as possible. . . . Their motto seems to be, "If I do not take all I can get, somebody else will get something. . . ." Notwithstanding the wholesale destruction which is thus going on, the salmon of Alaska are not in danger of actual extermination.

The biological implications of the uncontrolled exploitation of wild salmon are only one part of the story. Among the recurring political threads in Alaska's history are the conflict and tension between outside and local interests. The management of salmon is no exception. The owners of Alaskan canneries lived in Seattle and San Francisco; none were Alaskans. Because they were from "away," these absentee owners were immune to local Alaskan pressure to conserve the salmon resource. Compounding the problem was the fact that Alaska was not a state—it had no voting

FIGURE 16. *Fishermen unloading salmon from a lighter, Alaska, 1917. Credit: John N. Cobb.*
Source: Manuscripts Special Collections, University Archives, University of Washington Libraries, Cobb 4148.

representation in Congress—and thus had no local authority to enforce the protection of salmon.

As local frustration grew, arguments erupted before Congress, letter campaigns were initiated, and dueling reports staked out the positions of the federal Bureau of Fisheries, the territorial governor of Alaska, and Alaska fishermen. The Washington, D.C.–based Bureau of Fisheries reports exuded optimism; those from Alaska expressed growing concern and frustration. Economist Richard Cooley tells us that in 1914 Alaska governor Walter Clark reported to the secretary of the interior: "The waters of Alaska have been exploited for their wealth for many years, and they have yielded many millions of dollars, and large individual fortunes have been accumulated therefrom. At no time, however, have the exploiters contributed anything like an adequate return for the privileges they have enjoyed. . . . In the desire for gain on the part of most of the exploiters of the fisheries of Alaska, the conservation of these fishes seems to have been practically lost sight of." A critical point of controversy was the use of fish traps. As Cooley explained, "Although traps were frequently opposed on such grounds as their alleged ability to destroy entire runs of salmon, their wastefulness and their destruction of other species, the real reason for conflict was perhaps more basic. It was essentially a dispute between capital and labor." Traps were too expensive for local Alaskan fishermen to build and maintain; typically the traps were set up by Seattle and San Francisco cannery owners with deeper pockets.

The conflict continued, even to the point of gunfire, but the power of the cannery owners was not seriously threatened. In 1916, Congress was considering greater home rule for Alaska through bills that provided for a full territorial legislature as well as for statehood. The new legislature would be allowed to regulate and tax the fisheries, as was the case in all preceding U.S. territories. The cannery owners wanted none of it and were successful in persuading the Bureau of Fisheries and Congress to bar any local control of fisheries. Alaska was a colonial economy, as it still is to some degree today. Natural resources were extracted and sold elsewhere by absentee corporations. Those in power were happy to keep it that way.

By 1924, forty-two bills dealing with aspects of Alaska's salmon fishery had been introduced into Congress, but none overcame the absentee cannery owners' influence. The collapse of the fishery by the early 1950s alarmed even the cannery owners, but by then it was too late. The depletion of the salmon resource continued, with fewer than three million cases produced in 1953—a decline of 65 percent from the peak in 1936. Alaskans increasingly saw statehood as the only way to solve the problem; by the early 1940s control of the salmon fishery had become a major issue in Alaska's statehood campaign. As local political power increased and the statehood movement grew, salmon production continued to decline. Finally, in 1959, President Dwight D. Eisenhower proclaimed Alaska the forty-ninth state. Within a year, outside control of the salmon fisheries ended. The hated fish traps—symbols of colonial government— were soon abolished, with the exception of four operated by Alaska Natives.

With the significant benefits of statehood, and the conflict between outside interests and local concerns diminished, Alaska's fisheries were able to move into a new, more promising era. The territorial fisheries bureau soon emerged as the Alaska Department of Fish and Game, and it moved quickly to collaborate with other fisheries scientists. Not surprisingly, the introduction of science-based policies began to show results within two decades. Catches of salmon stabilized, then began to rise consistently, reaching 670 million pounds in 1985, from the low of around 200 million pounds in 1959. In the 1990s, landings were between 687 and 994 million pounds, making that decade truly the golden age of salmon productivity.

Despite their successes, Alaska's fisheries managers knew all the variables were not within their control, particularly with an anadromous fish that spends its adulthood beyond Alaska's territorial limits, in the open ocean. Alaska's managers joined forces with federal agencies, politicians, and diplomats to forge an international treaty with Japan in 1952 that reduced Japan's take of North American salmon on the high seas. By 1992, Japan stopped all its salmon fishing on the high seas.

Alaska's fisheries managers also had a little help from Mother Nature. In the mid-1970s there was a major change in ocean currents and temperatures. In contrast to the situation in the 1960s and early 1970s and perhaps in contrast to today, ocean conditions off Alaska's coast became more favorable to the survival and growth of young salmon, while becoming less favorable off the coasts of California, Oregon, and Washington. Because of these more favorable conditions and the efforts of fisheries managers, many Alaskan salmon runs during the 1980s and 1990s approached and exceeded all previous records. Salmon prices, especially for sockeye and Chinook, reached record levels during the same period. Life was good within the Alaskan salmon industry. But, despite Alaska's best efforts and the ocean's goodwill, clouds were on the horizon.

PRINCE WILLIAM SOUND and the Orca Cannery Museum were well behind us on August 8. For two days the *Clipper Odyssey* had been making its way out along the Alaska Peninsula, arriving at Chignik in the afternoon. The most striking feature of the shoreline was the fish-processing plant. Gulls and kittiwakes flocked around the buildings. Within them, cod, halibut, black cod, and salmon are frozen, packaged, and shipped out to markets around the world. Fifteen million pounds of salmon alone are shipped each year. A jet delivers thirty thousand pounds of fresh local fish to Japan each week.

I walked through the small town to a small stream nearby to fish. It was filled with pink salmon heading upstream to spawn. Every wave of the clear, green bay that broke in the river mouth seemed to carry another wave of migrating salmon. They showed no interest in my artificial flies, although I did fool a couple of large Dolly Varden chars that were following the salmon for a meal of their eggs. Soon the incoming tide chased me away. As I walked back to catch the last Zodiac to the ship, I wondered about the day's experiences and the contradictions I saw. The salmon seemed so abundant, yet the small town of eighty year-round residents, which swelled to one thousand at the peak of the processing season, was clearly facing economic hardship. Chignik, like so many small fishing towns in Alaska, had a company store. But in this one the shelves were almost bare. The new owner of the processing plant and the store had decided to close it down. Residents were deeply concerned about this loss and the possibility of others to follow as the economic dominoes began to fall. Certainly, this wasn't a reflection of any lack of salmon. Most salmon runs have continued to be strong in Alaska. In 2000–2001, landings of Alaska salmon averaged 738 million pounds. The difference is that they were worth barely a quarter to a third of the value that smaller landings brought in the period 1988–1992. Imagine the distress of fishermen, whose costs for boat maintenance, fuel, and salaries increased over the same period. Processing plants were hit hard as well, and the company stores began to close. What happened?

When Alaska's fisheries managers set out to rebuild salmon stocks, they never imagined that farm-raised salmon would sweep world markets so quickly. The economics of the highly efficient and controlled process of salmon farming and distribution quickly put fishing for wild salmon at a critical disadvantage. In 1981, only 26 million pounds of farmed salmon were raised around the globe. By 2001, production reached 2.5 billion pounds! Norway and Chile were the largest producers. Alaska wild-salmon landings went from constituting the majority of the world's salmon production to constituting less than 25 percent in two decades. Coho salmon, which fetched an average price in Alaska of $1.74 per pound in 1988, brought only 44 cents per pound in 2001. For the captains of the moored fishing boats in Cordova, it cost less to stay at the dock than to fish for salmon. Not surprisingly, salmon farming is illegal in Alaska.

THE INTERACTIONS AMONG the scholars, passengers, and Alaska Natives in Alaska were a world apart from the interactions that Harriman and his scholars experienced. The 2001 version had not one but two Alaska Native scholars, both women, and it included many Alaska residents as well. These two Native scholars, the expedition's anthropologists, and many of the Alaska Natives and even Russian Natives we met made clear how important subsistence hunting and fishing are in the region. Now subsistence issues have led to the return of much salmon management to federal control.

What is subsistence fishing? Roughly, it means the catching of fish for personal and cultural uses but not primarily for sale or for recreation. Subsistence fishing has a long history in Alaska. For Alaska Natives, subsistence fishing is an integral part of their culture and way of life; it is a connection to the land, rivers, and the sea. Should that give them a special right to subsistence fishing or at least give them priority? It's a controversial question and much too complex to discuss in detail here, but it affects decisions about salmon; the current troubles have arisen because of differences between a federal law and Alaska's constitution.

To make a long and complicated story short—a story that involves frontier attitudes, urban-rural differences, local versus outside control of resources, states' rights, diverse groups all wanting to preserve their rights to fish, and differing views about cultural and ethnic issues—Alaska's constitution guarantees equal access to Alaska's resources to all the state's residents. A federal law, however, gives priority to rural subsistence users (mostly Natives) in Alaska and thus potentially restricts urban residents (mostly non-Natives) from such access. The federal law also requires that Alaska law be consistent with it. Attempts to amend Alaska's constitution have failed in the legislature, and in the 1990s the federal land management agencies began a program to assume management of subsistence uses on federal lands and navigable waters (salmon rivers) in Alaska. Ironically, Alaska's long political journey has come full circle. Salmon politics, which led to state control over salmon with statehood in 1959, led to a reversion to federal control in 1999, although this time around there is cooperation between federal and state managers.

What will happen next? The external forces of fifty years ago—cannery owners in Seattle and Portland, who dominated the Alaskan salmon fishery in the years before statehood—have been replaced by new challenges from outside. Today a global market is dominated by salmon farmed in Chile, Norway, and elsewhere. Moreover, the ocean climate that shifted in Alaska's favor in the 1970s seems to be shifting back to earlier conditions more favorable to southern regions. The future is hard to know because so many unforeseeable factors can affect it.

It is interesting to speculate what the 1899 Harriman scholars would have thought of Alaska in 2001. The debates between conservationists and developers in 1899 seem familiar to today's readers. Grinnell's writings about the potential ruination of Alaska's salmon resource are not very different from commentaries addressing a host of environmental issues in today's magazines and newspapers. But Grinnell, who understood the issue of local versus outside control of resources, could have had no idea of the changes technology would bring. Muir could not have known how the military influx to Alaska in the 1940s and 1950s and the discovery of oil on Alaska's North Slope in 1968 would change the economics, lifestyles, and, above all, the size of Alaska's population. Human-caused climate warming was not even a concept in 1899, much less a measurable phenomenon. None of the 1899 scholars could have imagined how politically intense the issue of Alaska Natives' subsistence fishing rights would become. And none could have imagined that farmed salmon would so depress salmon prices that fishermen would be hard-pressed to cover their expenses even at a time of record-breaking catches. I have as little chance of predicting the future with any accuracy. Yet some things do seem fairly clear.

First, if Alaska maintains its commitment to scientific management, abundant wild salmon will remain in Alaska's oceans and streams. The abundance of salmon will fluctuate with climate change, and the climate will continue to change, but the future of Alaska salmon is assured—assuming that high-quality salmon habitats exist in the future. Much will depend on how vigorously Alaskans choose to protect those habitats.

Second, as long as there are salmon, a consumable resource, and people who want to consume that resource for a variety of reasons, there will be political issues and conflicts. Even if commercial fishing for salmon were to end in Alaska, tourists would continue to come to see salmon and the bears and other wildlife that depend on them. The future of recreational fishing is also hard to predict, but it seems likely to be important for at least several more decades. Native subsistence fishing is even more likely to remain an important part of the salmon fishery.

Third, national and global economic and political considerations will be ever more important in Alaska's future. The production of salmon farms in Chile, Norway, and other parts of the world has depressed the prices of Alaska's wild salmon. Events in faraway parts of the world influence Alaska's oil and timber prices. Environmental-protection concerns that have arisen mainly outside of Alaska have led to national legislation that affects fishing, oil exploration and production, and forestry within Alaska.

Perhaps more than those of any other state in the Union, Alaska's economic resources—timber, fishing, oil, tourism, and federal monies—are subject to a wide variety of factors outside its boundaries, and it is hard to imagine that changing.

Finally, I predict that Alaska will remain a global treasure, a place of matchless scenery, wildlife, and people. The 1899 Harriman Expedition helped to bring knowledge of this earthly paradise to other Americans at the beginning of the twentieth century, just as the 2001 Harriman Expedition Retraced has brought a refreshed understanding of Alaska to the rest of the United States at the beginning of the twenty-first century. I hope that knowledge will work to benefit Alaska, the nation, and the world.

Risk and Reward—
Prince William Sound

30 July 2001

Our call on Cordova and the neighboring village of Orca marked the easternmost boundary of our sail into one of the earth's special places, what John Burroughs described as a "feast of beauty and sublimity that stands out in the memory as unforgettable." Burroughs's rich prose aside, many people who intimately know Prince William Sound feel passionately about this place, where beauty and grandeur are gateways to the larger story. At first the magnificence of this landscape commands all your attention, its massiveness deceiving you into thinking that this world is static, never changing. Gradually the human imprint comes into focus and the story moves faster—Prince William Sound's rich and complex history is all about change and the people who are swept along in the process.

At this point in 1899, expedition members were both celebrating "beauty and sublimity" and shocked by the destitute condition of defeated gold miners straggling out of the Copper River region. The members visited Orca twice, the second time out of necessity. The *George W. Elder*, while sailing in Port Wells, struck ice and sheared off a propeller blade. This accident, as Burroughs explained, "had the effect of making our craft limp a little." The ship made its way back to Orca harbor and its soft bottom. When the tide dropped, the ship dropped with it; as it reached the soft bottom and listed to one side the propeller was exposed for replacement. While waiting for repairs and the rising tide, the expedition members spent time with the miners, listening to their harrowing stories. The miners lingered on Orca's beach with just the clothes they wore, awaiting the charity of any arriving steamer that might take them home. Hasty decisions driven by the prospect of quick money had proved fatal for many and ill-conceived at best for the survivors.

Leaving Orca to make our way deeper into Prince William Sound, Harriman Retraced's participants simultaneously celebrated the magnificence that surrounded us and grappled with questions about the future of the salmon fishery. The image of the old Orca Cannery reborn as a comfortable lodge for adventure travelers pushed our understanding of how dramatically circumstances can change.

In another leap, our focus shifted quickly to crude oil as we moved through Orca Bay on course for Valdez Arm and the Trans Alaska Pipeline Terminal. In Cordova, a delegation of Alaskans joined us for the sail to Valdez. They came to discuss the complicated and deep connections between oil and Alaska's contemporary economy, society, and environment. The perspectives they brought onboard were as diverse as the organizations they represented: the Alaska Federation of Natives, the Alaska Science and Technology Foundation, the Exxon Valdez Oil Spill Trustee Council, the Institute of the North, the National Park Service, and the state of Alaska's Community and Economic Development Commission and Department of Natural Resources.

Since 1977, thirteen billion barrels of crude oil have flowed through the 800-mile-long Trans Alaska Pipeline, from the North Slope at Prudhoe Bay to Alaska's most northern ice-free port, Valdez. This oil, 20 percent of the annual U.S. domestic crude-oil production, is loaded onto waiting tankers for transport to processing refineries on the west coast of the United States. With oil revenues constituting about 30 percent of the Alaska economy and almost 80 percent of the state budget, few Alaskans have not been touched by the political or economic impact of the state's oil.

The Alaska Native Claims Settlement Act of 1971 allowed the pipeline to be constructed over once-disputed Native lands. As a result, clear title to approximately 10 percent of Alaska's land was transferred to Na-

tive corporations, along with approximately $1 billion. This single act continues to have a profound and sweeping impact on the role of Native communities in Alaskan society.

Five years later, in 1976, all of Alaskan society benefited from the creation of the Permanent Fund. Designed to invest the new oil-revenue monies coming to the state, the fund was "to benefit all generations of Alaskans." Less than $1 million at its inception, in 2001 the Permanent Fund had assets in excess of $25 billion and paid a dividend of $1,850 to each man, woman, and child who was an Alaska resident for at least one year. With median family income at approximately $38,000 in 2001, the dividend could represent a significant part of a family of four's income.

With so much at stake and with oil and its costs and benefits so deeply ingrained in Alaskan life, emotions run high during dis-

cussions of oil and the future of Alaska, with the topics ranging from "what happens when the oil runs out" to national security, the Middle East, and drilling in the Arctic National Wildlife Refuge. Personal incomes, vast fortunes, global politics, ideologies, and environmental quality all become entangled.

Our discussion on the way to Valdez was no exception. At its outset, we generally agreed that, in developing Alaska, economic sustainability, ecological sustainability, and social equity needed to be balanced. Soon the details emerged, and someone pointed out, "Let's have a reality check; for the last twenty years, oil has paid for *everything* in this state. Oil and

FIGURE 17. *Head of Port Wells, College Fjord, including Smith, Radcliffe, Harvard, and Yale glaciers, named by the 1899 expedition members while in Prince William Sound. Credit: Edward H. Harriman. Source: Harriman family collection.*

FIGURE 18. *The Harriman Expedition's first view of the Barry Glacier, at the entrance of the soon-to-be-discovered Harriman Fjord. John Muir's instincts were correct, and an opening was found to the glacier's right, behind Doran Point. Moments later, Harriman Fjord and Harriman Glacier were named and charted. Credit: W. B. Devereux. Source: Harriman family collection.*

gas have tremendous benefits, but they also have a cost." Quickly the room erupted into talk about those costs, benefits—and environmental degradation. Diversifying the economy may seem an obvious path, but diversifying an economy so dependent on a single resource is no easy matter. During the discussion, some claimed that diversification is stymied because Alaska functions as an "economic colony" of corporations in the Lower Forty-Eight. Others reminded the group that diversification has its cost too. Tourism, for instance, brings people and development and can mean a loss of community and wilderness. Emotions rose, positions hardened, and people stared at the floor.

Edward Harriman was in the midst of protracted economic and political controversies when his doctor warned of exhaustion and prescribed a long vacation to Alaska. As a major player in shaping the fledgling U.S. corporate system, he was a master at assessing risk and reward; his wealth and power proved it—and so did his visit to Prince William Sound. On a luxury steamship owned by his company, Harriman brought his willingness to take chances with him. On July 26, 1899, the expedition explored what they named that day College Fjord, as well as all the glaciers along its length: Radcliffe, Smith, Bryn Mawr, Vassar, Wells, Amherst, Harvard, and Yale.

That afternoon they investigated another arm of Port Wells, off to the northwest. Assuming it was a dead end, they approached Barry Glacier at what appeared to be the fjord's terminus. The U.S. Coast Survey map showed they were at the end of charted, navigable waters. When Harriman and his colleagues saw what appeared to be an opening to the west, he instructed Captain Peter Doran to take the ship through it and into uncharted waters. Doran hesitated. Pilot Omar Humphrey objected; he could not be responsible for the ship or its passengers' safety "if we are going to take the ship into every little fishpond." Without hesitation, Harriman replied, "Go ahead, Captain; I will take the risk." Expedition members grew excited as Harriman exclaimed, "We shall discover a new Northwest Passage!" At the end of the day they had not discovered a new passage—which, by the way, the Eyak, Alutiiq, and Tlingit people who plied these waters had long known—but the expedition did explore and chart a section of coast that had not been formally documented by the Coast Survey. Of Harriman's risk taking and the naming of Harriman Fjord and Harriman Glacier, Burroughs declared, "It was one of the most exciting moments of our voyage." For Harriman, risk had again provided reward.

A hundred years later, the *Clipper Odyssey*'s charts tell a different story. Because of oil-tanker traffic, these are some of the most heavily documented waters on the Alaska coast. Unlike our fancy-free colleagues of 1899, we were required by the U.S. Coast Guard to report to the Vessel Traffic Center for approval to enter the Valdez Arm; radar surveillance there is constant, and all ships are required to have onboard a copy of the Prince William Sound Vessel Operating Manual. The *Admiralty Sailing Directions*, the bible for coastal navigation around the world, goes into great detail about Prince William Sound, including the once obscure Bligh Reef: "Bligh Reef, a long and narrow partially drying reef on a shallow ridge about 2 miles long lying 1½ miles off the W coast of Bligh Island. The area from the reef to the coast of Bligh Island is covered by the red sector of the Busby Island Light. Bligh Reef Light (60°50'02"N, 146°53'00"W, pile; red and white chequered diamond day marks) is exhibited near the SW end of the reef, and No. 6 Light-buoy (starboard hand) is moored 7 cables from the light."

Ninety years after the 1899 expedition, the vengeful side of risk thrust another mariner into a nightmare of inhuman proportions. On March 24, 1989, the tanker M/V *Exxon Valdez*, three-and-one-half times the length of the *George W. Elder*, hit Bligh Reef. Its hull tore open and spilled 260,000 barrels of oil into Prince William Sound. The 1899 expedition's triumphs were, in an ecological instant, dwarfed by an environmental and economic disaster that would forever change Prince William Sound and its people.

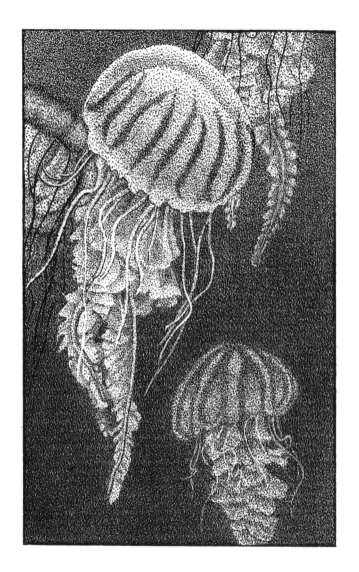

Purple Jellyfish

© PATRICIA SAVAGE

CHAPTER EIGHT

BEYOND SERENITY:

Boom and Bust in Prince William Sound

BRENDA L. NORCROSS

We entered the famous Prince William Sound . . . [with] one of the richest, most glorious mountain landscapes I ever beheld. Grandeur and beauty in a thousand forms awaited us at every turn in this bright spacious wonderland.

– *John Muir, "Notes on the Pacific Coast Glaciers," in vol. 1 of* Harriman Alaska Expedition

As the M/V *Clipper Odyssey* sails Prince William Sound, it strikes me once again: I am so lucky I go to sea for my job! I'm a fisheries oceanographer; in the wake of the *Exxon Valdez* oil spill, I spent ten years doing research on Pacific herring. Of course, I'm not always on such a large, comfortable ship. On the *Clipper Odyssey*, there's no smell of dead fish, and I am not up at all hours of the day and night sorting fish, elbow-deep in them. State-of-the-art stabilizers dampen every pitch and roll, so things don't have to be nailed down and we don't need sideboards to keep from falling out of our bunks.

Each visit, I marvel at the grandeur of this special place. This newest voyage brings the same joy, but I am also excited about sharing with my current shipmates not just the beauty of Prince William Sound but also its long, complicated story. For the first-time visitor, the sheer magnificence of the land and sea dominates the senses. But the serenity of the sound—with its three thousand miles of shoreline tucked into picturesque bays and fjords beneath the Chugach Mountains—gives no clue to the turbulence that the twentieth century brought to the region. All over Alaska, it was a century of natural disaster and human fiasco, a century of boom and bust, but perhaps nowhere were those ups and downs more pronounced than here. Certainly when Edward Harriman's expedition arrived in 1899, its members could not have foreseen the magnitude of events that would follow in the decades after the *George W. Elder*'s departure.

From the deck of the *Clipper Odyssey*, one has the strange illusion that the area is almost uninhabited. That's not true, and it's almost never been true; as much as seven thousand years ago, the Chugach people migrated from western Alaska to these rich shores. Today about seven thousand people live around the sound, most of them in Valdez and Cordova, towns named by Spanish explorers in 1790. In the entire 34,400-square-mile Valdez-Cordova Borough there are only about 10,200 people: just one person for every three square miles! No wonder the sound seems uninhabited.

Like many places on Alaska's coast, most of the towns around the sound are not even connected by roads; you can get to them only by boat or airplane. Valdez, the "big" town, is the exception; it has been connected to the world by a road since 1900. When gold fever struck Alaska in the 1890s, Valdez and, later, its new road became an important gateway to the Klondike gold fields and Alaska's interior. Thanks to the U.S. Army, Whittier has been accessible by railway since the early days of World War II, but not until the summer of 2001 did Whittier become connected by road to the outside world.

The weather in Prince William Sound often runs to extremes. It can be calm and beautiful or storming, blowing, and downright dangerous. This meteorological volatility has a parallel in Alaska's history, a story of economic extremes, of booms and busts and ups and downs. When the Harriman expedition visited Prince William Sound, several industries were already going strong: fishing, trapping, fox farming, mining, and salmon and herring processing. John Burroughs made note of the salmon canneries there, but neither he nor any of the others on the expedition included other fisheries in their commentaries. Notably absent is any mention of the Pacific herring, a fish species important to the sound's ecosystem and the people living within it. This oversight aptly reflects herring's lowly status at that time. Commercial herring fishing in the sound did not start until 1913. With marketable resources like salmon, furs, copper, and timber very much on the minds of the 1899 scientists, the noncommercial herring stocks drew little attention. Unlike the herring of the East Coast of the United States or of Europe, the Pacific herring was seldom used as food for humans in Alaska. It's not all that surprising that herring did not catch the attention of the scientists, even fisheries conservationists like George Bird Grinnell.

By the 1920s, the herring fishery had become large enough to support a scattering of pickling and fishmeal fertilizer plants around the sound. The peak catch of herring in Prince William Sound was 123 million pounds in 1938. In the decades following, herring catches declined, and fertilizer production ended in the 1950s. With the emergence of a herring egg, or roe, fishery in 1969, herring again become a commercially viable species. Herring roe has long been considered a delicacy in Japan.

Sound fisheries supplied that market until the recent downturn in the Japanese economy and the changing tastes of Japan's younger generations sent the industry into a decline again.

In the latter half of the twentieth century, communities on the sound grew and spread out. Today the natural resources from land and sea support people and their communities throughout the region, as they've done for centuries. Yet nature is not always benevolent. On March 28, 1964—Good Friday—an earthquake registering 9.2 on the Richter scale, the second-largest ever recorded on earth, smashed Prince William Sound. This literal "bust" in the earth's crust triggered tidal waves, killed at least 122 people, and caused more than $106 million in damage. The southwest end of Montague Island rose thirty-three feet above sea level. Latouche Island was lifted up by nine feet, and a forest long submerged along its shore rose to the surface. The Million Dollar Bridge across the Copper River forty-eight miles outside of Cordova, a potential road connection to the rest of the state, was destroyed and has never been reconstructed. Of the five towns on Prince William Sound, two were destroyed. Chenega Village was demolished; half of the forty-six residents perished when a ninety-foot wave swept over it. The island beneath it was raised five feet and moved fifty-two feet south. The village was not reestablished until 1983—and, then, it was moved to a different island.

A thirty-foot tidal wave hit the Valdez waterfront. But in contrast to Chenega, where the direct impact of the water caused disaster, at Valdez, calamity resulted from the town's being situated at the base of a glacier, on loose soil. The dock and other portions of the town slid into the sea. The slide generated another wave, called a seiche, which, like a wave in a bathtub, sloshes back and forth, end to end. As we discovered on the *Clipper Odyssey*, it's called Valdez Narrows for a reason. In 1964 the narrows acted like the end of the bathtub, and the wave that sloshed back along the sound has been estimated as being between 150 and 225 feet high. When it came back over Valdez, it wiped out the town and its fishing fleet. The Valdez that we visited in 2001 is, like Chenega, in a new location, four miles west of the original site.

The earthquake not only brought devastation to the people of Prince William Sound but also brought about changes that affected the fish on which they relied. The sound's famous pink salmon, like all salmon, swim upriver to spawn. Imagine how hard it was for them to make their journey after the earthquake turned streams into waterfalls. The salmon now have some of the shortest migrations of salmon anywhere; some migrate only ten to fifteen feet upstream. We do not yet understand the full impact of this abrupt environmental change on salmon spawning.

Salmon were not the only fish affected by the quake. Native elders recall that Tatitlek, on the east side of the sound, was the first area where herring spawned each spring, but they have not spawned there since the earthquake. Elders and longtime residents also remember herring spawning on the west side, but there has been no spawning there since 1973 or even earlier. One of the greatest challenges fisheries managers face is understanding whether these massive changes in spawning location are caused by events like the earthquake or the warming of the climate that occurred in the North Pacific in 1976.

Not all natural effects are as dramatic as earthquakes. Although seasonal influences on the biology of herring are subtle, they have far-reaching effects on the fish, the ecosystem, and the people of Prince William Sound. The spawning of herring is a massive ecological event, always attended by large aggregations of gulls, shorebirds, humpback whales, and Steller sea lions. Richard Nelson, my shipmate on the 2001 expedition, beautifully described the annual congregation in his 1989 book *The Island Within*:

> For several months around spawning time, the air and water teem with animals that live directly or indirectly on herring. These little fish are only six to twelve inches long, but they congregate in prodigious numbers, often a million in a single school. Not surprisingly, they are a key element in the whole marine community, and almost anyone who lives along this coast knows how important they are. . . . During the spawn, females eject their roe onto beds of kelp or other sea vegetation, and the millions of eggs naturally adhere. Males swimming amid the throngs of fish release their milt into the water to fertilize the eggs. At the height of the spawn, whole bays and stretches of coastline take on a turquoise cast for several days, and at low tides the entire shore is so layered with eggs that it turns light grey.

Perhaps it is unfortunate for the herring that their striking display allows predators, like gulls and shorebirds, to find them easily. What is easy for the birds is also easy for the herring spotter pilots, who fly around and guide the fishing boats to the herring congregations—a frighteningly effective method.

Despite the large numbers of herring in some years, spawning is not always a huge success. So much must work out for even a single herring to survive that their lives seem a game of chance. In reality, it is a numbers game. When more adult herrings spawn, more eggs will be laid. Greater numbers of eggs will survive if there are few storms, small waves, and few birds to eat them. Even if they beat the long odds, the baby herring (larvae) may suffer physical or genetic damage and die. In August through October they grow into juveniles and must avoid being eaten by other fish and birds. At the same time, they need to eat heavily themselves, to build the fat stores they must have to survive winter. Oddly, a warm winter is not what a juvenile herring needs. The warmer the water, the more active the juveniles become. Consequently, they prematurely use up the fat stores needed to survive until spring feeding begins. A young herring must survive all these threats just to reach its first birthday. Remarkably, for every one million herring eggs laid, as many as six thousand or as few as one single juvenile herring survives the first year. In other words, less than 1 percent make it, even in the best year. Even more remarkable is how Pacific herring have adapted within the Prince William Sound ecosystem. Despite the immense losses, this seemingly tiny percentage is usually enough to sustain a healthy herring population—while providing food for many other species along the way. Still, even with all the survival strategies that have evolved over thousands of years, there are no guarantees, particularly when humans and commercial fishing come into play.

In the years after the 1899 expedition, Prince William Sound experienced several economic ups and downs. During World War I, copper mines opened and flourished. Tourism, just underway, declined during the war but took a big leap when President Warren Harding visited Valdez and Cordova in 1923. During the Great Depression and World War II, tourism slumped again. In addition, the Katalla oil fields, which had supported Cordova, closed in 1933. Cordova was still the terminus of the Copper River and Northwestern Railroad, the place where copper ore that had been shipped by rail down from the Kennecott mine was then loaded on to waiting freighters. This economic bubble burst, too, with the closure of the Bonanza-Kennecott mines in 1938. Cordova then turned to herring and salmon fishing as the foundation of its economy—until uncontrolled industrialized fishing decimated the herring and salmon populations in the 1950s. As we saw from the *Clipper Odyssey*'s decks, the local economy today remains dependent on these highly variable fisheries. Unfortunately, the current situation is a bust, though luckily not as big as some in the past.

The biggest boom in Alaskan history was the discovery of massive amounts of oil in Prudhoe Bay on the North Slope. That discovery was critical to Prince William Sound, for Valdez was chosen as the terminus of the Trans Alaska Pipeline. In the mid-1970s, Valdez was transformed from a little fishing town into an oil boomtown by the construction of the Alyeska terminal facility, the station where North Slope crude oil comes out of the end of the pipeline and is loaded into tankers to be shipped out of Alaska.

Twenty-five years after the catastrophic earthquake, disaster struck again on Good Friday. On March 24, 1989, the tanker ship *Exxon Valdez* was leaving the Alyeska oil terminal in Valdez. Just after passing through Valdez Narrows, the tanker swerved out of the shipping lane to avoid an iceberg—and grounded on Bligh Reef near Tatitlek. The biggest boom ever to hit Prince William Sound—the oil pipeline—now became, ironically enough, the reason for its biggest bust. Nearly eleven million gallons spilled into the sound. Most Americans fifty or older remember where they were when President John Kennedy was shot. Since 1989, Alaskans have had their answers to a variant form of the question: "Where were you when you heard about the *Exxon Valdez*?" EVOS, short for *Exxon Valdez* Oil Spill, became a household word throughout the state.

I had only been in Alaska two short months when the *Exxon Valdez* foundered. Now my life and my career became engulfed in oil—literally. The immediate effects of the spill were devastating. As a scientist, I was dismayed that we had no solid information from before the spill to help us understand what was happening to an ecosystem now covered with crude oil. Yes, we could see that birds and otters were oiled, and killer whales were missing, but we could not see what was happening below the water's surface, and we had no way of knowing what animal and plant life had been like before the catastrophe. Lawyers would ask, "How many fish died, and how much money is each one worth?" I didn't know. I didn't even know what species of fish were there, besides salmon and herring—so how could I know how many of them were not there?

If I was frustrated, living four hundred miles away in Fairbanks, imagine the impact on the people who lived in Prince William Sound. In an instant, their way of life and livelihood were soaked in oil. The salmon and herring fisheries shut down. Even if the fish were not actually tainted with oil, they were tainted by association. No one would buy fish from Prince William Sound in 1989. The economic hardship caused by the fisheries' closing was unbelievable. Tension was rampant. In 1989, I spent my birthday stranded on a research vessel that was not allowed to dock in Cordova. We had arrived after hours, and our hull could not be inspected for oil contamination.

Bust often causes a certain kind of boom. Exxon signed a contract with a company to begin the cleanup, and its hiring of many fishermen and locals helped. But many nonlocals were brought in as well. Emotions ran high; there was a definite feeling of us versus them; which you were depended on who your employer was: the government or Exxon. In the midst of frustration and anger and hardship, a few people were making large profits from the spill; they were labeled "spillionaires." But many more people suffered from the catastrophe.

Scientists scrambled to design and conduct studies for comprehending this unprecedented environmental disaster but were often entangled in laws that permitted them to study only "injury"; as a result, the types of scientific questions that could be asked were severely limited. The state of Alaska and the U.S. government took Exxon to court. This litigation, too, complicated matters. Until there was settlement of the court case (and it took two-and-a-half years), all scientists were forbidden from publishing their results or speaking in public. Four years after the spill, in 1993, a symposium was held in Anchorage that finally provided scientists with an opportunity for open discussion.

Exxon was fined $150 million, the largest fine ever imposed for an environmental crime. They also paid $50 million each to the federal and Alaskan governments, as restitution for the injuries caused to the fish, wildlife, and lands of the spill region. In addition, there was a civil settlement, which required Exxon to pay $900 million over a ten-year period. The Exxon Valdez Oil Spill Trustee Council was established to administer these funds.

This settlement had positive outcomes. The scientific efforts (divided into research, monitoring, and restoration) received a total of $180 million. Part of this money supported hundreds of scientific studies involving both specific species and ecosystems. With the adoption of a Prince William Sound restoration plan, environmental studies were finally permitted to move past the reactionary "injury" stage of investigation. In addition, habitat protection, which meant the purchase of land to protect it from development, was allocated $392 million. Finally, $120 million was set aside to endow the Gulf of Alaska Ecosystem Monitoring and Research Program for future long-term monitoring of ecosystems.

After studying herring for many years, I was quite concerned about the future of the herring population and the fishery. A minimum number of spawning fish is needed to guarantee their continued existence in Prince William Sound. If the number of herring falls below the minimum, the commercial herring fishery is closed down, as happened from 1993 to 1996 and again from 1999 to 2004. There was a natural boom of herring juveniles in 1988, but juveniles have survived at a low rate ever since then. The oil spill occurred just weeks before herring spawning in 1989. Not surprisingly, the spill affected spawning and killed vast numbers of baby herring and their food. The survivors' resistance to disease was lowered, making them even more vulnerable. Herring came back to the sound at age four to spawn in 1992, but few of them returned the next year. Of those that did return, many died. Scientists discovered the presence of viral hemorrhagic septicemia, a disease found in fish exposed to oil. Without the necessary addition of young herring to their population, their numbers remained low, and the fisheries stayed closed. The fisheries finally reopened in 1997 and 1998, but with restricted harvest limits.

The population still wasn't stabilized. In 1999, disease again killed numerous herring. Though difficult to prove, the oil spill could have been the indirect cause of disease that year as well. In any event, the commercial herring fisheries will remain closed at least through 2004. Before the oil spill, the Prince William Sound herring industry was valued at $6 million to $11 million per year. For nine of the twelve years through 2004, the value was zero. Monetary value is not the only kind of measurement. In an ecosystem where humans are so intertwined with and dependent on their environment, the impact of the oil spill on human lives cannot be measured only in dollars and cents.

We could sense these other impacts as we walked around Cordova on a drizzly July day in 2001. In studies conducted in 1997, Arata and colleagues found that 40 to 75 percent of Cordova's commercial fishermen still had oil-spill–related symptoms of severe depression and posttraumatic stress disorder. Because the problem was created by humans, the researchers believe the people of Cordova never pulled together for mutual support as is typical in the wake of hurricanes, earthquakes, and other natural disasters. Residents still struggle with anger and outrage, lack of trust, and a sense of helplessness.

Unfortunately, the situation has gotten worse rather than better. For twelve years, more than ten thousand fishermen, Alaska Natives, business owners, and private landowners waited to receive their share of a $5 billion punitive-damage jury award levied against Exxon in 1994. Their hopes and prayers were dashed in November 2001, when the U.S. Court of Appeals in San Francisco ruled that the damage award was extreme, and the amount was reduced to about $1.2 billion.

In many ways, Alaska is a big small town. Most of us know people who were counting on the settlement for help. Banks had accepted notes against the promised settlement instead of foreclosing on boats and houses. In the wake of the 2001 court decision, people were losing everything they had. The Cordova community experienced more than one suicide following that ruling. "It is imperative," Picou and Gill wrote in 1996, "to recognize legitimate long-term human impacts resulting from . . . the *Exxon Valdez* oil spill."

I wish I could say the environment is recovering better than the people—but I can't. In fact, of the thirty critical species or resources that have been monitored, only seven, including the pink salmon, are listed as "recovered." The other twenty-three are listed as "recovery unknown," "not recovered," or "recovering." Pacific herring, the only fish species, four birds, and harbor seals are still listed as "not recovered." Our studies of juvenile herring show that many natural variables can affect the success of just this one species. Think how complicated it is, then, to understand how dozens of species are interacting with each other in an ever-shifting environment. The newly created Exxon-Mobil Corporation officially claims that no Prince William Sound species are in trouble because of the oil spill. The corporation suggests that the Exxon Valdez Oil Spill Trustee Council classifications are flawed because there are no pre-spill data for comparison. Many scientists and residents of Prince William Sound strongly disagree.

It is hard to know the direction the future will take. But we do know basic ways in which natural resources are affected: environmental conditions, pollution, and harvest. We cannot change the environmental factors brought on by nature, but we can learn to identify these factors and allow for them in our management policy. We also can control pollution. We know that accidents may happen, but there is no reason they have to be of the staggering magnitude of the *Exxon Valdez* oil spill. An accident is spilling a glass of water at the dinner table, not turning on a fire hose inside your house.

We want herring to return to support the ecosystem and to support the people. Herring not only are important to commercial fisheries but are critical to the survival of numerous marine mammals, birds, and fishes that rely on them as food. Unfortunately, no magic potions can bring about the herring's return. The policy of closing the fishery to protect spawning adult herring is the only tool we have to influence the Prince William Sound herring population. Though it does not guarantee that a certain number of juveniles will survive, it does increase the odds of survival. Although it is not locally popular, closing the herring fishery in Prince William Sound now will make for a better fishery in the future: the current population of Prince William Sound herring is at historically low levels. Again, it's a numbers game. To increase the herring population, more juveniles have to be produced. Many factors affect how many young herring will survive, and no two years will be the same. There will be good years and bad. Here we come to one of the greatest paradoxes of all: natural systems are by nature unstable, but contemporary society creates social systems that require them to remain constant.

FIGURE 19. *Columbia Bay and Heather Island, Prince William Sound.*
Credit: G. K. Gilbert. Source: Harriman family collection.

Alaskans are often said to be split into two groups: developers and tree huggers. Neither extreme is viable in today's world or in Prince William Sound. We need to preserve our resources, but at the same time we must use what we need, and sustainable management policies will help us to do so. We must also consider all factors, both natural and human. Our policy toward fisheries must acknowledge that in a complex environment a simple estimate of spawning fish is not a reliable predictor of future population size. Our education of students needs to reflect a holistic approach in which every species of fish is seen as part of the larger, interconnected ecosystem. Our ultimate goal should be a sustainable harvest of fish for human consumption that does not jeopardize other species. Extremes will not work. We have to find a balance, as precarious and ever-changing as it might be, in Prince William Sound, a place that has exemplified the astonishing changes in Alaska since the Harriman Expedition.

THE *CLIPPER ODYSSEY* makes a counterclockwise passage around Prince William Sound, a voyage of majestic beauty. We're in luck, in almost every way: we are in a region that averages two hundred inches of rain a year, and yet we find ourselves in bright sunshine, zooming around in Zodiacs at the base of glaciers. At this moment, in its midst, I can forget about the woes of this stunning place. A glacier thousands of years old makes a person feel small, insignificant. Yet I'm also exhilarated, almost giddy, because of the grandeur and my good fortune to have this time, among this beauty.

We will never know what the state of Prince William Sound might have been if the *Exxon Valdez* had not grounded on Bligh Reef. Perhaps the fisheries and the regional economy would not have failed. Perhaps some of our friends would still be with us. Fate cannot be changed, nor history reversed. But I do know that in the midst of a nightmarish catastrophe, I came to understand and love Prince William Sound.

From the Chugaches to the Chiswells

1–3 August 2001

W e anchored off Harriman Glacier the evening of August 1, after spending the afternoon exploring the lower portion of this mammoth river of ice and weathered shoreline. We had a feeling of accomplishment for having reached this spot, which had been so important to our colleagues in 1899. With so many differences between our world and theirs, this was a direct, precise connection. Just as they had, we could see the texture and colors of the glacier's ice, hear the quiet broken by its pops and cracks, and feel the waves of cold sliding off its face. Milky water seeped into our footprints, now mingled with those made by visitors from the *Elder*.

This day was an important, energizing one for our retracing. Geographically, we had so far sailed through the regions of Alaska with the largest cities and greatest numbers of people, complete with their political, economic, and social debates. Although we were only passing through, we could not help but be emotionally drawn in

and touched in one way or another. The miles traveled on the chart did not begin to explain the stream of human history we encountered as we spanned decades, centuries, millennia. Surrounded by magnificent, wild landscapes, we sometimes felt distanced from them by the force of human history. With all these experiences gathered in less than two weeks, sandwiched between daybreak starts and late-night endings, I could sense weariness among us. Being surrounded by the wilderness of Harriman Fjord could not have come at a better time.

At 10:00 P.M., with the sun on the horizon, we reluctantly weighed anchor to begin our sail out of the fjord. Toward the outlet we found traces of Edward Harriman's "people skills" as we entered Doran Strait, with Mount Doran and Doran Point to starboard—the three named after the captain of the *Elder*, who reluctantly but obediently entered these waters a century ago. No sign of Omar "Fishpond" Humphrey, the pilot who refused to go along with the scheme. The intense look on our own captain's face as the *Odyssey* entered the current and shallows between Barry Glacier and Doran Point nonetheless confirmed Humphrey's concerns. Our captain's eyes were fixed on the depth finder as he tersely reported depths to the quartermaster and pilot. The bottom rose up quickly from twenty-nine to seventeen to fifteen, then to nine fathoms (fifty-four feet). As the bottom rose, the ship's speed was reduced, settling at 3.5 knots. This speed was just fast enough to maintain control in the current but slow enough to minimize damage should the hull and the bottom abruptly meet. The conversation among the three navigators became quiet, succinct, and deliberate.

The current was easily visible as it rushed through the narrows. Ice from the face of Bar-ry Glacier was sucked into the current, forming long ribbons of slurry pulled by the accelerating water as it raced toward and eddied around Doran Point. Ribbons turned to lazy swirls when they hit the slower waters of Barry Arm and then drifted and melted away. Arctic terns exploited the food-rich mix of slower and faster waters, while families of sea otters, oblivious to the concerns on the bridge of the *Odyssey*, lazily floated along, socializing among themselves. In an instant, the scene was off our stern as the ship steered south into Port Wells and a period of transition.

With the morning twilight we entered the upper leg of Knight Island Passage, surrounded by the 5.6-million-acre Chugach National Forest. Chugach's spruce-hemlock forest surrounds much of Prince William Sound's coastline and is second in size only

FIGURE 20. *Captain Omar J. "Fishpond" Humphrey of the Pacific Steam Whaling Company with Yup'ik visitors. Credit: Edward S. Curtis. Source: Harriman family collection.*

to the Tongass within the national forest system. It is the most northern national forest, and it signaled changes to come. The towering temperate forest that had been with us since Prince Rupert would soon yield to climate and geology, giving way to the more diminutive tundra, grass, and shrubbery of the Alaska Peninsula.

As soon as we had enough daylight, the Zodiacs were in the water and scattered along the dozens of islets, coves, and bays of southern Knight and Squire islands. Unlike the sweeping, grand views of the Chugach Mountains across Prince William Sound, this place had an intimacy between land and water more reminiscent of the Maine coast. With no ocean swells to contend with, we cut the engine and floated in the intertidal zones that meandered with the shoreline and rock outcrops.

It is a marvel how the plants and animals of this ecological community survive in such an extreme environment. Here, the tide ranges between six and twelve feet, exposing many community members to fresh air and direct sun in one part of the day and the depths of saltwater in another. At low tide, nature's answers to this challenge were on full display. The brown seaweeds, such as kelp, dominated the plant life in the tidal zone. Red sponges, one of the more primitive animals we would encounter, were easy to spot clinging to rocks and boulders. A lionsmane jellyfish blithely floated by accompanied by its ecological partners, about a half-dozen small sculpin. The lionsmane's stinging tentacles allow it to capture and ingest zooplankton, or small fish, which the sculpin lure in. In return, what the jellyfish doesn't eat, it expels, to be scavenged by the sculpin. The sculpin's protective outer mucus membrane allows it

to travel free of predators within the safety of the lionsmane's otherwise poisonous tentacles. Sea stars, invertebrates that are found a little further up the evolutionary ladder, were all around in an array of colors, sizes, and shapes. True stars, sunflower stars, six-rayed stars, and red ocher stars had attached themselves to rocks and were feeding on barnacles and mollusks.

The world of marine invertebrates—sponges, crabs, sea stars, snails, and worms, to name a few—went largely unnoticed in the 1899 expedition's popular accounts; animals with spines—salmon, seals, birds, and bears—drew the attention. Ironically, when all the 1899 reports are lined up, it is clear that the invertebrates were surveyed most extensively. Throughout Alaska's tidal waters, Wesley Coe, Trevor Kincaid, and William Ritter had collected samples of a wide variety of invertebrates, distributing them on their return to universities and museums for analysis and classification. Their collaborative work resulted in four extensive volumes that cover species ranging from ribbon and segmented worms to starfishes and sea spiders. When land invertebrates are added, including a volume on insects and William Dall's study of mollusks, invertebrate taxonomy and surveys constitute over half of the 1899 expedition's final report: 2,345 pages!

During the 2001 expedition, we often wonder how the 1899 expedition members spent their time; this day, as we gazed into these tide pools, we had at least one answer. A number of them stood for a considerable time in cold, shifting waters, bent over at the waist, staring down into the ebb and flow, foraging in the sand, poking around and under rocks, looking for small, spineless creatures. They were clearly successful in their unsung efforts.

By noon the Zodiacs were back onboard the *Odyssey,* and we were bound for Montague Strait and the Gulf of Alaska. Our last landing in Prince William Sound was at the abandoned Beatson Mine at Sleepy Bay, on the northern end of Latouche Island. Here Harriman and mining engineer Walter Devereux went ashore to visit A. K. Beatson's new copper-mining operation, courtesy of another force of nature. Thousands of years ago, when Latouche was ocean bottom, deep-sea vents pressured by volcanic activity deep within the earth expelled superheated water containing dissolved minerals, including copper. When the solution hit the cold seawater, the minerals separated, forming ore deposits. The sea level then dropped, and these geological accidents became exposed as green oxidized copper outcrops, much like a copper roof that has turned green. These colorful patches of earth had attracted the knowledgeable prospector's attention. Latouche's deposits were so rich that it was second in copper-ore production only to the Kennecott mine in McCarthy. Harriman's interest in Latouche was more than casual. Alaskan minerals were attracting Gilded Age financiers like Daniel Guggenheim and J. P. Morgan, who were at the pinnacle of society back in Harriman's hometown, New York City. By 1925 the Beatson Mine was at its peak, supporting four hundred miners, bunkhouses, a general store, and a hospital. In 2001 only a few dilapidated wooden buildings and rusting hulks of machinery marked the spot.

As we clambered back into our Zodiacs, we looked across Latouche Passage to Evans Island, where the "Battle of Saw Mill Bay" had been fought because of another mineral from beneath the earth's surface. In 1989, as the Exxon oil spill migrated through the bays and islands of Knight Island Passage, the

fishermen of Cordova had struggled to "boom off" the oil moving toward the millions of three-inch salmon fingerlings being raised in the Saw Mill Bay hatchery. Unlike the tide pools and beaches surrounding us, which were ultimately covered with crude oil, the hatchery was saved.

Early on August 3, our restlessness gave way to anticipation as we looked over the charts and great distances ahead. Alaska's pressing social and economic issues would certainly not disappear, but from this point on scenes of human activity would gradually be separated by greater and greater distances, by vast stretches of ocean and uninhabited landscape. We were headed for an expansive maritime landscape and a run of coast that would take us from the Kenai Peninsula to Dutch Harbor.

On this stormy day, the Chiswell Islands first appeared as apparitions in the fog and mist that surrounded us. As their forms took shape, the cliffs and shorelines of these jagged uplifts of ocean bottom came alive with Steller sea lions, otters, and marine birds. In our Zodiacs once again, we explored just a few of the two hundred islands that make up the Chiswells. Their combined area is just thirty-three hundred acres, a tiny fraction of the Alaska Maritime National Wildlife Refuge, of which they are a part. But for a marine bird that spends most of its year on the open seas, island size is a secondary concern. The fact that these desolate outposts are so inhospitable to land predators is the reason marine bird populations thrive on their cliff faces and pinnacles. An estimated sixty-three thousand birds nest on the Chiswell Islands, about two-thirds of the population nesting along the Kenai Peninsula's six-hundred-mile coast.

Safe from predation and surrounded by fish to feed their young, birds—horned and tufted puffins, parakeet auklets, pigeon guillemots, common murres, cormorants, and black-legged kittiwakes—nest everywhere, in the jumble, on every cliff shelf and crag. As we sat in our boats, bobbing in the chop, craning our necks, scanning the cliff top with our binoculars, the radio called us back to the ship: time to move on. At that same moment a song burst out, so seemingly out of character for this spot that I questioned my hearing. There, in a patch of grass and bluebells barely three feet across, a song sparrow was foraging and singing away as if in a New England hedgerow. John Burroughs would have been pleased.

Had he been along for the next stage of our journey, the ever-seasick Burroughs would have been less pleased at the prospect of entering the waters directly ahead. The *Odyssey* rounded the Kenai Peninsula by way of the Kennedy Entrance for Homer, in Kachemak Bay. This confluence of the Shelikof Strait, Cook Inlet, and open North Pacific Ocean, where tides and gale winds are opposed, is notorious for its twenty-foot tide range, rip tides, and heavy seas. Fortunately for those of us with our own apprehensions, our passage was made under moderate conditions. In Homer, we would participate in community meetings at the Pratt Museum and in Halibut Cove. While we were on shore, the captain and crew would complete the reprovisioning necessary before beginning our voyage to Kodiak and, from there, westward out the Alaska Peninsula. On this stretch of coast, where there are few ports, ocean and volcanic forces join to dominate the landscape and shape human culture. This is also the coast to which Vitus Bering brought the Russian Empire.

Owl Mask and Short-eared Owl

CHAPTER NINE

ONE CENTURY AT A TIME:

The Alutiiq People of Kodiak Island

↣

ARON L. CROWELL

Close your eyes and visualize standing on a shore where a stream meets the sea. The tide has just begun to fall, and as it releases its hold on the river water you gaze into the clear waters of the stream at the multicolored stones in its bed, and at the bits of sea-weed and twigs that are being carried off to unknown destinations. Those bits and pieces are our Alutiiq culture as it has been pushed, shoved, jostled, and propelled from the time of our earliest ancestors to the present day.

— *Roy Madsen, Alutiiq elder, "Tides and Ties of Our Culture"*

T HE *George W. Elder* steamed south from Cook Inlet on the last day of June 1899. Gradually, the barren mountains and austere glaciers of the mainland fell astern. Ahead, just over the horizon, were the grass-cloaked hills of the Kodiak archipelago. Warmed by the Alaska Current, Kodiak Island shed its mantle of glacial ice more than ten thousand years ago. John Muir once marveled that "no green mountains and hills of any country I have seen, not even those of the Emerald Isle, can surpass these."

The principal settlement, today called Kodiak but known in the 1880s as Kadiak or Saint Paul, was a neat vision of European order against a sweeping prospect of sea, hills, and sky. John Burroughs described a quaint settlement of cabins and frame cottages "strung upon paths and grassy lanes, with its chickens and geese and children." Many of its five hundred residents, of mixed Russian, Alaska Native, and Euro-American descent, were employed in the sea otter trade. Saint Paul was one of

FIGURE 21. George W. Elder *docked at Kodiak.*
Credit: Edward S. Curtis. Source: Harriman family collection.

the oldest colonial towns in Alaska, with a blue-domed Russian Orthodox Church that signified an eighteenth-century legacy of Russian conquest and colonial rule. Russian traders had forced Native residents to hunt otters and to produce food and clothing for the Russian-American Company. Paul's Harbor (Pavlovskii Gavan), as the town was first called, was built in 1793. Central to the fur-trade empire, it served as the principal settlement of "Russian America" until 1804, when a new capital was established at New Archangel, or, as it is known today, Sitka.

By the time the United States purchased Alaska in 1867, more than eighty years of Russian occupation had indelibly altered the lives of southern Alaska's Native peoples, including the Alutiiq people (Alutiit) of the Kodiak region. The Alutiit, whose homelands also include the Alaskan mainland from Prince William Sound to the Alaska Peninsula, are closely related to more northerly Inuit (Eskimo) cultures. Nearly three-quarters of the original Alutiiq population perished under the harsh Russian labor conditions, food shortages, and epidemics. Survivors married Russian immigrants, learned the new language, accepted Orthodox baptism, and dressed in Western clothing.

At the time of the 1899 expedition, little of traditional Alutiiq culture was still evident, at least to the casual visitor. Echoing the sentiments of his time, Harriman ethnologist George Bird Grinnell wrote that the Alutiit had abandoned their "primitive ways" to be "Christianized and in a degree civilized." Indeed, the process of cultural change was continuing under the influence of Protestant missions and U.S. government schools, which banned both the Russian and Alutiiq languages.

Slightly more than a century later, the *Clipper Odyssey* approached Kodiak under glorious clear skies, and we too were greeted by the "pastoral paradise" and "grassy wilderness" that Burroughs described but also by a community far different from the one that Burroughs saw, a community transformed by the twentieth century. Visitors can still walk about the small town with its Russian-era warehouse, early cemeteries, and nineteenth-century Orthodox church, but Kodiak is no longer an isolated colonial outpost. The compact grid of houses, shops, and office buildings is a node on the global network of commerce and communication, home to six thousand people from the United States, Europe, and the Pacific Rim. Kodiak is Alaska's second largest fishing port, its harbor bristling with million-dollar salmon and crab boats and ringed by fish-processing plants, marine suppliers, and a large Coast Guard base.

The most striking contrast to 1899 is the contemporary visibility and prosperity of the island's First People. Alutiiq residents own businesses and fishing boats and have built successful cultural and political organizations. Native corporations established by the Alaska Native Claims Settlement Act of 1971 manage the interests of Alutiiq shareholders. The Alutiiq Museum, founded in 1995, is nationally recognized for the excellence of its cultural programs and archaeological research. The museum proudly presents an indigenous cultural tradition that would have been nearly invisible twenty years ago, its expression hidden by prejudice and uncertainty. The Alutiiq people of today are experiencing an era of strength and renewal after more than two centuries of loss, change, and oppression.

In *Walden,* Henry David Thoreau imagined that to look through another's eyes, even for an instant, would be miraculously to "live in all the ages of the world." Thoreau's words link identity to history, for the way each of us sees the world—and ourselves—is the legacy of previous generations, the distillation of ancestral experience. Alutiiq educator Gordon Pullar expressed a related idea in 1994: "To indigenous people, time is a circle. Those ancestors who may have died hundreds of years ago are still part of the circle. They are still members of the group of people living today." In tracing the path of five hundred generations of Alutiiq forebears, we may perhaps begin to understand this continuum of history, identity, and spirit.

More than thirteen hundred archaeological sites preserve an astounding record of Alutiiq history. One of the most dramatic discoveries came in 1984, at an old village site at the mouth of the Karluk River on Kodiak Island. Archaeologists uncovered the floor of an Alutiiq winter house that was built in the late seventeenth or early eighteenth century, several generations before Russian contact. The floor of the house was just as the occupants left it, covered with wooden artifacts, carving chips, and the bones of seals and other animals. In a wooden storage box, excavators found a wooden bird mask, placed face down among ordinary household tools.

The mask can be interpreted on the basis of Alutiiq spiritual traditions and historical information. Up until the late 1800s, Alutiiq communities held ceremonies each winter to assure an abundance of game and fish. Masked dancers portrayed bird spirits and other beings that descended from the sky worlds above or rose up from under the sea. Multiple hoops that surrounded the masks were a map of these worlds within worlds. Just as masked celebrants assumed animal form, so creatures in the wild could part their feathers or fur to reveal the "persons" who dwelt inside them. Traditional belief holds that all things in the universe have persons within—animals and plants as well as the stars, sea, sun, and moon. The entire universe is thus alive and aware. The relationship between hunter and prey, between community and cosmos, has always been regarded as one of mutual understanding and respect.

The roots of this tradition go back nearly twelve thousand years, to the arrival of Siberian migrants who settled first in the Alaskan interior and later along the shores of the Gulf of Alaska. Although coastal sites from the earliest times are rare—many were undoubtedly submerged by rising seas as the Pleistocene glaciers melted—there is evidence of an advanced maritime culture existing by 5500 BCE, evidence that includes oil lamps for burning sea mammal oils, barbed harpoons, fishhooks, and many other varieties of hunting and fishing tools. Settlements are littered with shells and the bones of seals, sea otters, small whales, sea lions, ducks, seabirds, and fish. Archaeologists have found fine bone needles that suggest the manufacture of warm, waterproof clothing made of animal skins and intestines. Occupation of the Kodiak archipelago, thirty miles offshore in one of earth's stormiest seas, confirms that these early coastal settlers had learned to construct and navigate seaworthy watercraft.

A dramatic cultural change took place about thirty-five hundred years ago. Communities became larger than they had been, and people built substantial houses of earth and wooden timbers. Objects and raw materials that must have been brought from other regions reveal increasingly distant trade connections and influences from around the North Pacific. Kodiak Island in particular appears to have been a crossroads for ideas and technologies, with contacts that extended east to the Indian cultures of Canada's Northwest Coast, west to the Aleutian Islands, and north to the Bering Sea. The art of this period was extraordinary: stone lamps depicting whales and humans, jewelry of polished coal, and bone carvings of people and spirits. Archaeological evidence suggests that about a thousand years ago Bering Sea Inuit people came to Kodiak Island, and oral traditions also tell about this migration. Linguists suspect that the arriving population spoke an early version of the Yup'ik Eskimo language that has evolved into the Alutiiq language of today. The fact that Bering Sea Yup'ik used masks much like those of Kodiak Island adds tantalizing evidence of a historical connection between the two regions.

The last centuries before Western contact were a time of social transformation. Houses grew still larger, communities expanded, and there were growing differences in wealth and social status. The classical Alutiiq society of this era included many

Exchange of greetings and gifts at Yakutat. Left to right: Rosita Worl, Tom Litwin, and Tlingit elders George Ramos Sr. and Lena Farkas. Credit: Kim Heacox.

On Cape Fox beach, Irene Shields Dundas (drummer) and Eleanor Hadden, both of the Saanya Kwaan Tlingit, begin the healing ceremony that marked the return of Tlingit objects taken in 1899. Credit: Kim Heacox.

Mist along Tracy Arm, southeastern Alaska. Credit: Kim Heacox.

Clear-cut forest near Hoonah, southeastern Alaska. Credit: Lawrence Hott.

Troller, Icy Strait, southeastern Alaska. Credit: Kim Heacox.

Admiring Margerie Glacier, Glacier Bay National Park. Credit: Kim Heacox.

Gulls on cannery rooftop and dock, Cordova, Prince William Sound. Credit: Kim Heacox.

Oil tanker loading at Valdez, the terminus of the Trans Alaska Pipeline. Credit: Kim Heacox.

Hikers on Harriman Glacier, Prince William Sound. Credit: Kim Heacox.

"Harriman Glacier," oil on paper. Credit: Kesler E. Woodward.

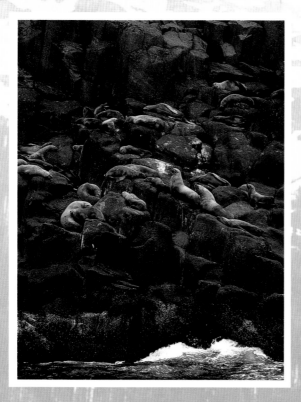

Steller sea lions (Eumetopias jubates) *on columnar basalt, Kak Island, Semidi Islands. Credit: Kim Heacox.*

Mother and cub, coastal brown bears (Ursus arctos), *Geographic Harbor, Katmai National Park. Credit: Megan J. Litwin.*

Fireweed in an abandoned village, Unga Island, Shumagin Islands. Credit: Kim Heacox.

*Thirty-million-year-old
petrified tree on the shore of
Unga Island, Shumagin Islands.
Credit: Megan J. Litwin.*

"Skimming," northern fulmar in wake of the Clipper Odyssey, *pastel. Credit: Patricia Savage.*

Old Russian church and village buildings, Dutch Harbor, Unalaska Island,
eastern Aleutians. Credit: Kim Heacox.

Northern fur seal (Californinus ursinus), *Pribilof Islands. Credit: Kim Heacox.*

Saint Paul Village, Pribilof Islands. Credit: Kim Heacox.

"Hunting Bunting," snow bunting on Saint Paul Island, pastel. Credit: Patricia Savage.

Walking on the beach, Saint Matthew Island. Credit: Kim Heacox.

*Whale and walrus bones from years of subsistence harvest, Gambell Village,
Lawrence Island. Credit: Kim Heacox.*

Robert Soolook Jr., Little Diomede Island, with drying walrus skins. Credit: Kim Heacox.

"Lorino Transportation," color pencil on paper. Credit: Kesler E. Woodward.

Chukchi dancers at Lorino Village, Chukchi Peninsula, Siberia. Credit: Kim Heacox.

Yup'ik longboat, Clipper Odyssey *in background, Lorino Village, Chukchi Peninsula, Siberia. Credit: Kim Heacox.*

Chukchi woman.
Credit: Megan J. Litwin.

Members of the Harriman Alaska Expedition Retraced and Tlingit hosts at Cape Fox. Credit: Kim Heacox.

Black-legged kittiwakes and the Clipper Odyssey, *Chignik. Credit: Kim Heacox.*

special roles: political leader, shaman, whaler, midwife, healer. Weapons, shields, and fortified village sites suggest that warfare and competition increased among villages and with other peoples of the northeastern Pacific.

On a late August evening, the *Clipper Odyssey* weighed anchor in Kodiak for a night crossing to the Alaska Peninsula. Out on Shelikof Strait, I thought of the earliest generations of Alutiiq ancestors whose journey had bridged two continents and ended at the edge of the sea. The coast was a rich environment for human life but also changeable and dangerous. Survival here demanded close knowledge of the ocean, the weather, and the complex web of marine life. Coastal people gradually elaborated tools and techniques for every circumstance and developed new forms of political organization and spirituality. The archaeology of Kodiak Island and surrounding regions provides a fascinating perspective on this endlessly inventive human response as it unfolded through ten millennia.

The next morning our vessel dropped anchor in Kukak Bay on the Alaska Peninsula. Perched on top of a steep-sided islet a seventeenth-century Alutiiq village site is visible today as a cluster of grass-covered house depressions and mounds of bone and shell. Kukak residents are said to have retreated to this refuge when threatened by enemies "from the west," most likely neighboring Unangan raiders from the Aleutian Islands. As we stared down the sheer rock walls and imagined ourselves in that distant time, I could think only of the invaders who followed the Unangan raiders across the horizon, outsiders from beyond the broad Pacific world that was already part of Alutiiq consciousness.

THE FIRST RUSSIAN SHIPS, captained by Bering and Alexei Chirikov, appeared in the summer of 1741. The consequences of their brief reconnaissance would be momentous. Before Bering's visit, the Russian fur trade had focused on acquiring luxurious Siberian sable pelts for sale to the Chinese aristocracy. A new maritime-trade era began when the Bering expedition returned with sea otter furs from the Aleutian Islands. The dense fur held the same commercial allure as sable, and Russian traders soon began to frequent the Aleutian chain. Unangan residents of the islands were forced to do the hunting, which required the ability to handle a kayak and to shoot the animals with a bow or dart. Violence broke out as Unangan communities tried to repel the Russians and to avenge their brutalities.

An Alutiiq oral tradition about one of the first Russian trading vessels to visit Kodiak Island recalls that time. Arsenti Aminak told ethnologist Heinrich Holmberg in 1851: "When we saw the ship far off, we believed it was a giant whale, and curiosity drove us to examine it more closely. We went out in baidarkas [kayaks], but soon saw that it was not a whale, but a strange monster, never seen before, which we feared and whose stench [of tar] made us sick. The people aboard it wore buttons on their clothes, we thought they were squid, but when we saw that they took fire into their mouths and blew out smoke—we knew nothing of tobacco—we could only believe that they were devils."

Well-organized Alutiiq fighters drove the first Russian traders from Kodiak Island despite their disadvantage in weaponry—wooden armor and arrows against muskets. But in 1784 Siberian merchant Grigorii Shelikhov succeeded where others had failed. Armed with muskets and small cannon, his crew attacked and slaughtered hundreds of men, women, and children who had gathered at a defensive site similar to the one in Kukak Bay. The massacre site at Partition Cove on Sitkalidik Island is remembered today as Refuge Rock or by its Alutiiq name, *Awa'uq*: "to grow numb." This defeat marked the beginning of a dark period for the Alutiit.

Shelikhov subdued Native resistance throughout the archipelago and established a brutally efficient fur-production system. He took the offspring of local chiefs as hostages to ensure the chiefs' cooperation. Within a few years Russian forts and work stations had been established from the Alaska Peninsula to Prince William Sound. In 1799, the Russian-American Company successfully consolidated its control of the entire trade. The Russian companies forced Alutiiq men to join large sea otter hunting expeditions each summer. In the first decades of the 1800s the Kodiak fleet included up to five hundred kayaks and traveled all the way to Southeast Alaska to hunt in areas where the otters were still numerous. Many hunters failed to return home, lost to accidents at sea or to Tlingit attacks. Back on Kodiak, Alutiiq women harvested food and sewed clothing for the Russians, while the elderly, young, and disabled trapped birds, foxes, and ground squirrels. Starvation stalked the villages because there was little opportunity for normal food-gathering tasks during the summer months. The weakened population suffered deadly epidemics of influenza, measles, dysentery, and smallpox, the worst being the smallpox outbreak of 1837–1838, which killed over seven hundred people on Kodiak Island. The total Alutiiq population, estimated at about nine thousand before Bering's arrival, was reduced to less than two thousand by 1840.

The social consequences were devastating. Alutiiq wealth, social vitality, and political autonomy vanished. Many survivors of the great smallpox epidemic were displaced from their home villages and moved by the Russian-American Company to consolidation settlements on Kodiak Island. Other Alutiit were shipped to far-flung Russian outposts, including Fort Ross in northern California and the Kurile Islands north of Japan.

Russian Orthodox missionaries, who arrived in 1794, pushed the Russian-American Company to ease work requirements and to increase payments to Native hunters. Many Russian men married Alutiiq women, and generations of their bicultural children learned skilled trades and received educations in Russian-American schools. Most Alutiiq people learned to speak the new language, and some elders today still use Slavonic to conduct Orthodox services.

When the United States purchased Alaska in 1867, the Alaska Commercial Company and other U.S. firms quickly moved in to take over Russian assets. They concentrated first on the sea otter trade and then on new enterprises that included salmon canning, logging, mining, fox farming, and commercial whaling. New waves of immigrants arrived in the region, including Scandinavian fishermen, who married into local communities. In an effort to acculturate the Alutiit to "American" ways, the government enforced a strict English-only policy for students in village schools. This policy continued into the mid-twentieth century. Many elders today remember being physically punished for speaking a few words of Alutiiq in the classroom. Martha Demientieff remembers her days as a student in a mission school: "It was very easy to understand the objective of school . . . it was to 'civilize' you. To civilize meant you had to speak English, you had to give up your Native ways and wear Western clothing and live in Western housing and be Christian. It was, you know, displace and replace. As a student I knew I was there to learn white man's ways."

The very name *Alutiiq* signifies some of the changes in cultural identity that resulted from two centuries of Western contact. Alutiiq people originally called themselves "Sugpiat," or "real people." The Russians called them "Aleuts." This was a convenient general term that fur traders applied to Native coastal populations from the Aleutians to Prince William Sound. Aleut was pronounced "Alutiiq" in the local language of Kodiak Island and surrounding areas, and this new name was eventually

FIGURE 22. *Native boys in required Western clothing, Metlakatla.*
Credit: Edward S. Curtis. Source: Harriman family collection.

accepted by the people themselves. Today, Native residents call themselves Aleut, Alutiiq, or Sugpiaq, depending on personal preference or local village custom. These and other variations—for example, "Russian Aleut" or "Scandinavian Aleut"—reflect the many facets of a multicultural identity.

IN 1997, elders from eighteen Alutiiq villages gathered in Kodiak for a conference to plan the exhibition *Looking Both Ways: Heritage and Identity of the Alutiiq People.* They joined staff from the Smithsonian Institution's Arctic Studies Center and the Alutiiq Museum to discuss museum collections, photographs, and oral traditions that represent the history and culture of the region. The elders sought to answer a deceptively simple question: What does it mean to be Alutiiq? During the conference and in the months that followed, the conversation came to include hundreds of Alutiiq people of all ages. There was an urgency to these discussions, a sense that learning about their cultural roots had become a critical part of younger people's survival.

Elders talked about the cultural importance of subsistence life—the harvest, sharing, and consumption of wild foods. Fish, seals, shellfish, bird eggs, and plants make up a large part of the diet in many villages today and are shared widely with urban relatives. The process of teaching children how to hunt, fish, gather carries a host of meanings and lessons. College student Shauna Lukin remembered summer chores that sometimes seemed tiresome to her as a child: netting salmon with her father, cleaning the fish, and putting up with swarms of annoying flies as she worked. Yet, she concludes, "I've come to learn that all those mornings when I had to get up early, my father was teaching me . . . how to survive the harsh Kodiak climate and how to feed my family and myself. I have come to understand that although my family gathers and preserves our subsistence food differently than our ancestors . . . we are still sustaining a main component of our Alutiiq culture."

Many traditional values, beliefs, and practices are cherished expressions of Native heritage. Children learn respect for elders and the rules of Native social grace. The Alutiiq language, now spoken by few people under the age of sixty, is beginning to reenter the classroom through bilingual-education programs. Artists and performers are revitalizing traditional arts, from dance and skin sewing to beading and basketry. Alutiiq people are proud to highlight their heritage today, even if for many it is only one aspect of busy contemporary lives that pull in varied directions. Pullar finds that being Alutiiq in today's society is a combination of inheritance and outlook, a complex mixture of culture, kinship, and genetic makeup that has been shaped and defined by history. As Pullar said in 2001, ultimately, Alutiiq people "maintain the ability to decide who they are despite outsiders' attempts to decide for them. The right to decide who they are and what they will be called is clearly the exercise of self-determination."

These thoughts highlight one of the most striking contrasts between our visit to Kodiak in 2001 and that of the 1899 expedition. Reflecting the values of their times, Grinnell and other members of the earlier voyage seemed comfortable defining Alaska's indigenous peoples in arrogant if not racist terms. At the time government policy and popular sentiment attached only negative values to Alaskan languages and cultures, and attempts by missionaries to lift Alaska Natives from a state of "low savagery" were applauded. In effect, no Alutiiq voice was heard in the Kodiak of 1899.

In 2001, our Alutiiq hosts welcomed us to a Native community that tells its own story, maps its own course, and defines its own image. Traditions once lost or repressed are now a source of strength. Kodiak elder Sven Haakanson Sr. said, at the 1997 conference, "You've got to look back and find out the past, and then you look forward." In just a few words, he shares with us the aspirations of Alutiiq communities. After one hundred centuries, you learn to take them one at a time.

Sad to Go, Crossing the Shelikof Strait

7 August 2001

Like our colleagues in 1899, we were sorry to leave Kodiak. From the moment we arrived, we understood why John Burroughs said that Kodiak was "a mingling of the domestic, the pastoral, the sylvan, with the wild and the rugged." Yet, as we discovered, its geography has placed it at a turbulent crossroads of culture and history. Even Burroughs's "world of emerald heights and verdant slopes" can be transitory and violently transformed. Change on Kodiak Island can be, and has been, swift beyond imagination. Geologic forces there have seized the landscape and reshaped it many times.

After 1899, the village of Kodiak literally rose from the ashes, only to be drowned later by giant ocean waves. Just a day after our Kodiak visit we would sail to Katmai National Park, where the largest volcanic eruption of the twentieth century occurred. According to the U.S. Geological Survey, the result for Kodiak was cataclysmic:

On the afternoon of June 6, 1912, an ominous cloud rose into the sky above Mount Katmai on the Alaska Peninsula. The cloud quickly reached an altitude of twenty miles, and within four hours, ash from a huge volcanic eruption began to fall on the village of Kodiak, one hundred miles to the southeast. . . . During the three days of the eruption, darkness and suffocating conditions caused by falling ash and sulfur dioxide gas immobilized the population of Kodiak. Sore eyes and respiratory distress were rampant, and the water became undrinkable. Radio communications were totally disrupted, and with zero visibility, ships couldn't dock. Roofs in Kodiak collapsed under the weight of more than a foot of ash, buildings were wrecked by ash avalanches that rushed down from nearby hill slopes, and other structures burned after being struck by lighting from the ash cloud.

A half-century later, the 1964 earthquake that demolished Valdez ravaged Kodiak. A resident standing on the hill above Kodiak watched thirty-foot-high earthquake-generated tsunamis break and roll across the waterfront: "It was about the third or fourth wave that really stirred things up. It hit the boat harbor and it was like a thousand guns going off as moorings and lines snapped like toothpicks. Everything moved toward town. The boats hit the stores and the stores hit each other, and they all moved up the creek away from the bay." Other parts of the island reported fifty-foot waves. It became obvious to us aboard the *Clipper Odyssey* that we were moving deeper into the infamous Ring of Fire, which encircles the North Pacific Rim. This volatile region of grinding tectonic plates has had four times as many volcanic eruptions as anywhere else on earth, with ten major eruptions occurring in the Katmai region in the past seven thousand years. I had to wonder what our small ship would do should one of the fifteen active volcanoes along Shelikof Strait decide to erupt.

For the 1899 expedition, this was all part of a past they did not know about and a future they could not see; they were fully occupied with their own zany stay at Kodiak. E. H. Harriman had many reasons for sponsoring the expedition, and shooting a bear was very high on the list. In fact, Harriman cut short the explorations of Cook Inlet when he learned at Seldovia that Kodiak was known for its bears. He immediately ordered Captain Peter Doran to take the ship to Kodiak in pursuit of his prize.

There were differing opinions among the *Elder*'s party about Harriman's quest. En route, a group of scientists diplomatically negotiated being dropped off at Kukak Bay to survey plants and birds. On reaching Kodiak, Merriam, feeling the weight of his host's previously failed bear hunts, quickly made plans for a two-day hunting trip led by a Kodiak resident and Russian bear guide. The majority of the ship's party stayed behind, but the controversy continued.

Harriman triumphantly returned to camp to announce he had gotten his bear. Much to Merriam's relief, it was "a real big genuine Kodiak Bear." The hunting party, committed to bringing Harriman's quest to closure, had carefully driven the bear toward a waiting Harriman, who, with one shot, dispatched the animal. It was later noted that Harriman's fellow hunters had enough firepower to assure that there would be no confusion as to who was the hunter and who the hunted. John Muir, Trevor Kincaid, and others were dismayed by the whole episode. Burroughs's understated account summed up the event: "Mr. Harriman had the luck to kill the long expected Kadiak bear. He . . . found her grazing in true bovine fashion. . . . She was eating grass like a cow, Mr. Harriman said. She was a large animal, but below the size of the traditional Kadiak bear."

Undeterred by the details, many in the party were pleased that Harriman achieved his goal so that the Fourth of July festivities planned for the next day could commence. The expedition's Committee on Music and Entertainment outdid itself. The *Elder* was decorated with bunting; its cannon was fired throughout the day; and the schedule of events was filled with poems and orations. A "huge" gramophone played patriotic songs from the *Elder*'s deck, including John Philip Sousa's "Stars and Stripes Forever." The party attended a baseball game on shore and joined in the traditional small-boat races

FIGURE 23. *Stepan Kandarkof,*
Russian bear hunter and guide, Kodiak.
Credit: Edward S. Curtis. Source:
Harriman family collection.

hosted by the Kodiak community. The only controversy came with Charles Keeler's surprise poetic rebuttal to William Brewer's unquestioning support of U.S. involvement in the Spanish-American War. In this polite company, some questioned Keeler's politics, others his timing. Fortunately young Carol Harriman was next on the program, reading her patriotic poem "Our Banner." A child's charm moved the afternoon forward beyond the faux pas, and any hard feelings were left for another time.

Although Harriman Retraced arrived well after the island's annual Fourth of July celebration, the community gathered again to extend an enthusiastic, day-long welcome. With a postcard sunrise over Saint Paul harbor, our Zodiacs ferried a delegation of community leaders, scientists, and students to the ship for a morning of exploring along Kodiak's northeastern coast. Once underway we immediately began to share information and

stories, ranging from data on bear biology to the hair-raising rescues undertaken by Kodiak's U.S. Coast Guard Station, the largest in Alaska. In Marmot Bay, the Zodiacs were lowered to explore The Triplets and its island rookery of over a hundred thousand nesting seabirds. Hundreds of loafing tufted and horned puffins bobbed in the intertidal waters with Steller sea lions, sea otters, and harbor seals. It was a privilege to see into the lives of these creatures, lit by the warm August sun, the air filled with the smell of saltwater and the sounds of wildlife busily making their way.

By noon we returned to the dock and a waiting crowd of well-wishers. The rest of the afternoon was spent visiting with townspeople, exploring Kodiak's many museums, and talking with marine scientists about their research and the state of Alaska's fisheries. The day ended with a conversation-filled dinner for Kodiak's leadership aboard the *Clipper*

Odyssey. It was a sad moment at 10:00 P.M. when I announced to our guests that the ship would soon be leaving for the Alaska Peninsula, by way of Kupreanof Strait. As the gangway was raised and lines cast off, we lined up along the *Odyssey*'s rails to exchange waves and shouts of goodbye with our Kodiak hosts on the dock below.

By fate or by coincidence, one of the more passionate controversies that engaged the scholars of Harriman Retraced involved bears and an early morning visit to Geographic Harbor at the end of Amalik Bay. We had crossed the Shelikof Strait during the night to Geographic Harbor on the report that the area was known for bear sightings! Entering the bay, I was immediately stuck by the expansive patchwork of stark gray earth interspersed with shrubby vegetation clinging to the mountainsides. Just over the ridge to the west were the remains of the Novarupta Volcano, which had exploded in 1912, sending seven cubic miles of superheated rocks and ash across the landscape—an infinitesimal fraction of that amount had been enough to destroy Kodiak. Almost ninety years later in this section of the Alaska Peninsula, the aftermath of Novarupta continued to dominate the land in countless shades of gray.

On pumice-littered beaches we encountered the Alaskan coastal brown bear. With the falling tide, the beach flats had become exposed and inviting to foraging bears and scavenging glaucous-winged gulls. Soon a sow and two cubs arrived in search of Nuttall's cockles, a large clam found buried in mud—mud that not too long ago was vol-

FIGURE *24. Fourth of July aboard the* Elder, *off Kodiak.*
Credit: Edward S. Curtis. Source: Harriman family collection.

canic ash raining from the sky. From our Zodiacs we watched the family follow what seemed a familiar routine. The sow in the lead, the trio pawed at the mud, stuck their noses in the scrapes, and continued along until they found their prey. The bears keyed in on squirts that the cockles made when expelling seawater, some of which shot six inches above the mud. When one of the bears zeroed in on a cockle, the digging and biting in the mud began in earnest. After a while the milk-chocolate-colored fur on their paws, legs, bellies, and faces was covered with gray caked and drying mud.

Most remarkable was the process that followed the excavation of a cockle. After the experienced sow pulled it from the mud with her front paws, she set it on the flat. With her front paws together, the cockle beneath them, she put the entire weight of her body on her paw pads, and with quick jabs of pressure, cracked the cockle open. The hard part done, using one paw to steady the clam on the slippery ground, she gnawed on it, pulling out meat piece by piece. The cubs, having not yet mastered the technique, would resort to biting the shell, with mixed results.

In addition to feeding, the sow was also teaching her young. The method of smashing clams for food is learned and passed from adults to the young through practice and the reinforcement that comes with success. After a while, the lesson got old for the cubs and distractions became more enticing. The second cub in line eventually gave up on the lesson completely, lying out flat on its belly in the mud. The cub just behind the sow more or less kept up for a time but began to fall behind as it became engrossed in a rock and all the playful opportunities it provided. By the time it had finished playing, a mud mask

spread from the tip of its nose to the base of its ears.

With Zodiacs scattered around Geographic Harbor, we, and others, spent the morning watching brown bear. Also in this small bay were two floatplanes and two private yachts, all here for the same reason: to watch bears. Two National Park Service rangers in a small skiff watching the behavior of the bear watchers signaled to some of us that the wildness of Geographic Harbor might be in question. Although this may have been just a typical day of bear watching on the bay, the buzz of Zodiacs, private yachts, and floatplanes challenged some of our party's ideas of what an Alaskan wilderness bay should be.

The now familiar television images of Yellowstone bears in search of food, with their haunches sticking out of car windows, would have been inconceivable to Muir. How did that bear behavior come about, how did they learn it? Couldn't happen here, right? The debate on the *Odyssey* started to heat up. Like the 1899 expedition, we too were just short-term visitors, albeit with no intention of shooting a bear, but we couldn't help asking ourselves certain questions. Were we—in our Zodiacs, yachts, and floatplanes—making a subtle but nonetheless important impact of a different kind? How many bear watchers had come before us, how many would come in the years to follow? What information were the bears processing as they watched us?

At midday it was time to move on. One by one, Zodiacs began clustering off the *Odyssey*'s stern. We quickly exchanged observations; those exchanges became discussions. Clear differences of opinion emerged, and hardened, as we debated the role of humans in the future of bears and wilderness. Some of us without hesitation voiced our opinion that the bears were reacting to the presence of humans and adjusting their behavior in response. Others saw no difference at all, and some who did felt that bears react all the time to events in their environments that cause them to make adjustments. What's the big deal? No one knew how a bear living in Yellowstone when it was established in 1872 as an isolated wilderness park came to have descendants prone to, and comfortable with, ransacking cars for food.

Of all the debates we had aboard our "floating university," this one hung on and may have changed some relationships. But our journey and ship required us to move on and anticipate what lay ahead. We had great distances to cover, and, after backtracking to the Kukak Bay Refuge Archeological Site, the *Clipper Odyssey* began the journey westward toward the Aleutians. With some "big" water before us and alluring place names like Semidi, Chignik, and Shumagin ahead, any hard feelings would have to be left for another time.

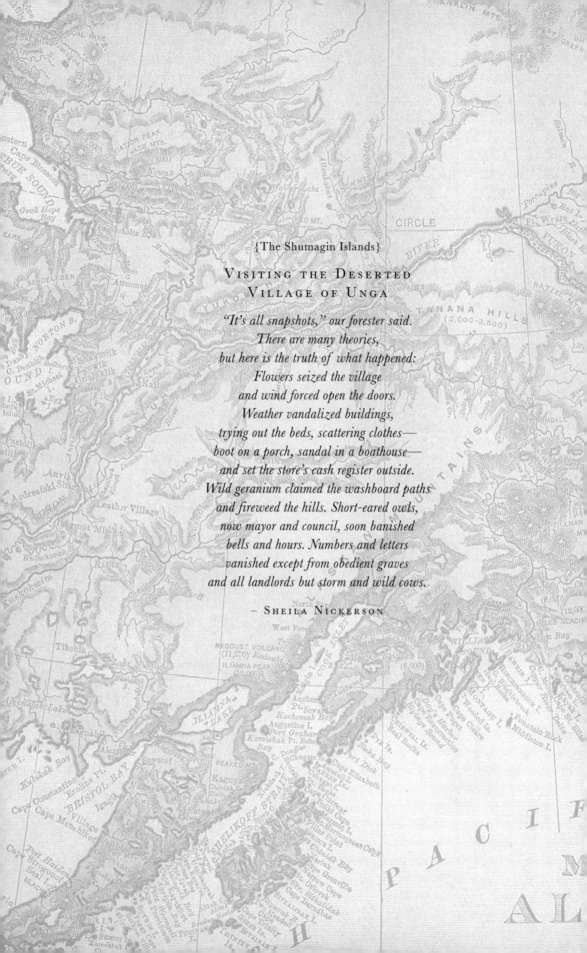

{The Shumagin Islands}

Visiting the Deserted
Village of Unga

"It's all snapshots," our forester said.
There are many theories,
but here is the truth of what happened:
Flowers seized the village
and wind forced open the doors.
Weather vandalized buildings,
trying out the beds, scattering clothes—
boot on a porch, sandal in a boathouse—
and set the store's cash register outside.
Wild geranium claimed the washboard paths
and fireweed the hills. Short-eared owls,
now mayor and council, soon banished
bells and hours. Numbers and letters
vanished except from obedient graves
and all landlords but storm and wild cows.

— Sheila Nickerson

Westward, the Alaska Peninsula off Starboard

8–9 August 2001

As we passed Chirikof Island and sailed farther into the North Pacific on the shoulders of the Alaska Current, a comment by Henry Gannett, the 1899 expedition geographer, began to make sense: "Alaska is not a country for agriculture, nor homemaking. It has paid us many times over for its purchase price, and in the future will pour much wealth into our laps, but it will never pay, as other accessions to our territory have paid, in making homes for our people. At present, few people go to Alaska to live; they go merely to stay until they have made their stake." Up to this point in our voyage, Gannett's statement seemed a historical description that did not jibe with the contemporary life we observed during our port calls.

Surely, the communities of the well-settled Southeast and Gulf regions would take exception to his characterization in 2001. Modern "homemaking" is now an established way of life for many, many people there. Towns and cities that were once iso-lated frontier outposts are today part of regional networks complete with daily flights and Express Mail. The passage of a hundred years has brought improved transportation, commerce, expanded markets, rapid communication, and closer ties with the world beyond—all the things a community needs to take hold.

But now, from the deck of the *Clipper Odyssey*, we were seeing a new kind of landscape and a new reality unfolding. The Semidi and Shumagin islands are remote places like no others we visited, and outpost towns like Chignik, Unga, and Sand Point marked our entry into a different Alaska—socially, ecologically, and economically. This was the Alaska that Gannett described a century ago. The forests that had softened the violent twists of the earth's crust were left behind, and a bold, raw landscape, beautiful in its starkness, stood revealed. In contradiction, lush grasslands appeared, covering river plains and rolling hills and flaunting brilliant,

FIGURE 25. *A restless earth: stratification, uplifting, and lava intrusions.*
Credit: Edward S. Curtis. Source: Harriman family collection.

blooming wildflowers in improbable places, like the tops of basalt columns piercing the ocean's surface. The region's cooler temperatures and persistent cloudy weather may not support the amount of photosynthesis needed to grow a cedar tree, but vibrant grasslands flourish and unhesitatingly fill the niche with emerald green.

Before us was a landscape that quietly engenders a deep, instinctive wariness. Kristine Crossen, our shipboard geologist, enthusiastically announced that we had reached a place on the planet where tropical tectonic plates that have been drifting north from the equator for 250 million years collide, with spectacular results, into the North American Plate. Throughout this leg of the voyage we were mindful of the fact that between our starting position near Chirikof and the end of

the Aleutians were dozens of volcanoes. In fact, Chirikof and the Aleutian Islands are volcanoes that rise thirty thousand feet or more from the ocean's floor. The epicenter symbols on the earthquake map for this section of coast, indicating eruptions reported since 1896, so crowd and overlap one another that it is impossible to count them all. At this pitch of activity, the numbers are secondary, and the smear of ink running along the coast is simply sobering. A report of the University of Alaska Geophysical Institute by Larry Gedney matter-of-factly stated that the Shumagin Islands' last major earthquake was in 1848, and they were long overdue for another. That report was written in 1983, and we're still waiting.

Signs of past tension in the earth's crust are all around, once you see past the thousands of seabirds that nest on them. We found Aghiyuk Island in the Semidi National Wilderness area and, later in the day, Kak Island covered with horned puffins, common murres, northern fulmars, black-legged kittiwakes, ancient murrelets, and parakeet auklets. Parasitic jaegers worked the skies, harassing food away from parent birds of other species inbound to nests perched on the shelves and in the fissures of basalt columns.

This improbable relationship between seabirds and basalt lava has its origin in ancient eruptions of lava from volcanic vents in the ocean floor. Seawater and air cooled and hardened the molten basalt into columns that Crossen described as looking like "a bundle of pencils." Sections of the columns cooled at different rates, resulting in cracking and fissures. Over geologic time, with the relentless pressures of weather and climate, pieces of the "pencils" fall off, the bundles crack and shift, and countless shelves and crannies appear. The resulting rugged nooks and crags

are the nesting sites of choice for millions of seabirds along this coast.

For humans, the story is more complicated. Our charts showed us deep into the Alaska Peninsula's maritime wilderness, a place where human communities are separated by great distances and the temperament of the North Pacific Ocean. Our visits to Chignik and Unga Island gave us a sobering look at what it takes for a community of people to attempt "homemaking" in this environment. Chignik, with its year-round population of 103, was remarkable in its contrasts. The residents we talked with said that temperatures don't get much above sixty degrees in summer or below zero in winter, when heavy winds and wild seas can isolate the village for days and weeks at a time. In the Koniag language *chignik* means "big wind."

Within this small, weathered village, the Norquest Seafood fish-processing plant and adjacent bunkhouses for seasonal workers are a hub of activity during the salmon fishing sea-

FIGURE *26. Pavlof Volcano. Credit: Edward S. Curtis. Source: Harriman family collection.*

FIGURE 27. *Geologist G. K. Gilbert viewing a basalt column. Credit: Edward S. Curtis. Source: Harriman family collection.*

son, which lasts about five months. Norquest is based in Seattle; its web site urges applicants for seasonal employment to sign on with their eyes open:

Coming to Alaska to work can be a tremendous experience, but it is not for everyone. Please read this information carefully to be sure this is the right experience for you. Working on a seafood processing line can be wet, cold, boring work. Most positions on the line require long hours of standing in one place and performing the same repetitive tasks over and over. During the peak of a season we may work fourteen or more hours per day seven days per week. We may go several weeks without a day off. By the same token, we may go for periods of time without fish to process. During these times there will be little or no work, hence little or no pay. Remember, work is

dependent on fish and there are no guarantees to anyone how much fish there will be or when it will arrive.

But the salmon do come, and the seiners arrive at the dock. Depending on the boat's size, the seiners off-load between thirty-five thousand and two hundred thousand pounds of fish. The fish are vacuumed through a large tube that runs down the length of the dock and end up in the plant's brine tanks, where they are kept fresh. From there they move onto an automated, laser-operated conveyor that separates fish by species and size. Next the eggs are harvested, and every pound the plant processes is sent to Japan by jet. The fish, after a quick detour through the automated "de-header," continue along the conveyor to the processing line, referred to as the "slime line" by the workers doing the gutting and cleaning. Observing this stage of the process, you completely understand Norquest's cautionary note to the college student or footloose adventurer in search of an Alaskan experience. More than a few romantic notions have left this building along with barrels of discarded fish entrails. At the end of the season twelve to fifteen million pounds of salmon—up to 250,000 pounds of individually handled fish per day—have gone through the plant. About thirty thousand pounds of fresh salmon are flown to Japan each week; the rest is frozen and loaded on freighters for distribution around the world.

Residents tell us the plant and its workers are segregated from the village, which is populated by Aleut, Alutiiq, Yup'ik, and non-Native peoples. Off the main gravel road, boardwalks lead to homes scattered along the meandering path. For this shipload of visitors from suburbs and cities, a home-business doughnut shop and the post office were destination points. Kathy Frost, our marine mammalogist, has spent years visiting remote communities. She reminded us, sometimes sternly, that if we wanted to understand this community and the others ahead, we needed to see it through the eyes and the values of the people here, not those in Juneau, Seattle, or Chicago—or Washington, D.C., 4,106 miles away. In Chignik, if you want medical care, you can wait for the doctors who fly in for short visits, or you can travel to Anchorage, 450 miles away. The arrivals of supplies, food, and mail are events that define a day, week, or month. Subsistence on caribou and fish is not a romantic ideal but a daily routine. The corporation that recently sold the processing plant to Norquest still runs the small grocery store. With its stake in the community sold off, the corporation plans to close the store, the

shelves of which are nearly bare. Waiting on the dock to catch the last Zodiac back to the ship, a small group of us marveled at the wild, expansive beauty of Chignik's coastline along Anchorage Bay. Looking back to shore as we headed out to the ship, we saw a small community perched on the edge of Alaska's vast maritime frontier.

By day's end on August 9, we had left the Shumagins and resumed our westerly voyage toward Unalaska and Dutch Harbor. I had anticipated the coarseness of this volcanic landscape but was surprisingly touched by the stories of fragile human endeavor we came upon. Just hours before we had left the abandoned village of Unga. During our visit, we had imagined what it must have been like when fishermen and miners labored there, children went to school, families went to church, and people shared the latest news on the steps of the post office. Except for the shell, it was all gone, people and companies having made their stake and moving on—or just moving on. Was there a point in Unga's slide toward abandonment when the grocery-store shelves were almost bare? Could the future have been changed by different decisions, or do fish stocks, remoteness, and a tempestuous ocean always have the final say? Just across a narrow strait on Popof Island is prospering Sand Point, whose inhabitants proudly point to its small airport, modern boat harbor, and school system as signs of vitality and growth. The Sand Point community expanded during the king-crab boom of the 1960s, then successfully switched to processing Tanner crab and shrimp when the king-crab fishery was depleted. Maybe this is a place along the Alaska Peninsula where homemaking will take hold.

Abandoned Building in Unga

© PATRICIA SAVAGE

CHAPTER TEN

GHOSTS OF UNGA

↷

WILLIAM CRONON

THE MOST VIVID MEMORIES we bring back from a journey are often of the places and moments we least anticipated remembering: the destinations we stumble on by accident, the encounters that were never on our original itinerary. One might think that the Harriman Expedition Retraced was at a special disadvantage in acquiring unexpected memories of this sort. After all, our ostensible purpose was to follow as closely as we could the route of the *George W. Elder* a century earlier. Unlike our illustrious predecessors, we supposedly knew just where we were going long before we departed. But despite all our planning, despite all the charts and navigational aids that enabled us to anticipate our route far better than Harriman and his companions could anticipate theirs, we still found plenty of surprises along the way.

Some of the most moving surprises in fact occurred in just those places where we strayed from the original route. When we did not gain permission to disembark at a Tlingit village site on the 1899 itinerary, we instead made an unplanned cruise up Tracy Arm, sailing past granite cliffs enshrouded in mists so delicately layered in the dawning light that we felt as if we had suddenly been transported into a landscape painting from the Sung Dynasty. A similar scene unfolded at the aptly named Surprise Bay in Kenai Fjords National Park, which we learned about almost by accident. Harriman never went anywhere near the place, but, like Tracy Arm, Surprise Bay became an indelible memory for all who witnessed it. With the moon hanging low in the west as the sun rose in the east, our Zodiacs passed through the fog bank at the narrow mouth of the bay, and we found ourselves in a magical world where mist and dew transformed everything they touched. Tidal pools became mirrors for the golden peaks on the high horizon; spruce trees sent up clouds of steam to greet the warming sun; salmonberries and devil's clubs glistened in the morning light. None of us had

FIGURE *28. Popof Island in the Shumagins.*
Credit: Edward S. Curtis. Source: Harriman family collection.

ever heard of Surprise Bay before we happened on it, but none of us will ever forget it either.

One of the most memorable of these unplanned detours took place on August 9. Little on our official itinerary suggested that anything remarkable might occur on this day. Our schedule said only that we would be anchoring off Popof Island in the Shumagin group. On July 7, 1899, the Harriman Expedition had dropped off several of its scientists here so they could collect specimens while the rest of the party headed north into the Bering Sea. But knowing this didn't tell us very much about what we should be doing at this site.

In fact, we never made it to Popof. We cruised right past the substantial fishing community at Sand Point on the northwest corner of the island, anchoring instead on the other side of Popof Strait, off Delarof Harbor on Unga Island. Members of the Harriman Expedition had not bothered to stop at Unga in 1899, even though (or perhaps because) it was much the more populous of the two islands at the time. We made a similar choice by not stopping at Sand Point. What unfolded over the next several hours was among the most profound reminders of our entire trip that the journey we were making was not just through space but through time. Wandering amid the ruins of Unga, we could glimpse the full sweep of Alaskan history in a single afternoon.

Unga having been added to our itinerary at the last moment, none of us knew much about the site when we stepped onto the rocky beach of a little cove just east of the village. Some of our more avid birders raced up the hill in hopes of glimpsing a rare species of owl that was supposed to live on the island, and only after their quest was frustrated did they begin to realize that the human landscape of this place was at least as rewarding as the ornithological one. A decaying boardwalk led up from the beach past a collapsing warehouse and a small shed containing a rusting diesel generator. From the top, most of the village lay spread out before us, dropping down toward the protected waters of Delarof Harbor, which had been invisible to us until now. Dozens of wooden buildings in varying states of disrepair stood scattered about the slopes. Whatever paint they might once have possessed had long since vanished; their clapboards were weathered to a uniform gray, their windows gaped unglazed onto the weedy jungle that surrounded them. Most were small one- or two-story structures that had served as dwellings or shops or both, but a few were more substantial. Down toward the harbor was a large meeting house with a bell tower, evidently a church or a school. It had shifted on its foundations and lost a full story by slipping weirdly sideways, so that only the roof and the tower still resisted the remorseless pull of gravity. Off to the northwest stood a large blocky building that looked rather more modern and institutional, windowless but otherwise in comparatively good shape: some kind of factory, perhaps, or maybe this was the school?

Because we knew so little about what we were seeing, most of us began groping for clues that might help us understand what had happened here. The more we wandered, the more our questions deepened, and the more mysterious Unga became. How long had this community existed before it was finally abandoned? What had these people done to support themselves? What were their lives like? And, most intriguingly, where had they gone and why had they left? What we were seeking, of course, were stories—stories that would render this place meaningful, connect its past to our present and thereby give us access to the human beings who had preceded us here. Although Unga's residents had clearly departed years before, we could still sense their presence so palpably that it was hard not to feel like uninvited guests in a ghost town that had not so long ago been a much-loved home. Unlike those on the 1899 expedition, some of whom apparently felt no compunction about dismantling the Tlingit village at Cape Fox, we walked through Unga almost as if on tiptoe, taking nothing and disturbing as little as possible as we sought to reconstruct its past.

Even the simplest questions seemed remarkably hard to answer. Many just had to do with dates. All these structures and artifacts: When had they been built or brought here? When were they abandoned? What time was this place? The answers to such queries accumulated gradually as we practiced the most basic of history's crafts: constructing a timeline. Through the window of one old house, we glimpsed a moldering but still readable textbook that had evidently served to teach at least one immigrant the basics of the English language. It looked like it might date from the

1920s, though when it might have arrived in Unga was harder to say. The diesel generator on the walk up to town undoubtedly placed us somewhere in the first half of the twentieth century. Down by the harbor, the transom of a collapsing wooden dory held up an ancient outboard motor, with gas tanks still attached. It seemed to place us in the 1940s or 1950s. So did the propane-powered stoves and refrigerators in a few of the houses, the newest of these displaying the characteristic streamlining that marked them, quaintly, as "modern." The large building on the northwest side of town did turn out to be a school. The rusting mimeograph machine visible through a basement window seemed likely to have been purchased in the years immediately following World War II.

The more clues we gathered, the more they seemed to point to a community that was no longer accumulating new things by the early 1960s. At about that time, it seemed, the residents of this village had left their homes for good. Pop-top aluminum beer cans, tossed into various corners of some buildings, clearly dated from a later period, perhaps the 1970s or 1980s. But were they the debris of a still-inhabited town or, more likely, the litter of subsequent visitors? Less ambiguously, the shiny new chain-link fences surrounding the two cemeteries on the hill north of town had dated plaques on them, declaring that they had been erected just a short while before our visit. These fences almost surely dated from long after the time that Unga's inhabitants had moved elsewhere. The boundaries protected by these fences signaled quite clearly that the village and its cherished dead were far from forgotten by those who had moved away.

The graves themselves offered the most definitive clues, though only a few of us visited them, out of respect for their hallowed ground. We were seeking historical clues, but we also meant to honor those who had worked and finally given their lives to create this place called Unga. The most poignant grave stood all by itself on a little hill overlooking the harbor. Although we had not seen trees since Kodiak Island, the Aleutians being devoid of forests, here was one of the last trees we would see before sailing north, standing as a sentinel beside this final resting place. A little white marble headstone, transported from some distant quarry, ornately carved and partly covered with lichen and moss, commemorated the early death of one Morna P. Wilson. Born on September 29, 1911, she had lived little more than five years before dying on October 10, 1916. "Rest in Peace, Our Darling Child," the stone said. Across all these years, it was still possible to feel the pain—and love—that had caused this alien piece of marble to be brought to Unga and these darkly familiar words to be inscribed on it. The stone offered nothing but the beginning and end of Morna's story, yet that was enough. She somehow gave Unga a human face, a vivid reminder of the joy and tragedy that eventually mark all human places and histories.

To the north, the first of the two cemeteries had a number of other gravestones whose inscriptions were still legible. These too spoke of the tragic deaths of young children, as well as the passing of beloved fathers and mothers. The names were Norwegian, suddenly throwing light on whole realms of history about which refrigerators and outboard motors were silent: the extraordinary journeys people had made to get here, traveling halfway round the planet to live in this remote corner of Alaska. The most recent grave dated from the 1940s, confirming all the other evidence of Unga's declining years. The second cemetery offered no names or dates, but its decaying wooden markers with their distinctive triple crosses—the lowermost crosspiece set on a diagonal to the upright—told an entirely different story. If the first cemetery was mainly Norwegian and therefore Protestant in its Christianity, this one was Orthodox. The dead who slept here were Russian and Aleut, bearing witness to a history more ancient than that of the immigrants who had come here from Scandinavia during the late nineteenth and early twentieth centuries.

That might have been the last we knew of Unga, but in mid-afternoon a small fishing vessel suddenly appeared in Delarof Harbor. Two of our leaders went out in Zodiacs to talk with the skipper, who had come to investigate the sudden appearance of a large ship in the waters off his old hometown. It turned out that the residents of Unga had not moved far away at all: many still lived just across Popof Strait in Sand Point. When we got back to the *Clipper Odyssey* late in the afternoon, I learned that one of our student scholars had brought with her a wonderful book entitled *Unga Island Girl* by Jacquelin Ruth Benson Pels. Filled with memories, documents, and photographs of Unga from the first half of the twentieth century, it began to supply the human stories we had only glimpsed during our day's exploration. When Pels's recollections are combined with an invaluable history of the Aleutian East Borough written by anthropologist Lydia Black, it becomes possible to reach back into Unga's past to see how remarkably it reflects and echoes Alaska's larger history.[§]

Archaeological finds have been relatively scanty in the Shumagins, perhaps because of the volcanic eruptions that occasionally blanket these islands with ash. The best available evidence suggests that the Shumagins have been inhabited on and off by Aleut peoples for thousands of years. One of the earliest and most intriguing archaeological finds was made by a young Frenchman, Alphonse Louis Pinart, who visited Unga Island in the autumn of 1871. An elderly man took him to the site of an abandoned native village and showed him a nearby burial cave filled with a number of Aleut ritual masks, three bodies, and a carved human figure. Pinart recorded these finds and took with him a number of the finest masks, so that, curiously, some of Unga's oldest native artifacts now reside in France, in the City Museum of Boulogne. Shortly after Pinart's visit, William Dall, who would later be among the scientists on

§ Because my direct knowledge of Unga is limited to the brief time we spent there during the Harriman Retraced Expedition, I have had to rely for background information on two important secondary works: Jacquelin Ruth Benson Pels, *Unga Island Girl* [*Ruth's Book*] (Walnut Creek, Calif.: Hardscratch Press, 1995), and the superb historical accounts in Lydia T. Black, Sarah McGowan, Jerry Jacka, Natalia Taksami, and Miranda Wright, *The History and Ethnohistory of the Aleutians East Borough*, Alaska History Series 49 (Fairbanks: Limestone Press, 1999). In this volume, Lydia T. Black's essay "Unga: The People and the Community, an Ethnohistory," pp. 113–141, has been an especially important source for this essay, and I would like to acknowledge my debt to Black's fine work.

Harriman's 1899 expedition, made a visit to the burial cave, confirming its archaeo-logical importance. And yet, two decades later, he evidently did not think it suffi-ciently interesting to take the railroad magnate for a tour.

The Shumagins entered written history with the arrival of Vitus Bering's expe-dition in 1741. In August of that year, after returning from their landfall at Kayak Island, one of Bering's ships, under the command of Sven Waxell, made its way to these islands. Aleuts in kayaks greeted the Russians, and the two groups exchanged gifts. This encounter marked the beginning of a trade relationship that would bind the Russians and Aleuts for over a century. Bering's men landed on Nagai Island, southeast of Unga, to replenish their water supplies. While they were doing so, a sick sailor, Nikita Shumagin, died and was buried on shore. Thus did the whole group of islands gain its modern name: Bering's map would be the first in European carto-graphic history to show the Shumagin Islands. Unga Island, as yet unnamed, is crudely but recognizably outlined on that map.

The next recorded Russian visit to the Shumagins did not come until Potap Zaikov made a systematic exploration of the area in the years 1776–1778. He reported that only Unga Island was inhabited. (Its being inhabited is undoubtedly the reason that Captain James Cook made landfall in Unga in 1778 during his famous voyage around the world.) Russian traders had been operating in the Aleutian chain following Bering's discoveries, but the Shumagins were not brought into the trade economy until the final decades of the eighteenth century. In 1784, Evstrat Delarov began operating from a new base located beside an exceptionally well-protected cove at the southeastern corner of Unga Island. Delarof Harbor, beside which little Morna Wilson now lies in her grave, still bears the name of this Russian sea captain and trader. The settlement he established there, initially named Greko-Delarovskoe, would be the local center of operations for the Russian-American Company until the United States finally purchased Alaska in 1867.

Through these Russian adventurers, Unga Village became tied to one of the greatest economic, cultural, and ecological transformations in all of Alaskan history. As the Revolutionary War against Great Britain was coming to a close and the new United States was being formed, Russian traders were encouraging a massive slaugh-ter of seals, sea otters, and other fur-bearing mammals along the Alaskan coast, including the Aleutians. The Russians often used brute force and coercive means, including kidnapping and severe punishments, to compel Native involvement in their fur and ivory enterprises. Aleut communities were significantly disrupted as the Rus-sians shifted them from one location to another in pursuit of sea mammals.

At Unga, local Aleuts were additionally devastated by a tsunami that swept the island on July 27, 1788, after a huge earthquake shook the entire Alaskan peninsula. Their numbers were, in part, replaced by Aleuts from Kodiak and elsewhere. New arrivals included male employees of the Russian traders, and the Native women with whom they lived and worked.

Unga soon became a base for hunts in the Shumagins and on the Alaska Peninsula. Foxes were trapped on Unga itself, while otters and sea lions were taken on the mainland. Walrus ivory was an especially prized commodity, and Unga played a key role in the walrus trade throughout the Russian period. In all these ways, the little outpost by Delarof Harbor helped link the ecosystems of coastal Alaska to the devastating demands of distant markets.

However tenuously, the Russian empire in North America eventually reached as far south as California. On our journey, we first encountered its legacy in Sitka, originally called New Archangel, which in 1804 became Russian Alaska's capital. As the eastern headquarters for Aleksandr Baranov's Russian-American Company, Sitka became the center of the fabulously profitable sea otter trade in Southeast Alaska. Sitka was linked by a series of outposts westward along the coast to Kodiak, where in 1791 Baranov had initially made his headquarters. The trade links continued to Unalaska and the Russian Far East, from which furs traveled on to Moscow and to the rich markets of China. The settlement on Unga Island became an important way station between Kodiak and Unalaska, providing a stopover for Aleut hunters as they paddled small, skin-covered boats along the coast for their Russian masters.

Along this route too would travel the Russian Orthodox priests who first introduced Christianity to this land. For us, the most visible signs of their legacy were the ornate, onion-domed churches we encountered first in Sitka, then in Kodiak, Unalaska, and finally in the Pribilof Islands. To this day, the large majority of Aleuts, many of them part Russian in ancestry, are Orthodox Christian in faith. Unga itself had an Orthodox chapel by the end of the eighteenth century, though we found no sign of it during our visit. The old cemetery on the hillside above the village, with its triple wooden crosses and neatly fenced plots, stands as the only visible reminder of the turbulent period when Russia sought to extend its empire westward across the Bering Sea.

The years of Russian rule came to an abrupt end in 1867, when the United States purchased Alaska in the aftermath of the Crimean War. Russia was willing to sell its easternmost colony partly because it needed the money but also because Alaska's marine mammal populations had declined precipitously since the fur trade's heyday. Sea otter populations in particular had plummeted in numbers nearly to extinction, which meant that Baranov's Southeast trading empire no longer looked nearly as profitable as it once had. The Pribilofs and their fabulous seal rookeries seemed to be the greatest prize Alaska could offer its new owners.

The United States passed a law in the 1870s limiting sea otter hunting to Aleut Natives or their spouses, thereby providing a powerful economic incentive for white hunters to marry Native women. This helped explain an aspect of Unga that had initially puzzled us. Although the names we encountered in our explorations of the village were mainly Scandinavian or English, the faces we saw in several of Unga's old photographs—including those of Morna Wilson's family—were of mixed racial

FIGURE 29. *Alder thickets near Sand Point, Shumagin Islands.*
Credit: Edward S. Curtis. Source: Harriman family collection.

ancestry. Intermarriage of this kind gradually reduced the number of Aleut names
and Russian names as well. By the middle of the twentieth century, a fair portion of
the town's Native inhabitants carried Norwegian or English surnames. Our maps
showed similar shifts in place names. Delarof Harbor retained its Russian name, as
did the Shumagin Islands themselves. But the village of Unga returned to a Native
name and ceased being Greko-Delarovskoe. Across Popof Strait, Sand Point became
the English name for a new fishing village on Popof Island. It would eventually grow
to surpass Unga because of its larger and deeper harbor and would draw residents
away from the old village.

The early years of U.S. rule brought much change to the Shumagins. Already
places like Unga were beginning to look toward new commodities that would eventually overshadow fur as the center of Alaska's economy. Although the Klondike
Gold Rush would not come until 1898, leaving in its wake the romantic artifacts and
stories that now draw so many tourists to Skagway, little Unga already had gold
mines by the 1880s. The most important of these Unga mines was the Apollo Consolidated. In fact, much of what we witnessed as we wandered the overgrown walkways of Unga was a product of this San Francisco–based company. Apollo
Consolidated hired an architect to lay out wooden houses for its employees and to
design the network of boardwalks that served as the village's streets. By the early

twentieth century, Unga had a school, hospital, Methodist church, dance hall, several successful stores, and regular U.S. mail service. For a time, it even had a limited telephone network. It was a bustling little community and seemed slated to remain one of the more important settlements in coastal Alaska.

Unfortunately, it was not to be. Apollo Consolidated completed its last full year of production in 1904. Although a cyanide-processing plant was eventually constructed to extract gold from the tailings of the original mines, production essentially ended with the conclusion of World War I. And so the town turned its attention to various other industries to sustain itself. Foxes were raised and hunted during the 1920s and 1930s, but this market had collapsed by the start of World War II. Island-based canneries and fishing camps operated for a time but were abandoned during the Depression, when Alaskan fisheries fell on hard times. Unga continued to rely on fishing as its economic mainstay, but doing so was becoming more difficult as profits shrank.

By 1930, Unga's population had fallen to just 150 people, half of the 300 who had lived there just a decade earlier. The downward spiral was now more or less permanent. A growing number of residents moved across the strait to Sand Point. There, better harbor facilities and greater capital investment meant larger canneries and more reliable jobs, to say nothing of better stores and government services. World War II brought a suspension of mail delivery to Unga, shutting it off from the outside world at a time when Japanese forces were occupying western portions of the Aleutian Islands. Although mail service resumed after the war, it was only for a few more years: the post office permanently closed in 1958. Because so few children were now living in the village, the school shut down shortly afterward. Any parents seeking a formal education for their offspring had no choice but to move elsewhere, usually to Sand Point. A handful of inhabitants hung on through the 1960s, but even the holdouts were gone by the end of the decade. Abandoned at last, Unga gradually weathered and collapsed to become the ghost town that greeted us so hauntingly on August 9, 2001.

Unga was never one of the most important communities in Alaska, yet that very fact gives its history an archetypal quality. Although it was a significant regional center for the Russian empire, it was far overshadowed by Sitka and the Pribilofs. U.S. traders and miners expanded its role in the closing decades of the nineteenth century, but new transportation networks and economic opportunities elsewhere sealed Unga's fate. Dramatic shifts in geopolitics—most especially the coming of World War II and the explosive growth of Anchorage—all guaranteed that Unga would remain on the margins of Alaskan history. No one writing a textbook about the state's past would bother to devote much more than a footnote to its story.

And yet, so much of Alaskan history has left traces here: the Native settlements that existed for thousands of years, the early assault of the Russians on the marine mammals of the coast, and the introduction of Orthodox Christianity to Alaska's original inhabitants. The transfer of power from Russia to the United States and the gradual discovery of gold and other minerals as commodities to be developed by corporations thousands of miles away. The rise of the fishing industry and the canneries that prepared the catch for shipment to distant markets. And, not least, the cycles of boom and bust. Too often in U.S. history, the temptation of seemingly endless resources and the dream of instant wealth have encouraged ruthless exploitation of natural systems and organisms that ultimately could not sustain the pressure they were asked to bear.

As we wandered amid the ruins of Unga, it was hard not to wonder how many other corners of this remote and starkly beautiful land might eventually suffer this same fate. In places where resources are so scarce, and economic opportunities so transient, how can people hope to build sustainable communities? Yet Unga offers another lesson as well. Although the island and this ghost town have certainly been much changed by the human history that has transpired here, the land and its creatures still survive, often displaying a surprising resilience if only they are given the protection they so obviously deserve.

The same can be said for the human communities here. Although Unga is now a ghost town, the descendants of many who built and sustained it live just across the strait on Popof Island. They have never really left and still make their homes in these islands. Like so many Alaskans before them, they are shifting with the times, accommodating themselves to the changing circumstances of the modern world even as they continue to make homes in this great land. Unga is not the end of their story—just one more chapter along the way.

PART FOUR

BERING SEA

↜

{After Dutch Harbor}

ENTERING THE BERING SEA

We never know what we have left behind.
Along with driftwood from the south—
even as far as Ketchikan—we enter
the Bering Sea, that kingdom of cold riches.
First, at the 200 fathom mark,
come humpback whales and Dall's porpoises,
then Bogoslof and other rookeries of fur and wing,
leading us up the route of bloodlust.
A scientist said: "With ecosystems, once they change,
they don't go back. They change into something else."
Under us, seals and pollock and orcas roll
and the cages for crabs gape.
Let go now of faraway things.
Turn your tag as you disembark.
Leave your name at the open gate.

—SHEILA NICKERSON

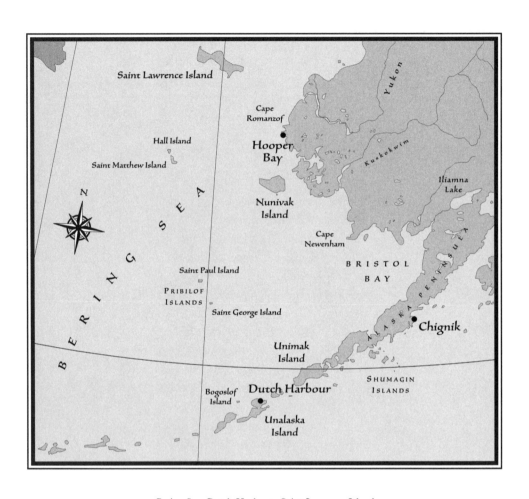

Bering Sea, Dutch Harbor to Saint Lawrence Island

Starting North

10–11 August 2001

What a difference a day makes! As I stood on the *Odyssey*'s bridge on August 10 at 6:30 A.M. in preparation for our landing at Otter Cove, the sun rose below a solid ceiling of cloud cover. Spectacularly dramatic light poured across the landscape; a beautiful summer day was about to unfold. Earlier I had reviewed the *Admiralty Sailing Directions* for Unimak Island, the first island in the Aleutian chain after the Alaska Peninsula. Its description of the Aleutians was consistent with our recent experience: "The weather is characterized by persistently overcast skies, and the whole area is very stormy, suffering almost continuous variations of wind and weather as it is traversed by one depression or another. . . . The poorest visibility in the Alaska area occurs along the Aleutian Islands; clear weather is seldom experienced. . . . In summer extensive fog occurs and is often not dissipated by the sun . . . particularly in July and August when it can reduce visibility below 2 miles for 10 to 20 days a month throughout the chain." For Otter Cove in particular, the mariner is advised, "The cove is open to ocean swells, owing to which there is always heavy surf, and north winds blow with violence over the low isthmus[;] . . . for these reasons Otter Cove is not recommended as an anchorage." In 1899, Henry Gannett declared that the area "was unrivaled for bad weather."

Not on this glorious day. From the bridge, Unimak's volcanoes—Roundtop (elevation, 8,135 feet), Isanotski Peaks (8,135 feet), Shishaldin (9,372 feet), and Pogromni (6,520 feet) off to the west—were all clearly visible. Shishaldin, its snowfields serenely awash in the pink morning light, is, despite appearances, the most active volcano in the Aleutians, last erupting in 1999. Steam and volcanic gases drifting from its cone and into the clouds are a subtle reminder. Under these clear conditions, the Aleut name for Shishaldin, *Sisquk*, required little interpretation, "mountain that points the way when I am lost."

FIGURE 30. *Lupines on sand dunes. Credit: Edward S. Curtis. Source: Harriman family collection.*

As our Zodiacs approached the beach, blue holes formed in the cloud cover, and the sun streamed through to the ocean's surface. The notorious North Pacific surf was replaced by a glassy surface that rippled only occasionally with a passing breeze. Cape Cod could not have offered a nicer, gentler day at the beach, absent the black volcanic sand. As the temperature steadily climbed, layers of polar fleece were enthusiastically stuffed into backpacks as we made our way along the beach.

The dunes that paralleled the beach and coastal plain behind them were extravagant. The foredune of black sand rose steeply thirty to forty feet from toe to top. We gained access to the back dune swale through a breach, a blowout created in the dune by the surging waves of some past, anonymous storm. Jammed in the breach was a large, chaotic pile of driftwood in all sizes, from trees to small pieces, interspersed with many types of gear or parts that a ship might lose or cast away. Our shipboard anthropologist, David Koester, saw all this material not merely as ocean-going debris but as evidence of a supply chain powered by the Alaska and Aleutian currents. For the Native peoples inhabiting this treeless environment and the settlers who followed, driftwood—of fir, spruce, hemlock, cedar, redwood—which catches the westward current as it passes the southern coastal forests, was an important source of building material and firewood. The pile had also provided a well-placed perch for a bird of prey, possibly an eagle, based on the size of the tracks in the sand below. Talons bursting into the sand, a small mammal chased, a scuffle—the tracks told the story, marked the spot where the predator finished the strike. Other prints, of an investigating fox, veered from lower down on the beach to the scene, circled the mix of smells, and continued on their way along the beach.

Standing in the breach, we did not realize it doubled as a gateway to one of the most beautiful landscapes nature could offer on such a rare Aleutian day. As we climbed the back dune, we looked back to see a beach-grass–filled swale the size of six football fields and, beyond, the *Clipper Odyssey* drifting at anchor in placid Otter Cove. Continuing to climb, looking back frequently, not wanting to miss a moment of the scene behind us, I reached the top of the dune. The view literally stopped me cold in my tracks. As far as the eye could see, a plain thick with sunlit grass lay below the bluest of skies. From the distance a river a hundred yards wide snaked through the plain toward us, the grass blurring its banks. The plain unfolded toward Shishaldin and Isanotski volcanoes to the west and toward False Pass and Ikatan Peninsula to the east. Beyond False Pass in the distance was the Bering Sea. All my adult life I have wanted to see the Bering Sea, and here, quite by surprise, it appeared off the fringe of a great grassy plain filled with tall grass, blueberries, strawberries, and rainbows of wildflowers in full bloom. In the midst of this profusion, a red fox loafed in the midday sun, shorebirds foraged along the river's bank, and the loudest sound was a ground squirrel calling to its neighbors. As time passes and many of life's experiences drift away, these images will continue to travel with me.

At 5:00 P.M. the sighting off starboard of the Scotch Cap cliffs, with Pogromni Volcano rising above them, marked another milestone for Harriman Retraced. All afternoon we had sailed west until we reached the end of Unimak Island and Unimak Pass. The pass would take the *Clipper Odyssey* from the North Pacific into the Bering Sea. For days our course had been west-southwest, but with this passage we would shortly turn north toward the Arctic Circle. Although some of the more exotic parts of the voyage still lay ahead, with well over a thousand miles to sail, this was the leg that would end in Nome, our final destination.

Almost every person onboard marked this occasion by lining up along the *Odyssey*'s rails, looking out over the Bering Sea in wonder and disbelief: a body of water renowned for its violent, life-threatening weather and waves was flat as a lake, the crystal-blue skies, puffy clouds, and sun all mirrored in its surface. Making our way to the international port of Dutch Harbor and adjacent city of Unalaska, we sailed along the north shores of Akun and Akutan islands. Every scene—of deep marine caverns scattered along twisted volcanic cliff faces, plunging waterfalls hundreds of feet high, grassy emerald-green cliff tops, snow-covered peaks—was reflected and reinterpreted by the Bering Sea's surface. With hundreds upon hundreds of floating and flying black-legged kittiwakes between the ship and shoreline, whiskered auklets scattered among them, we could not help but think that our Yakutat friends' prayer for fair weather had taken hold.

A magnificent sunset at 11:00 P.M. accompanied our sighting of Priest Rock on Cape Kalekta and Princess Head, marking the *Clipper Odyssey*'s entry into Iliuliuk Bay and Dutch Harbor. At 5:45 the next morning, we would tie up to the dock and welcome aboard a group of Unalaska residents.

Visiting some of the remote settlements along the Alaska Peninsula, one has to won-

FIGURE 31. *Tliuliuk Village, Unalaska Island near Dutch Harbor.*
Credit: Edward S. Curtis. Source: Harriman family collection.

der, "Why did they pick this spot?" For Dutch Harbor and Unalaska, the answer is obvious. A large bay and harbor are protected from the Bering Sea to the north by Amaknak Island and shielded from the North Pacific to the south by Unalaska Island. For sailors traveling between the Far East and the Arctic, at the top of the world, it is a safe harbor in the midst of a maritime wilderness where winds have been recorded at 172 miles per hour and waves regularly exceed thirty feet. For centuries, regardless of which industry has been booming or busting, Dutch Harbor has held on because it is the maritime equivalent of "Last Chance for Gas and Water!" Dutch Harbor played a strategic role in the eighteenth- and nineteenth-century otter and fur-seal industries, the massive gold rush into Nome and blue-fox farming along the Alaska Peninsula at the turn of the twentieth

century, the thriving herring fishery of the 1930s, the king-crab boom of the 1950s, and today's bottom-fish industry. The strategic location of Dutch Harbor was of enough concern to the Japanese in World War II that they mounted an air raid and bombed it. Whether the need was for coal for a northbound steamer filled with gold miners or for refrigeration repair for an offshore fish-processing factory ship, Dutch Harbor and Unalaska fulfilled it.

It was for these reasons that the *Elder* called on Dutch Harbor in 1899. Captain Peter Doran, knowing the ship would have to be self-sufficient once it began its voyage into the Bering Sea wilderness, used the call to fill the coal bunkers and top off the water barrels. The supplies Doran needed were readily available because the North American Commercial Company was using Dutch Harbor as a supply depot for its fur-seal operations throughout the Bering Sea and Aleutians. While the crew went about supplying the ship, the expedition party, including John Burroughs, toured the village. Rumors had been circulating on the ship that the voyage might be extended to include Siberia. Burroughs, suffering from seasickness and homesickness, wanted no part of it. So when, in the course of his stroll, he came upon a guesthouse, he decided to forgo the Bering Sea adventure and stay in Dutch Harbor. He returned to the ship, quietly packed his belongings, and started down the gangplank, satchel in hand, only to meet Charles Keeler and John Muir coming aboard. Muir, the curmudgeonly tease, was the last person Burroughs wanted to encounter at this moment. "Where are you going with that grip, Johnny?" asked Muir.

Burroughs was talked out of his plan; that afternoon, Burroughs wrote, "The ship was off to the Bering Sea headed for the Seal Islands, and I was aboard her, with wistful and reverted eyes."

Today commercial sealing is long gone, replaced by an international fishing industry that is at the core of Dutch Harbor and Unalaska's current prosperity. The environmental and social issues that surround this fishery are as complex as any we have yet encountered. For this reason we had asked community members to join us onboard for breakfast and discussion about the future of the Bering Sea. As the visitors were introduced, I sat between Harriman Retraced scholars Kathy Frost, marine mammalogist, and oceanographer Vera Alexander, who has studied the Bering Sea for most of her career. The diver-

FIGURE *32. Ships at Dutch Harbor. The* George W. Elder *tied to dock for reprovisioning.*
Credit: Edward S. Curtis. Source: Harriman family collection.

sity of groups represented spoke to the complexity of the issue: the mayor of Unalaska moderated the discussion and was joined by representatives from the city's Budget Office, the Pacific Seafood Processing Association, the At-Sea Processors Association, the Aleutian Native Fishermen Association, the Alaska Marine Conservation Council, the Convention and Visitors Bureau, and Alaska Public Radio.

It became clear early on that local, state, and international economics have to be an intimate part of any discussion about sustainable fisheries and marine conservation. The port of Dutch Harbor ranks first in the United States in the volume of onshore seafood processed: seven hundred million pounds a year, worth $123 million. In addition, offshore seafood processing in the Bering Sea and Aleutians has an estimated annual value of $500 million. Wild ocean stocks of pollock, cod, sole, halibut, salmon, turbot, herring, Pacific Ocean perch, and crab contribute to these values, species by species, pound by pound. Dutch Harbor seafood products make there way into the markets of Malaysia, Japan, Taiwan, Korea, China, the United Kingdom, Israel, Spain, Portugal, and Norway.

The port of Dutch Harbor accounts for over half of Alaska's commercial fish value, and approximately 90 percent of Unalaska's forty-one hundred residents are employed in some capacity by the fishing industry. In 2001, 42 percent of Unalaska's tax revenues were tied to fish, meaning that schools, highways, hospitals, airports, water and waste facilities, and the electric plant are all heavily dependent on wild populations of fish, fish that nobody owns but everyone owns. These are the same fish that co-evolved over thousands of years as the Bering Sea and Aleutian Islands developed into the marine ecosystem we see today—one population using or being used by another to survive. Watching the body language of some panelists and members of the Harriman Retraced party, I knew we were about to enter the heated controversy surrounding the dramatic population declines of the endangered Steller sea lion and overfishing in the Bering Sea. There was no avoiding the issue; pollock, the preferred prey of the Steller sea lion, also represents 85 percent of the commercial catch. "Isn't it clear," I whispered to Frost and Alexander, "that overfishing of pollock is the problem?" Simultaneously they both replied, "No, it's not."

CHAPTER ELEVEN

CROSSCURRENTS AND DEEP WATER:

Alaska's Marine Mammals

◦⌒◦

Kathryn J. Frost

A small spot in the Bering Sea about . . . forty miles west of the northern corner of Unalaska, has been in recent years the seat of more violent volcanic activity, and has undergone greater changes of form than any other part of North America. In this spot, early in May 1796, accompanied by thunder, earthquake, and steam, a volcanic island was suddenly thrown up from the depths of the sea. . . . No longer ago than the summer of 1883, the waters were once more convulsed, and shrouded in steam and fog, a companion volcano was born.

– *C. Hart Merriam, "Bogoslof, Our Newest Volcano," in vol. 2 of* Harriman Alaska Expedition

IT WAS LATE in the afternoon on August 11 when we approached the craggy spires of Bogoslof Island, two volcanic cones joined together, teeming with seabirds, sea lions, and fur seals. In this remote corner of the Bering Sea it was gray and windy, and the swells were heaving—not much of an afternoon for a boat ride. Yet almost everyone onboard the *Clipper Odyssey* loaded into the Zodiacs for the opportunity to see the fur seals and Steller sea lions hauled out on the beach. We bobbed in the swells and chop at five hundred yards offshore, as required by our permit. At this distance, we couldn't see much of anything but a tawny brown line just above the surf zone. Only the cries of seabirds, the roars of territorial bulls, and the bleats of pups floating above the wind confirmed that, indeed, those distant specks were alive.

FIGURE *33. Bogoslof volcano and island.*
Credit: Edward S. Curtis. Source: Harriman family collection.

In the days before, there had been much discussion about this isolated place and the permit required to visit it. Bogoslof Island is a rookery where sea lion and fur seal pups are born each summer. Steller sea lions are listed as an endangered species, and the National Marine Fisheries Service has created a three-mile no-entry zone around their rookeries to avoid disturbance of breeding adults and pups. The Harriman Expedition Retraced had requested permission for the *Clipper Odyssey* to enter Bogoslof's no-entry zone to land a team of scientists, as the 1899 expedition did. When the permit was issued, the terms were clear: the ship could approach no closer than one nautical mile, and our Zodiacs would have to stay five hundred yards from shore. Our naturalist's curiosity came face to face with regulatory reality.

Truth be told, Bogoslof is just a small piece of the Steller sea lion picture. Only 2 percent of the sea lions in the area of decline are from Bogoslof, although almost one in ten pups is born here. But Bogoslof, its rookery, and the permits surrounding it are tangible symbols of a much broader debate over marine mammals, fish stocks, fisheries economics, and the overall health of the Bering Sea ecosystem. Unlike volcanic islands, ecosystems are hard to see and even harder to understand. The health of an ecosystem is even more nebulous.

How different was our experience from the landing of 1899, when the original Harriman voyagers ran their wooden power launches ashore amidst the bellowing, territorial sea lion bulls to explore the island and collect specimens of nesting seabirds. John Burroughs described "great windrows of [sea lions] upon the beach." For C. Hart Merriam, the Bogoslof sea lions were a high point of the expedition: "Dozens of adults . . . were sporting like porpoises in the breakers, moving side by side in schools[,] . . . shooting completely out of the water. These small squads behaved like well-drilled soldiers, keeping abreast, breaking water simultaneously, making their flying leap in the air side by side. . . . This they did again and again, evidently finding it great sport. It was a marvelous sight and one to be long remembered. Indeed, our momentary stop at Bogoslof in the fog and rain of that July evening proved one of the most interesting and exciting events of the cruise." For that first Harriman expedition, disturbance buffers did not exist, and no permits were required. There were no laws about depleted, threatened, or endangered species, and yet even a century ago the sea mammals of Alaska were not unaffected by humans.

One of the most striking aspects of the 1899 Harriman Alaska Expedition reports is the absence of a chapter discussing marine mammals, even though the expedition spent days and weeks at sea without landfall. Burroughs and Merriam briefly note the sea lion and its apparent abundance—but their reports do not approach the in-depth discussion of subjects like forestry and salmon. Merriam, the expedition's scientific coordinator and mammal expert, was responsible for describing the mammals they encountered but was kept so busy getting others to do their reports that his own was never completed. But I wonder: Was a beleaguered chief scientist the only reason for the lack of a marine mammal report? Or, perhaps, was it partly because Alaska's marine mammals had already been touched heavily by the hand of people, and the story was no fun to tell?

The Harriman volumes contain no descriptions of the large and small whales they must have seen during the many hours at sea, but they do mention the whaling industry and the havoc wrought by the fur trade. In William Dall's essay on the discovery and exploration of Alaska he mentions the first U.S. whaler "to venture through the Bering Strait" in 1848. Word of the trip's success spread so quickly that by 1849 a seasonal fleet of 144 U.S. whalers was established north of the Strait. The pressure on these whale populations was intense. Geographer Henry Gannett evaluated the status of the marine mammal fur trade in 1899: "The natural resources of Alaska are enormous. . . . Some of these, however, have begun to suffer from the drain to which they have been subjected. The gathering of furs and skins, which has been in progress since the early Russian occupancy[,] . . . has been prosecuted so actively that the fur trade is now of comparatively little consequence. . . . The sea otter has become very rare, and the fur seals . . . are now reduced to a small fraction of their former number." M. L. Washburn of the Alaska Commercial Company talked of the remnant fur seal population and also noted, "The beautiful sea otter is . . . practically extinct."

It is easy to think of the Alaska traveled by Harriman and Merriam as a pristine wilderness, but in fact by 1899 many species had already been overhunted and were

FIGURE 34. *Whaling fleet at Port Clarence.*
Credit: Edward S. Curtis. Source: Harriman family collection.

no longer easy to see. People came to this vast new land not to see it but to use it, and use it they did. By the time Harriman transited the Bering Sea, the Steller's sea cow had been hunted to extinction—not just hard to see, but gone forever. Sea otters, once so numerous that they, along with fur seals, prompted the purchase of Alaska, were so few by 1899 that the Harriman expedition rarely saw them. Walruses were gone from the Pribilofs and greatly depleted in other areas. Bowheads were depleted by mid-century, gray whales by the 1880s. From a marine mammal's perspective, this was no untouched wilderness.

A hundred years later, is the world for marine mammals any better? Through science and a "new" environmental conscientiousness have we fixed the situation? Gray whales and walruses have recovered. Gray whales are probably as numerous as they ever were, with more than twenty thousand plying the waters between Baja California and Alaska each year. Walruses—at least when we last counted them almost twenty years ago—were thought to be at or near historically healthy population levels. Sea otters are now numerous throughout much of their former range, although recent, unexplained declines in the Aleutian Islands are causing great concern. Certainly, the cessation of overharvesting has played a significant role in their recoveries, but these species share another common link: they are all benthic feeders, getting food from the bottom of the sea. They don't find their food within the pelagic food web of the Bering Sea, the world of floating plankton and forage fish—and of large-scale commercial fisheries.

What has happened to the marine mammals that do depend on this pelagic food web? Have the fur seals, sea lions, and seals that depend on the ocean's fish recovered? Are they healthy? When we left Bogoslof Island and journeyed on to the Pribilofs, we had a rare treat, the opportunity to see the largest northern fur-seal rookeries in the world. The boulder beaches were alive with scampering pups and males jostling to protect their harems, while young males cavorted in the waves. The bleats of fur seal pups looking for their mothers and the sound of thousands of barking females filled the air above the surf. Today there is no unregulated commercial hunting of fur seals, and visits to the rookeries, even by scientists, are highly controlled. Almost eight hundred thousand fur seals come to the Pribilofs each year to breed and have their pups—up from a few hundred thousand when Harriman was here. Yet, today's population is a far cry from the three to four million that biologists estimate were present two hundred years ago, or the two million recorded as recently as the 1950s. With all the safeguards and protections, how can this be? What other factors have complicated the story—entanglement in human debris, food-altering changes in ocean conditions, competition with commercial fisheries for food? Are the factors that caused earlier declines still in play, or has a new suite of factors entered the picture? Likely there is no single cause, and thus it is even more difficult to determine what measures might reverse such declines.

The story of Steller sea lions, also once abundant in the western Gulf of Alaska and the Bering Sea, is even more confusing. Unlike many of Alaska's natural resources, Steller sea lions are a relatively new subject in Alaskan conservation politics. Because their fur is coarse and sparse, sea lions were ignored by early fur traders. Until the 1970s, sea lions were abundant in the Gulf of Alaska and the Bering Sea; more than two hundred thousand inhabited Alaska waters. Then, a startling decline began that has reduced sea lion numbers in western Alaska and the Bering Sea by more than 80 percent. Counts of pups—an index of overall abundance and population health—have dropped along the Alaska Peninsula and the Aleutian Islands, at the Pribilof Islands in the Bering Sea and the Kurile Islands of Russia. At Walrus Island in the Pribilofs, only fifty pups were born in 1991—a vivid contrast to the twenty-eight hundred pups per year that were once born there. At Bogoslof Island, the counts of pups are down almost 50 percent in just ten years. There is no straightforward explanation for this drop in numbers, as there was for the hunting-caused declines of Alaska's other marine mammals in the nineteenth century.

This dramatic decline prompted review under the federal Endangered Species Act. In 1990, Steller sea lions were listed as threatened; by 1997, their status was revised to endangered in the western portion of their range. With endangered species listing, the Steller sea lion became entangled in a debate engulfing a huge area of coastline, from eastern Prince William Sound through the entire Bering Sea. The

National Marine Fisheries Service established ten- and twenty-mile no-fishing buffer zones around many sea lion haulouts and rookeries in order to protect important supplies of sea lion food from intensive, industrialized fishing. For commercial fishers, however, once-profitable fishing grounds are now off-limits. Lawyers, governmental agencies, and congressional delegations hotly debate the scientific data and the merits of the resulting regulations.

In the midst of all the politicking, scientists search for explanations. Government agencies and universities are spending vast amounts of money—more than $40 million on 150 projects in 2001 alone. Every aspect of sea lion biology is being examined, not simply because of the decline but also because their endangered status directly influences commercial fisheries. And what might be the cause? There is no indication that disease or accumulations of contaminants in body tissues are significantly involved. In the not-so-distant past, sea lions were killed intentionally (and accidentally) in conjunction with fisheries, but this no longer seems to be a significant concern. Entanglement in ocean debris occurs but is not common. Little is known about the impacts of predation by killer whales and sharks. All these factors can affect sea lion abundance and may not be trivial effects in relation to today's small population. It is unlikely, however, that they caused the large initial decline in a sea lion population that numbered almost two hundred fifty thousand in 1960 and has since declined to fewer than fifty thousand.

Many biologists think that the problem may lie in the food supply, especially for juvenile sea lions, which are just learning to feed independently. Evidence that the size and weight of sea lions declined between the 1970s and 1980s suggests that food was somehow involved. In the late 1970s, ocean temperatures warmed by several degrees and caused dramatic changes in fish populations. Some species, such as walleye pollock, became much more abundant. Others, such as shrimp and capelin, became far less abundant. Did these population shifts make it more difficult for sea lions, especially the young, to get enough calories to thrive? Although changing ocean conditions almost certainly did affect sea lions, as well as seabirds, fur seals, and other marine mammals, it is not the whole story. A natural experiment of sorts has occurred in recent years. Ocean temperatures have cooled again, and many of the forage fishes important to sea lions are now abundant. Even so, the sea lion population continues to decline.

What else could it be? Sea lions live in a world affected not only by climate shifts, predators, and other marine mammal or seabird competitors but also by their ecological relationships with humans. Sea lions and commercial fisheries compete directly for the same fish. Commercial fisheries in the Steller sea lion range remove huge quantities of fish each year—more than two billion pounds per year of pollock alone. That is enough to feed hundreds of thousands of seals and sea lions and millions of seabirds. Although fisheries managers calculate that these yields are "sustainable" for the fisheries themselves, they cannot foresee the impact on other, ecologically related species. What is left over after the fisheries remove their harvests may not be enough to support the nonhuman members of the food web at their pre-fisheries abundance.

Over the last two hundred years, people and their fisheries have vastly altered the Bering Sea ecosystem, changing the balance of who eats who and how much. Species like Pacific ocean perch and yellow fin sole were overfished and the great whales seriously depleted. Removal of these and other species, which were significant consumers of both fish and plankton, has undoubtedly greatly altered the way creatures of the sea interact. The aftermath of such changes may be part of the unexplained, continuing declines we see. And even climate change may be mediated or exacerbated by what we humans put into the atmosphere.

As we Harriman voyagers of 2001 struggled to understand the Bering Sea on which we sailed, I was struck by shipmate Vera Alexander's comment that things don't necessarily go back to the way they were just because humans stop doing something. Changes we make may be forever. What makes the sea lion problem so hard to decipher is that the ocean they live in is constantly changing. Factors responsible for the decline more than two decades ago may not be the source of recent declines. Despite sophisticated modern technology that can measure almost everything, we cannot recapture the past.

WHEN THE *ODYSSEY* STOPPED at Saint Paul Island, I was excited to find my friend Terry Spraker waiting. The last time I'd seen Terry was when we worked in the trenches together in the aftermath of the *Exxon Valdez* oil spill in Prince William Sound. Terry is now the veterinarian on duty during the subsistence harvest of fur seals by Aleut residents of the Pribilofs. For sixteen years he has been coming to Saint Paul and watching the Bering Sea and its animals change. I was completely surprised by his urgent concern about the fur seals and the impact of commercial fisheries on their future. We talked a long time about possible causes for marine mammal declines and the political problems we face because we do not have clear-cut scientific evidence pointing to one cause or another. Terry told me a story that goes right to the heart of the problem we face in the Bering Sea.

A man and his dog were walking. The man decided to cross a lake, so he got into a boat and called his dog to swim alongside. The dog was wearing a pack, so partway across the lake the man decided to put a rock in the dog's pack to test its ability. The dog just kept swimming, so the man decided to add another rock. The dog swam a little bit slower, but the man was impressed by the dog's strength. The man added a third rock and was again pleased at the result. The dog slowed down but was still able to keep its head above water with no problem. Finally, the man concluded that the dog was so amazing, he would put one last rock in the pack. When he did, the dog sank to the bottom and drowned. Which rock killed the dog?

Whatever the cause of the declines in sea lions and fur seals, clearly we must do whatever we can to prevent further human-caused problems. We can do little about naturally occurring events like the earth's cyclical climate changes or killer-whale predation, but we can make a difference in other ways. We can protect habitat and reduce competition from commercial fisheries. Through education and enforcement, we can curtail intentional and accidental killings. We can reduce ocean dumping and debris and control emissions that exacerbate climate change.

We need to be better stewards of our environment because we just don't know which factor is the rock that will cause the next species to sink. If we don't come to respect the complexity of our ocean ecosystems, which species will be the next to sound the alarm: spotted seals, ribbon seals, bearded seals, ringed seals, walruses? When the alarm sounds, as it has for the Steller sea lion, will we rush in and spend $40 million a year in a hurried attempt to understand our mistakes and patch together a belated response?

The marine mammal problems we face today are more complex than those that were apparent when the Harriman Expedition visited Alaska. It is no longer a matter of simply stopping the commercial overexploitation of these animals or any of our other resources. Many of the problems we face today have no clear-cut causes or solutions. In an environment of uncertainty, it is critical for all of us, no matter how different our value systems or our philosophies, to work together to find solutions that extend beyond special interests.

Soon after leaving the Pribilofs, the *Clipper Odyssey* took us to the Eskimo village of Gambell on Saint Lawrence Island. We watched Eskimo men stretching a walrus hide to cover a boat. In a modern, supermarket world, Gambell hunters still go out in skin-covered boats each spring to harvest bowhead whales. Gambell children eat whale muktuk (skin) and seal meat and oil. The next day we traveled on to Little Diomede, a community of about one hundred, precariously perched on a small island in the middle of the Bering Strait. At first glance Diomede is desolate; the land is steep, there are no trees. We were greeted by the sights and smells of weathered houses, drying seal meat, seal skins stretched to dry, and walrus-hide skin boats stored on wooden racks. Yet these people are not poor. They live in the middle of a river of marine mammals flowing north and south with the seasons.

Much has changed in these two tiny communities since the Harriman Expedition voyaged across the Bering Sea, but basic elements remain the same. Four-wheelers and outboard motors have replaced the sled dogs that village residents once used, and schoolchildren learn their lessons on computers. Helicopters bring the mail, soda pop, and diapers. But the people living here are still fundamentally dependent on what the ocean provides. They clearly understand that they are part of their environment and

FIGURE 35. *A homestead at Dutch Harbor.*
Credit: Edward S. Curtis. Source: Harriman family collection.

that their actions have direct consequences on the world around them. We could learn a lot from them about seeing ourselves as part of the ecosystem we exploit.

How can it be that seals and walruses, so important to daily life in these communities, are the focus of so little scientific attention? How can we have no idea of population status for these marine mammals? The funding bodies say there are no "issues," no problems, no documented declines. How would we know? We haven't looked in more than twenty years. Things have changed dramatically for sea lions and fur seals in twenty-five years. For just ten years, we didn't look at sea otters, and we woke up to a sea otter population reduced by half. What has happened to other marine mammals in the same ocean? One of the unanticipated consequences of the sea lion decline in particular—which has affected how a multimillion-dollar fishery for pollock is conducted—is that vast monetary as well as human resources are now directed at solving the "Steller sea lion problem." The total research budget for all other marine mammal species in Alaska and, equally important, the availability of scientists to conduct that research are small compared with the resources allocated to sea lions.

Although subsistence cultures may offer important lessons, Alaska remains a place of differing value systems and a complex modern history. Many people who come here take things from the environment to sell and use in other places. They may either miss or ignore the consequences of their actions, including the impact of these removals on the larger environment. When a resource is gone, they simply move to another place to find another resource. As Gannett observed in 1899, this approach is also very much part of Alaska's historical fabric: "Alaska is not a country for agriculture, nor for homemaking. . . . At present, few people go to Alaska to live; they go merely to stay until they have made their stake."

For twenty-seven years, I've traveled Alaska's waters studying its marine mammals—ice seals and harbor seals, beluga whales and walruses—from temperate Prince William Sound to the Arctic north. During these years, I have heard the singing of bearded seals, seen beluga whales jammed in a stream mouth like salmon, experienced mystical mornings among ice floes and moments of fear when storms raged and we were too far from home in a very small boat.

I know firsthand Alaska is a magnificent place, beyond the comprehension of most people who haven't seen it. Its volcanoes and glaciers, islands and mountains, vast seas and abundant wildlife are almost beyond imagination. But Alaska is far more than beautiful scenery and abundant wildlife. It's not manicured, it's not orchestrated. It is wild and special in its wildness. It is not just another fishery to be developed or oil well to be drilled. It is not a place to be taken lightly and used up.

It is time we realize that Alaska is not simply a place to make a stake, a one-dimensional land that exists only to "pour much wealth into our laps," as Gannett predicted. It has been a home to its Native people for thousands of years and is now home to those who have come since. With due respect to Gannett, Alaska *is* a place for homemaking, but, far more important, Alaska is a home for the soul of wild America. It is a place where not every piece of land or every stretch of coast has been irrevocably touched by people in pursuit of a stake. To safeguard this place and this larger view of what Alaska represents may be the greatest gift we can give ourselves, our children, and our grandchildren—if only we have the foresight to do so.

Only on Earth!

11–13 August 2001

A fast-moving meteorological depression followed us the forty-nine miles from Unalaska out to Bogoslof Island. During our brief visit to the waters off Bogoslof, the unsettled weather and restless volcanoes foreshadowed our introduction to the "hardball" political world of the Bering Sea fishery. In hindsight, I marvel at the wonderful naiveté underlying our goal to visit Bogoslof.

The circumstances of our visit could not have been more different from those of the 1899 expedition. "Bogoslof, Our Newest Volcano," C. Hart Merriam's account of their visit to this remote island, is enough to arouse any naturalist's curiosity. In his journal Merriam describes one volcanic island thrust up from the ocean floor a hundred years earlier, at the turn of the eighteenth century, and another created in 1883; together they made a wilderness breeding ground for sea lions and fur seals and a nesting site for thousands of seabirds. With E. H. Harriman in the lead, Merriam and the landing party wandered freely along the shore exploring the raw, unstable landscape, where vegetation had not yet got a foothold. Even for an experienced explorer like Merriam, this place was different: "It seemed remarkable that birds should voluntarily take up quarters in places where hot steam and fumes were almost suffocating."

By today's standards for both science and tourism, the 1899 party's visit was disturbingly disruptive. At its approach, thick clusters of sea lions "became restless and began to show signs of alarm," Merriam wrote. As the boats came still closer, the sea lions were "now thoroughly frightened and rushed through the shallow pool in wild confusion, making the water surge and boil and throwing the spray high in the air." At the sound of ornithologist Albert Fisher's gunshots—he was collecting specimens—"millions [of murres] shot out into the air and darkened the atmosphere like a great cloud, and roar[ed] like thunder—a roar that completely drowned out the bellowing of the sea lions. . . . Many green eggs fell when the birds left too hurriedly."

At this sight and others, John Muir became increasingly critical of the expedition's heavy-handed intrusion into wilderness. Just days before, we had had our own heated debates about the impact of our own journey and the influence we had had on Geographic Harbor's coastal brown bears. Although Muir's concern and ours were the same, the dramatic shift in sensibilities that has evolved over a hundred years was undeniable: it was inconceivable that our group would fire a shot into a colony of murres or provoke panic in a sea lion haulout. This shift is obvious progress in one area of wildlife protection, but we would become aware in the days ahead of larger, more complex problems without clear solutions.

Surrounded by whitecaps, bobbing in our Zodiacs on the growing chop, we wistfully watched from five hundred meters offshore a colony of Steller sea lions stretching along Bogoslof's shore. Having worked for many months to obtain a permit from the National Marine Fisheries Services to get even this close, I knew we were not denied permission to land on Bogoslof for fear that we would stampede sea lion harems or gun murres off the cliffs. At issue was not the limited activity of a group of scientists in inflatable boats. Larger forces were at work; our request to land had become entangled in fisheries politics. Permission to land on Bogoslof might be perceived as a special privilege or precedent, with some unforeseen legal consequence. Our request was thus involved in the tug-of-war over the future of the Bering Sea.

The "total allowable catch" of pollock in the Bering Sea, Aleutian Islands, and Bogoslof District approached three billion pounds in 2001. At the core of a contentious debate and a series of legal actions is the question, Is that too much? The commercial fishing industry is lined up on one side, and on the other are such conservation organizations as Greenpeace, the Environmental Defense Fund, the Sierra Club, the American Oceans Campaign, and the Trustees for Alaska. As we learned in Dutch Harbor, there is a lot to lose financially or ecologically, depending on how the question is answered. The National Marine Fisheries Service, which oversees the research used to create regulations and to set catch limits, and its parent agency, the National Oceanic and Atmospheric Administration, are at the center of the storm.

Back onboard the *Clipper Odyssey*, oceanographer Vera Alexander explained the workings of the ecosystem that supports the economics, which ignite the politics.

The Bering Sea is the world's third largest semi-enclosed sea. The wide eastern shelf along Alaska makes up about half of its total area. Most of the shelf is extremely shallow, less than two hundred feet in depth in many places, while the basin extending toward Russia and the western Aleutians can drop off to depths that exceed ten thousand feet. As a result, about half of the Bering Sea is underlain by the shallower continental shelf, and the other half is a deep basin. Several huge undersea canyons run up from the basin onto the shelf, channeling deeper water up onto the shallower shelf. If you look at a color satellite image of ocean-plant distribution during the spring season throughout the entire northern hemisphere, you notice immediately that there is no other region as rich as the Bering Sea.

Why? The western part of the Bering Sea upwelling currents move nutrients from the deeper to shallower waters, where waters moving up from the south meet cold northern waters. In this region, water moving up onto the shelf is supplied in part from the deep Pacific Ocean and carries with it a very high nutrient content. A major driving force for this northward movement of water is the ocean current that passes through the Bering Strait over the Chukchi Sea shelf and into the Arctic Ocean, eventually making its way into the North Atlantic Ocean. This massive movement of water is, in reality, water running downhill, driven by the difference in height between the Pacific and Atlantic oceans. For the area along the more western deep basin and continental shelf, this flow of nutrient-rich water produces the so-called "green belt," a zone of high plant growth along the outer Bering Sea shelf.

In the southeastern area of the Bering Sea, which sits atop the continental shelf, ocean water flows into this region from the Gulf of Alaska, powered by the Alaska Coastal Current and the Alaska Coastal Stream, whose fingers diverge off through Unimak Pass and the countless other passes along the Aleutian chain. Aided by both currents and tides, these waters continue northward and westward up onto the Bering Sea continental shelf, bathing the Pribilof Islands and the outer portions of the shelf with nutrient-rich Gulf of Alaska waters.

All these factors combine to create one of the most productive marine ecosystems on earth. It is home to at least 450 species of fish, crustaceans, and mollusks; 50 species of seabirds; and 23 species of marine mammals. Contributing to this rich diversity are the Bering Sea's eelgrass beds, which are the most extensive in the world, serving both as a massive source of plant food and nursery grounds for a wide variety of marine species.

At the conclusion of Vera's lecture, I marveled at the improbability of it all. Ancient geological accidents and a vast diffuse system of global currents and ocean chemistry had together produced an environment so conducive to supporting life that it is one of the most productive ecosystems on the planet. To no one in particular, I uttered a variation on the late-night comedians' refrain: "Only on earth!" For the plant eaters of the Bering Sea, this environment provides a tremendous supply of food. In turn, well-fed, reproducing plant eaters are ample food for the predators higher up the food chain: murres and puffins, sea lions, killer whales, fur seals, humans.

The issue gripping Bering Sea policymakers is how to balance the take—a moving target because of environmental variability—so the ecosystem benefits all shareholders, humans and wildlife alike, in a sustainable manner. What restraint is required to prevent a bust? What are the warning signs that tell us the boom is about to end? Are they ecological? Or is the signal the point at which the smart money pulls out? Is it too late once the grocery-store shelves are empty?

If the Bering Sea's very existence seems improbable, it seems equally improbable that answers to these questions and a resolution of the debate about how best to care for this unique place will come soon. During our discussions, we could not avoid a growing concern. Although no quick resolution seems likely to emerge, irreparable damage to the ecosystem, both unintended and manufactured, could be underway. Left with this dilemma, some of us recalled the conservative approach simply stated in the 1998 *Wingspread Statement on the Precautionary Principle:*

> There is compelling evidence that damage to humans and the worldwide environment is of such magnitude and seriousness that new principles for conducting human activities are necessary. . . . Corporations, government entities, organizations, communities, scientists and other individuals must adopt a precautionary approach to all human endeavors. Therefore, it is necessary to implement the Precautionary Principle: when an activity raises threats of harm to human health or the environment, precautionary measures should be taken even if some cause and effect relationships are not fully established scientifically. In this context the proponent of an activity, rather than the public, should bear the burden of proof.

As if waking from a dream, we saw Tolstoi Point appear out of the fog. A short overnight sail north from Bogoslof brought us early on August 12 to the eastern side of Saint George Island in the Pribilofs, or Seal Islands as they are sometimes called. With the aid of modern navigation, we avoided the fate that Henry Gannett warned about in 1899: "It is no uncommon experience for vessels bound for the Pribilofs to miss the islands in the fog, and to spend days searching for them, as for needles in a haystack." Although the mist and fog chilled us that day and the next as we visited the largest Pribilof Island, Saint Paul, forty-five miles farther north, the Seal Islanders' hospitality toward us was heartwarming. During our visits, groups of students and teachers from both Saint George and Saint Paul hosted our Young Explorers Team. They traveled the islands together, explored the *Clipper Odyssey,* and shared stories about their experiences and way of life.

On Saint George we visited the old sealskin plant, a centerpiece of the community's cultural education and outreach program. The plant and a locally developed teaching guide, *Teaching with Historic Places: The Seal Islands,* provide the children of the Pribilofs and visitors with the inseparable histories of the islanders, their religion, and the fur seal. At the center of spiritual life is the beautifully restored Saint George Russian Orthodox Church. On Saint Paul, the history and traditions of the Pribilofs intersect with today's world. The Pribilof School District, out of concern for cultural identity, created the Pribilof Islands Stewardship Program. In a world of competing values, the program is intended to "empower island youth with *both* western concepts and indigenous ways of knowing as taught by elders, sealers, scientists, and artists." As a statement of respect for their natural island world, the Aleut Tribal Government of Saint Paul created the Ecosystem Conservation Office. It actively engages the entire community in environmental-protection and wildlife-management programs that range from recycling to marine mammal research.

During our two-day Pribilof visit we met with church deacons, elders, tribal-council and Native-corporation members, government scientists, and fishermen. Before long we came to understand that the people of the Pribilofs have been intimately part of the tumultuous history of the Bering Sea and its marine mammals for centuries; they are the human face of the controversy that we saw shadowing the wild volcanic cones of Bogoslof. The responsibility they show toward the resources they critically depend on is both a practical matter and one of cultural pride. They also know that over 70 percent of the world's fur seals live in the Pribilof Island rookeries, and that population has been steadily declining despite the best local efforts. The problem is much bigger; ending commercial seal harvesting is no longer enough.

Although much has changed in a hundred years, some things have not. C. Hart Merriam had been to the Pribilofs in 1891. In preparing for the 1899 expedition, he used his influence to secure a special permit from the secretary of the treasury to again visit the islands. On his return, he was shocked to find that the number of fur seals had dramatically declined to just 20 percent of the population he had observed eight years earlier.

Fur Seals

© PATRICIA SAVAGE

CHAPTER TWELVE

CONSERVATION
COMES TO ALASKA

~~

R OBERT M c C RACKEN P ECK

T HE SALT HOUSE on Saint George Island is quiet now. The long, windowed room that once glistened with the red and white of blood and blubber seems almost shrinelike in its disused state. Its weathered wood tables, fog-muted light, and chilly dampness reminded me, when I first entered, of an English country church. Another in our group, haunted by the building's gory past, found its ambiance closer to the morbid halls of Auschwitz. To Andronik (Andy) Kashevarof, who has lived on this Pribilof Island all his life, this was simply a place where families like his once earned a living from the skins of seals. As he explained to me and other members of the Harriman Expedition Retraced, until the 1970s, here and in other, comparable buildings now destroyed, the raw pelts of countless slaughtered animals were stripped of their fat, "pickled" in salt, and packed for export to furriers around the world.

Andy's account of how the seals were routinely herded from their gathering places along the beach and bludgeoned to death on the "killing fields" near town was offered without sentiment or regret. To a man who has worked the line and knows what it means to eke a living from the land and sea, the story of processing the fur seals, from beach to cargo, is as matter-of-fact as the harvest of corn or soybeans is to a Kansas farmer. At the end of his talk and our salt-house tour, he passed around some finished pelts. The sensuous feel of the dark brown fur was enough to explain its enormous popularity. Second only to sea otter fur in its softness and warmth, pelts from the Pribilof fur seals were once so desired by the rest of the world that their sales helped the United States to pay itself back for the purchase of Alaska. But the harvest

FIGURE 36. *Fur seals at Saint Paul Island, the Pribilofs.*
Credit: C. Hart Merriam. Source: Harriman family collection.

came at a heavy price. At the height of their fur's sartorial popularity, the seals themselves came perilously close to disappearing forever.

To conservationists, historians, and a growing number of ecotourists who visit
the Pribilofs (primarily Saint George and its larger sister island, Saint Paul) in search
of wildlife, the survival of the northern fur seals represents something of a miracle.
It is certainly one of the great success stories in wildlife conservation. While the Harriman Alaska Expedition of 1899 did not play a direct part in forging the international treaty that ultimately saved the fur seals from extinction, it may have played a
pivotal role in drawing public attention to their plight.

When Edward Harriman arranged with the U.S. Treasury Department for the
expedition to visit the Pribilof Islands, the North American Commercial Company, a
private concession, held exclusive rights to harvest the Pribilofs' fur seals for their pelts.
Millions of these seals congregated each summer, as they do today, on the islands'
rocky beaches to breed and rear their pups. To guarantee the stability of the seal population, company workers were supposed to obtain furs by killing only bachelor males,
or *holluschickie,* thus leaving the breeding members of the colony unharmed and able
to perpetuate the species. At the time of Harriman's visit, the rules governing the fur
seals' land harvest were being ignored to make up for increasing competition from
pelagic (seagoing) harvests by unregulated Russian, Japanese, and Canadian sealers.

The combined pressures from land and sea had a seriously negative effect on the seal population. It was not the first in the boom-and-bust cycle of fur sealing, but it could easily have been the last.

COMMERCIAL INTEREST in the Pribilofs began in 1786, when the Russian explorer G. L. Pribylov and his crew found these storm-lashed islands and their abundant sea mammals some three hundred miles off the Alaskan coast. Although the harvest of sea otters first attracted Russian traders to the Pribilofs, it was the fur seals (varyingly called "sea dogs," "sea cats," and "sea bears"), calving by the millions on the islands, that ultimately sustained the attention of Russian fur traders, or *promyshlenniki*, and their Aleut conscripts. Some of the Aleuts were forced to settle on the Pribilofs in order to facilitate the annual harvest of pelts. Some of their descendants still live there today.

By the time the Russian government sold the Pribilofs (along with the rest of Alaska) to the United States in 1867, millions of fur seals had already been killed for their pelts. This lucrative trade was one of several factors contributing to U.S. interest in acquiring the territory in the years following the Civil War. Senator Charles Sumner of Massachusetts, arguing on behalf of Alaska's purchase in 1867, speculated that Russian profits on sealskins from the Pribilofs between 1817 and 1838 alone might have exceeded 85 million rubles (about $63 million). Such proceeds— and the prospects of similar profits in the future—dwarfed the mere $7.2 million paid by the United States for the acquisition of all of Alaska. Just three years after the Pribilofs came under U.S. protection, the Alaskan explorer (and later Harriman Expedition participant) William Dall observed that "the fur trade is the only branch of industry which has been fully developed in Alaska, and all others have been forgotten in the enormous profits which have attended its successful prosecution. . . . From a pecuniary point of view it is at present the most important business in the territory."

Like Dall, C. Hart Merriam, the scientific dean and provost of the Harriman Expedition, was familiar with the history of the fur trade in Alaska. He was especially knowledgeable about the harvest of fur seals on the Pribilofs, for he had visited the islands in 1891 as one of two representatives appointed by the U.S. president to an international commission on pelagic sealing in the Bering Sea. At that time the seal population had appeared stable and the harvest of pelts indefinitely sustainable.

When Merriam arrived at Saint Paul with the rest of the Harriman party on July 9, 1899, he expected to see the fur seals in their multitudes going about the business of procreation as they had for millennia. Instead, he found a beleaguered seal population—one-tenth the size he had recalled from eight years before. He quickly recognized that, despite federal guidelines intended to regulate (and thus indefinitely sustain) their harvest, the herds were suffering from serious overhunting on both land and sea.

On his return to Washington, Merriam sought out the Treasury officials responsible for the Pribilofs to express his concern over the deteriorating conditions he had observed. Fellow expedition member George Bird Grinnell was more outspoken and more public in his expression of alarm. An articulate defender of public resources, Grinnell had made a career of exposing the mismanagement of the national parks and their use for personal gain. As the editor of *Forest and Stream* magazine, he wielded considerable influence in shaping public opinion on matters relating to resource protection and wildlife management. To Grinnell, the fur-seal decline was a clear case of greed superseding common sense, and he was determined to stop it. He used what he had learned in the Pribilofs to editorialize in his magazine against the "destruction" of the fur seals.

Grinnell gave his readers a historical perspective that echoed Dall's observations of more than three decades earlier, but with a distressing update: the days of unlimited resources for the fur trade, he warned, were fast coming to an end. "When Alaska first came into the possession of the United States," wrote Grinnell, "the only thing of value that it was supposed to possess was its fur. . . . The yield of the seal islands [the Pribilofs] in value far exceeded anything else in the [Alaska] Territory. . . . Today [1900] the fur trade of Alaska is hardly worth considering. The fur seals have travelled a long way on the road to extermination; the sea otter is practically wiped out."

Eschewing sentiment and moral persuasion, Grinnell used practical applications of economic theory to support his argument for tighter regulations on the harvest of seals. "It would seem a wise policy to protect these animals," he wrote, "[so] that they may thrive and increase, and in due time [again] yield their valuable furs." This kind of down-to-earth thinking would earn him a sympathetic hearing in U.S. homes, if not in the halls of Congress. Unbeknownst to Merriam, Dall, or Grinnell, certain members there were turning a blind eye to the excessive fur harvest on the Pribilofs in exchange for some lucrative (kickback) harvests of their own.

Grinnell correctly put the blame for the fur seals' decline both on the North American Commercial Company (which had the exclusive rights to fur harvesting in the Pribilofs), for ignoring its quotas and abandoning the practical harvesting traditions of the *holluschickie*, and on sealers from Russia, Japan, and Canada, whose indiscriminate and wasteful pelagic harvest took the lives of many pregnant and nursing seals. These combined pressures, he explained, had reduced the population of fur seals to less than a quarter of what it had been just two years before. Grinnell went on to predict the extermination of the species within four years unless immediate action was taken to enforce a limit on the number (and sex) of the animals killed. An astute politician in his own right, Grinnell called on the United States and Great Britain (which represented Canada at the treaty negotiations on pelagic sealing) to do the right thing and make both countries proud: "It is probable that today the fur seal herd is only about one-tenth as large as it was when the United States took possession of these islands, and it rests with the two great English-speaking nations of the world to say whether this herd shall increase or whether it shall be exterminated."

Although Grinnell's article did much to draw public awareness to the issue, it would take many people, working in the back halls of Congress, to expose and eliminate the corruption and mismanagement that were allowing the decimation of the seal herds. The combined effort helped to stave off the imminent extinction of the species and ultimately led to the first international treaty to protect wildlife, which was enacted in 1911.

The empty salt-house and the modest homes that cluster around the onion-domed Church of the Great Martyr in Saint George today give no hint of the vast fur fortunes that were made here. The money went elsewhere. The harvesters and their descendants stayed. Although local residents still kill a few hundred seals for their own use each year, there has not been a commercial harvest on Saint George since 1972 or on Saint Paul since 1984. As a result, the seal population has returned to the size it may have been when Pribylov first saw the islands in 1786. The estimated one to two million healthy fur seals that still bleat, croak, and roar from the rocky beaches of the Pribilofs each summer give no hint of how close the species may have come to being hunted to extinction.

When Harriman planned his 1899 trip to Alaska, he had not anticipated that he or any of his guests would become involved in the international politics of fur sealing or any other contentious environmental issues. He had organized the trip with an eye toward "pleasure and recreation," not politics. But given the makeup of the scientific faculty in Harriman's "floating university," it was perhaps inevitable that some would become more deeply involved than even they could have imagined.

John Muir was already one of the best-known environmental activists in the United States when he joined the expedition. His primary focus was then on California, but he quickly and happily redirected his energies to Alaska during the course of the trip. A veteran of several previous trips to Alaska, he used the ship's captive audience as a forum for his lectures not only on glaciers (his official area of expertise) but on the territory's many other "gloriously wild and sublime" features as well. Muir saw the wilderness as sacred and worth protecting in its own right and took every opportunity to share his opinion with others.

Although some members of the expedition agreed with Muir, others, notably Grinnell, Merriam, and Bernhard Fernow, held a fundamentally different view of nature. They saw Alaska's wilderness as a reservoir of natural resources that could—and probably should—be used for the common good, as long as it was not abused for private gain. Such differences of opinion must have led to many lively discussions aboard the *George W. Elder*, not unlike those we had on the *Clipper Odyssey*. At the end of the expedition, Muir characterized the interactions of its participants in appropriately geological terms. "I enjoyed the instruction and companionship of a lot of the best fellows imaginable," he wrote in a letter to the Misses Harriman and Draper (quoted in Bade), "culled and arranged like a well-balanced bouquet, or like a band of glaciers flowing smoothly together, each in its own channel, or perhaps at times like a lot of round boulders merrily swirling and chafing against each other in a glacier pothole."

The conflicting philosophies voiced during the "chafing" part of the group's discussion reflected a fundamental split in the nascent conservation movement in the United States. This split was to continue throughout the twentieth century and is still with us today. As we hosted various visitors aboard the *Clipper Odyssey* for discussions of current environmental and social issues affecting Alaska, we heard the same conflicting views that formed a basis for debate by Harriman's party one hundred years before: whether to protect nature or to use it; whether to preserve nature in its pristine state or to consider it a renewable resource and, through an aggressive policy of "multiple use," allow as many people to enjoy it in as many ways as possible

Harriman, who might have fallen into a third camp at the start of the trip (to use natural resources for maximum economic gain), ultimately found value in the views of both groups and maintained his interest in Alaska long after he returned from its wild shores. He never played a public role in Alaska's politics, but he profoundly, if indirectly, affected the course of Alaskan history by organizing the expedition of 1899 and sponsoring its subsequent publications. The expedition's thirteen-volume report, which Harriman and his family financed, established a comprehensive baseline for the future study of the flora and fauna of the Alaskan coast.

A full set of the original report, borrowed from the Smith College library and carefully shipped to Prince Rupert, was with us for the entire Harriman Retraced expedition. I wondered how many other books had ever visited the sites of their conception. Excerpts of John Burroughs's narrative, read aloud at our daily gatherings from these well-worn volumes, refreshed our memories of places we had visited or built our expectations of places we would see in the days ahead. The technical portions of the report—detailed accounts of starfish, sea worms, fox farming, atmospheric conditions—went unread, although their existence was often cited by our naturalists. Some of their beautifully detailed illustrations found their way into our special-subject lectures.

Before the Harriman trip, accurate scientific information about any of Alaska's natural resources was hard to come by. In a report to the U.S. Treasury Department written soon after the purchase of Alaska, the naturalist and artist Henry Wood Elliott observed: "On the subject of Alaska, it is safe to assert that no other unexplored section of the world was ever brought into notice suddenly, about which so much has been emphatically and positively written, based entirely upon the whims and caprices of the writers, and, therefore[,] . . . the truth in regard to the Territory does frequently come into conflict with many erroneous popular opinions respecting it." The Harriman Expedition and its widely distributed reports went a long way toward changing the misconceptions Elliott described. They also served as a baseline against which we could measure our own observations a century later.

Although Harriman's was by no means the first or last expedition to make important scientific discoveries in Alaska, it was the most highly visible and thus one of the most influential. The status of the scientists enlisted by Merriam for the trip ensured that any expedition findings would be shared with a large public audience and would thus extend the impact of the undertaking well beyond the scientific community or the government bureaucrats responsible for administering the new territory. No one who participated in the Harriman Alaska Expedition could have been unaffected by the experience. The long period of intense, confined contact between figures of such intellect with a shared interest in the subjects at hand was without precedent in the annals of scientific investigation.

A tight network of social contacts between Harriman Expedition members ensured that Alaska and its resources would be the topic of conversation at many a gathering for years after Harriman and his guests returned from the "snapping, snarling[,] . . . hissing, spitting[,] . . . treacherous" Bering Sea, as John Burroughs described it (quoted in Peck, "A Cruise for Rest and Recreation"). The Cosmos Club in Washington, the Century Club in New York, the Explorers Club, the Boone and Crockett Club, and the Campfire Club of America each provided an unofficial forum in which the Harriman Expedition participants could communicate their impressions of Alaska to others. Because so many important opinion leaders either had been on the trip or had heard about it firsthand from a participant, the territory's natural resource issues, which otherwise might have been ignored, overlooked, or given low priority in Washington, were given a high level of visibility. Thanks to the knowledge and insights obtained by the Harriman party, the discussions that surrounded these issues were unusually well informed.

How much networking went on following the trip can't be quantified, but a review of some post-expedition correspondence between the participants suggests that it was extensive. "The H.A.E. [Harriman Alaska Expedition] (termed in full—Ham and Eggs) has resolved itself into the Ham and Eggs Club with Mr. H[arriman] as president," wrote Louis Agassiz Fuertes from Seattle at the end of the trip. The club, he explained to his family in Ithaca, New York, was "to meet in full as possible once a year in New York and as often as it wants in 2's and 3's and anywhere" (quoted in Peck, *A Celebration of Birds*).

Burroughs was a frequent host to members of the expedition on the East Coast, while Muir kept the club alive by hosting its traveling members in California. "Already I have had two trips with Merriam to the Sierra Sequoias and Coast Redwoods," he wrote to the Harriman family within a month of their return from Alaska. "And last week [Henry] Gannett came up to spend a couple of days. . . . I hope to have visits from Professor [G. K.] Gilbert and poet Charlie [Charles Keeler] ere long, and Earlybird [William] Ritter and possibly I might see a whole lot more in the East this coming winter or next" (quoted in Bade).

Perhaps the most important contact Muir made during the course of the expedition was Harriman himself. Not only did Harriman help to support Muir financially in the years following the trip, but he became an invaluable ally in Muir's fights for wilderness protection in California. "I wish I could have seen you last night when you received my news of the Yosemite victory," wrote Muir to his friend and fellow activist Robert Underwood Johnson in February 1905. "About two years ago public opinion [about preserving the Yosemite Valley as a national park], which has long been on our side, began to rise into effective action. On the way to Yosemite [in 1903] both the President [Theodore Roosevelt] and our Governor [George C. Pardee] were won over to our side. . . . But though almost everybody was with us, so active was the opposition of those pecuniarily and politically interested, we might have failed to get the bill through the Senate but for the help of Mr. H___, though, of course, his name or his company were never in sight through all the fight" (quoted in Bade).

We may never know how many other conservation issues were invisibly supported or advanced by Harriman. Nor can we know what he hoped to achieve by inviting such an extraordinary roster of guests on his family vacation. Whatever his intent, by assembling many of the greatest scientific minds of his day for an intense period of thoughtful exchange, Harriman played a pivotal role in advancing the cause of science and conservation at a critical time in history. The Harriman Expedition came as a welcome capstone to the already long and distinguished careers of such participants as William Brewer, Dall, Burroughs, and R. Swain Gifford. For some younger members, like Keeler, Edward Curtis, and Fuertes, it opened important new doors and provided a launching platform for careers just ready to take off. Regardless of age or experience, everyone who participated in the Harriman Expedition agreed with Merriam's prediction that it would be "the event of a lifetime" (quoted in Peck, "A Cruise for Rest and Recreation").

Retracing Harriman's expedition route, we saw much of what Harriman and his companions saw from the deck of the *George W. Elder*. In some of the wilder parts of Alaska, the changes have been so few as to be barely noticeable. In many others, the changes have been profound. Our visit to the Pribilof Islands revealed an interesting mix of continuity and change. Except for the greater abundance of fur seals and some modernization in technology and architecture, relatively few outward changes have been made here since the Harriman visit. Politically and philosophically, however, the Pribilofs of today are very different. Although they were once considered the property of a commercial concession and managed by the U.S. Treasury Department, the seals and other wildlife on the islands now fall under federal agencies whose missions are more directly focused on the protection of wildlife. The seabirds, walruses, and sea otters are under the jurisdiction of the U.S. Fish and Wildlife Service. This branch of the Interior Department grew directly from the U.S. Biological Survey, which Merriam created and led (with Harriman's financial support) shortly after his return from Alaska. The fur seals, whose economic importance for Alaska continued until recent times, fall under the control of the National Marine Fisheries Service.

Descendants of Aleut conscripts who once killed seals for their Russian masters or, in Harriman's time, worked for the North American Commercial Company, now monitor and protect the islands' abundant bird colonies and the very seal calving grounds that were harvested to the brink of extinction by their ancestors. Where tourists were once banned, except by special permission, they are now encouraged. (The magazine on my Alaska Airways flight from Nome was advertising nature tours on the island of Saint Paul.) The kind of disruptive or destructive human activities that were once permitted on the islands are today carefully controlled in the interest of wildlife conservation. There is even an aggressive campaign to prevent rats from establishing themselves on the Pribilofs, lest their presence cause harm to the bird life.

The Russian Orthodox church on Saint George, still a center of spiritual activity to the 150 people who live there, now sells postcards to off-island visitors, and the abandoned salt-house is being reconditioned to serve as a museum of local history. The story it will tell is one of greed and altruism, excess and restraint, adversity and triumph. In all its fascinating complexity, the Pribilof story holds elements of a much broader conservation story: the long and continuing history of the United States's struggle to regulate itself.

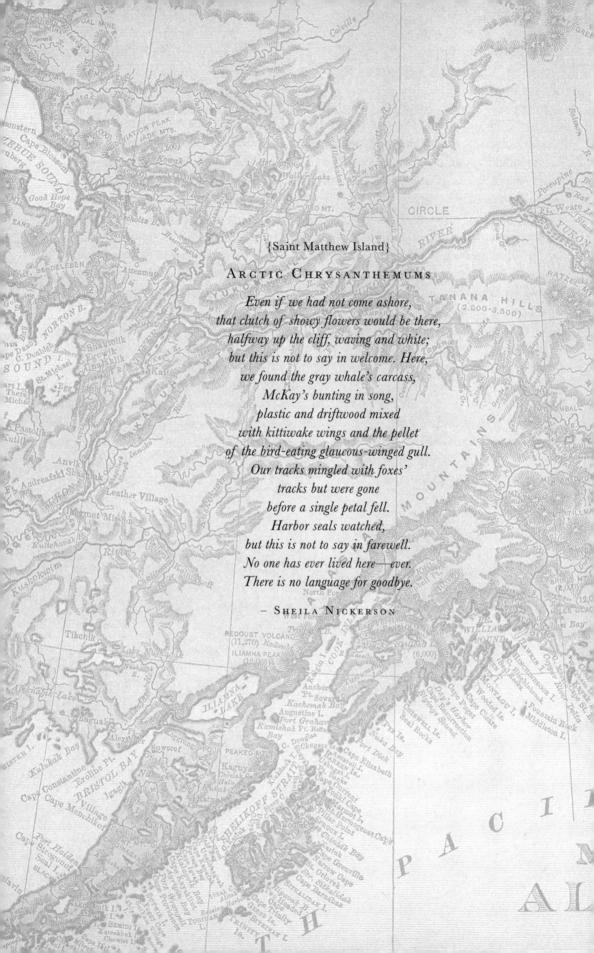

{Saint Matthew Island}

ARCTIC CHRYSANTHEMUMS

Even if we had not come ashore,
that clutch of showy flowers would be there,
halfway up the cliff, waving and white;
but this is not to say in welcome. Here,
we found the gray whale's carcass,
McKay's bunting in song,
plastic and driftwood mixed
with kittiwake wings and the pellet
of the bird-eating glaucous-winged gull.
Our tracks mingled with foxes'
tracks but were gone
before a single petal fell.
Harbor seals watched,
but this is not to say in farewell.
No one has ever lived here—ever.
There is no language for goodbye.

— SHEILA NICKERSON

Wilderness Islands—
Hall and Saint Matthew

14 August 2001

Late in the afternoon of August 13, Saint Paul disappeared off the *Clipper Odyssey*'s stern. Sailing deeper into the Bering Sea, we were beginning our 196-mile sail north/northwest to Saint Matthew and Hall islands. We would arrive the next morning at these uninhabited islands, some of the Bering Sea's most isolated and remote maritime wilderness areas. For thousands of years no permanent Native villages have existed on these islands, and the era of exploration did not produce Western settlements. Not surprisingly, though, the islands were well known to the explorers, whalers, and fur traders who navigated these northern waters. The islands' large year-round population of polar bear provided a ready supply of fresh meat—while it lasted. When they explored the islands, the hunters of the 1899 expedition found only traces of bear.

Between 1942 and 1945, a temporary outpost was set up on Saint Matthew, with a few chosen members of the U.S. Army and the U.S. Coast Guard keeping watch over the country's westernmost frontier. Their stay had no lasting effect on Saint Matthew—with one exception, the importing of twenty-nine reindeer to be used as an emergency food supply. The reindeer introduction was a classic, albeit accidental, experiment in population ecology. At introduction, the reindeer had no natural predators and an abundant, pristine supply of lichen to keep them in prime breeding condition. With no constraints, their population exploded 20,000 percent between 1945 and 1964, their numbers growing to six thousand animals! In no time, the huge herd overgrazed the tundra habitat of the 128-square-mile island, and the population crashed to just forty-two animals by 1966. Today just a few animals remain, and the habitat continues to recover from overgrazing.

The only other serious threat to these islands was a federal proposal to construct an industrial complex for servicing oil-exploration companies, a proposal that did not reach fruition. The first governmental protection for Saint Matthew and Hall islands came about in 1909, when President Theodore Roosevelt declared them bird sanctuaries; later they became part of the Alaska Maritime National Wildlife Refuge.

Federal protection notwithstanding, the continued preservation of these islands has a lot to do with their location. In the midst of summer, when the islands are covered with vibrant congregations of breeding wildlife and wildflowers in bloom, their isolation is alluring. Our ship has proven its ability to deal handily with challenges posed by both the seas and the distances that otherwise isolate these islands. But, in ways that few of us onboard can imagine, winter is a different story. Each winter sea ice forms in the Chukchi Sea above the Bering Strait, breaks into large floes, and is driven through the strait by prevailing northerlies. In the season's depths, when there is little or no sunlight and brutally low temperatures, the ice floes collide and crash into one another to form a jagged puzzle of ice that attaches to the ice growing from the shoreline. By March of each year pack ice covers much of the Bering Sea's continental shelf, extending hundreds of miles south from the Arctic Circle and enveloping Saint Matthew and Hall islands. Historically, the ice reached eighty to one hundred miles past Saint Matthew Island. And it has had, and continues to have, a profound effect on the ecology of land and sea and on the human cultures that depend on both.

For this extraordinary leg of our trip we can thank Mary Averell Harriman. The 1899 expedition's outward voyage was to have ended at the Pribilofs, but Mrs. Harriman expressed an interest in seeing Siberia—an exotic place that would provide wonderful stories for her to share back in the rarefied social circles of New York City. The ever-seasick John Burroughs, who at this point would rather have been in a Dutch Harbor guesthouse, sto-

ically reported, "According to our original program our outward journey should have ended at the Seal Islands, but Mrs. Harriman expressed a wish to see Siberia, and if all went well, the midnight sun. 'Very well,' replied Mr. Harriman, 'we will go to Siberia,' and toward that barren shore our prow was turned." Burroughs was not alone in his misery. In the approach to the Pribilofs aboard the "Geo. W. Roller," both of the expedition's artists, R. Swain Gifford and Frederick Dellenbaugh, took to their cabins to suffer in private.

A near calamity provided only fleeting hopes that the expedition would turn homeward. Leaving Saint Paul in the dark and fog, the group sat down to dinner. In his journal C. Hart Merriam recounts the interruption that rocked the ship: "Just before leaving the table, the ship scraped on the bottom, and a few seconds later struck hard on a reef and struck again with a fearful rasping, bumping crash. We thought the bottom smashed in, but the engineer told us she didn't leak. Going on deck, we were astounded to see a stretch of low green land close by on the port bow. . . . As the tide was rising we swung off, put about and took a south by southeast course before shaping our course again for St. Matthew Island. . . . We were going full speed when we struck. A great day—the Pribilof Fur Seal rookeries and tundra gardens, and promise of a shipwreck all in one day!" Burroughs's assessment was less cheerful: "Some of us hoped this incident would cause Mr. Harriman to turn back. Bering Sea is a treacherous sea; it is shallow . . . and in summer it is nearly always draped in fog. But our host was a man not easily turned back; in five minutes he was romping with his children again as if nothing had happened."

Further unnerving the already reluctant

members of the expedition party, the next day brought another surprise. In the fog, the *Elder* sailed past Saint Matthew and Hall islands. Captain Peter Doran concluded it would be too dangerous to turn back and continued on to Siberia. They would have to wait for the return voyage to visit these islands.

Our overnight sail from Saint Paul to Saint Matthew was more reminiscent of the 1899 expedition than some of our party would have preferred. As we dined that evening, the seas picked up, and a good swell swayed the ship. Even with the ship's high-tech stabilizers, we found ourselves swerving and stutter-stepping from one spot to the next as we made our way about the ship. During the course of dinner, a number of shipmates grew silent and reflective. With polite but hasty "good evenings," some retreated to their cabins to await calmer seas. Our wish was partially granted the next morning when we dropped anchor off the northern, leeward side of Saint Matthew. The Bering Sea, which just hours ago had been pitching and rolling, was now flat-calm and glassy.

At least that is what it seemed in the water just around the ship. Knowing we were anchored a half mile off Saint Matthew's shore was more an act of trust in the green glowing radar screen than direct knowledge—the fog was so thick we could not see much beyond the ship's bow. Before committing all the Zodiacs to a landing, we launched a scouting party to assess the beach and the surrounding terrain. My fellow expedition leader and seasoned voice of experience, Mike Messick, handed out signal flares as we boarded the scout boat. Flares are useful for signaling in the fog, but, should it be necessary, they are also useful for distracting a polar bear surprised by equally startled human visitors.

Polar bears wander the pack ice in winter, and in the past they were able to reach and colonize Saint Matthew. In more recent years, with a thinning and retreating of the more southern pack ice, the bears have been cut off, and a stable population has failed to materialize. Here, even in this most remote wilderness, we could not escape the larger issues facing the Bering Sea. Although the role of human activity in promoting global climate change is passionately debated, the facts remain that the Arctic is warming and sea ice is melting at record rates. Winters are growing shorter; the expanse of winter sea ice is dramatically shrinking. Polar bear migration, walrus breeding cycles, the nourishing spring marine-plant blooms that follow the annual retreat of ice— the pack ice affects all these natural events. Given the integral role of the ice in the functioning of this ecosystem, it is anyone's guess what the future holds if global warming continues at its current pace. We already see serious changes underway, changes that are well beyond the grasp of short-term local management plans and courtroom wrangling.

For the moment, we had to set aside consideration of such questions. We were in a boat, surrounded by fog, preparing to land on an unfamiliar beach. We had had a report that a bear had been stranded on the island after last spring's pack ice retreated, so our first task on reaching shore was to search the beach for tracks and scat. Looking for bear signs in thick fog quickly enlivens instincts seldom needed in the settled world. Our attention was fixed on small pieces of information—sights, sounds, smells—that in our other lives would go unnoticed. With a mixture of relief and disappointment, we found no sign of bear, and we radioed back to the ship to send along the rest of the Zodiacs and the waiting party.

FIGURE 37. Saint Matthew Island.
Credit: Edward S. Curtis. Source: Harriman family collection.

The fog began to lift by 8:30 A.M. For the first time we could see the full breadth of our landing area—a cove with a long gravel beach with mountainous bookends of jagged volcanic rock at each extreme. Bull Seal Point, anchoring the southeastern end of the cove, was alive with seabirds. Between the rocky points, the land rose to a green, flower-filled terrace of tundra, the first true tundra we had encountered. The outward appearance of this place had changed little in one hundred years. We felt we were seeing exactly what Burroughs saw in 1899: "ground covered with nature's matchless tapestry . . . a thick heavy carpet of variegated mosses and lichens had been stretched to the very edge of the cliff, with rugs and mats of many colored flowers."

Just below this lush mat of vegetation is a zone of permafrost whose coarse soil, as the name implies, is permanently frozen. This frozen layer of soil is key in distinguishing Arctic tundra from more southern plains of mixed plants and shrubs where the subsoil freezes and

thaws with the seasons. As I pressed my palm into it, the cold, wet mat felt like a sponge, and the water seeped around my fingers with the pressure. The frozen layer below blocks the penetration of rain and surface water, and so the tightly vegetated mat is truly "gushy." Tundra is sometimes described as lacking biological diversity; in the worst description, it is called a "barren." On the contrary, this place, on top of a volcanic rock surrounded by pack ice in winter and just four hundred miles from the Arctic Circle, is very much alive. Within this community of plants and wildlife a wide variety of ecological strategies are in play.

Making my way up the slope from the shore, I found the footing at first quite wet, but it became dryer with every step up slope. As I went along, the plants sorted themselves out according to their tolerance for "getting their feet wet." A zone of herbs gave way to a mix of herbs and grasses, and a little farther up lichens joined the mix. At the ridge, grasses gave way to moss; lichens became more dominant. The view from the top, across the expanse, can only be described as impressionistic: a rolling field of greens, brown, and grays was dotted with thousands of red, blue, and yellow wildflowers in all directions. When I tried to imagine tundra before this visit, *impressionistic* was not a word that ever occurred to me. Seeps and rivulets emerged from the ground, surrounded by lush carpets of red and green cushion mosses and stunningly green algae-covered rocks. The colors were all the brighter for being set against the moody silver and gunmetal ocean that flowed from the shore toward Russia.

A small flock of adult and young McKay's buntings and snow buntings hopped in and around tussocks in search of food; a Lapland longspur, perched on one of the higher tufts, called "peetooyou" to its neighbors. In an instant, calls from three or four directions responded to the inquiry. About two-thirds of the way up the slope, as the soil grew dryer, brown-lemming mounds appeared, increasing in number with elevation. Not surprisingly,

signs of Arctic fox also increased. Like polar bear, Arctic fox travel great distances over pack ice. With ample supplies of lemmings, seabird chicks, and eggs, wandering fox have had good reason to colonize Saint Matthew.

If the ocean was the backdrop for the island's array of color, the cliffs at Bull Seal Point were the source of the island's sound. From half a mile away, the cacophony of cries, "hahahas," squawks, and croaks suggested an avian riot in progress. More than two million seabirds nest on Saint Matthew and Hall islands, a number that is hard to comprehend even when one sees the birds tightly packed and endlessly unfolding into flight along the cliffs. With each step we took closer to the point, the details of the scene—the territorial squabbling, the precarious acrobatics, the juveniles' fussing—became more extraordinary. Farther ahead, her binoculars fixed on the cliffs, was Vivian Mendenhall, our expedition ornithologist. I picked up my pace to join her, eager to learn what she was thinking.

FIGURE *38. Saint Matthew Island tundra.*
Credit: Edward S. Curtis. Source: Harriman family collection.

Tufted Puffins in Glacier Bay

© PATRICIA SAVAGE

CHAPTER THIRTEEN

SEABIRDS AT THE EDGE
OF THE WORLD

VIVIAN M. MENDENHALL

This was our first visit to uninhabited land, and to a land of such unique grace and
beauty that the impression it made can never be forgotten. . . . The first thing that
attracted our attention was the murres. . . . Their numbers darkened the air. As we
approached, the faces of the rocks seemed paved with them, with a sprinkling of gulls,
puffins, black cormorants and auklets.

   – *John Burroughs, "Narrative of the Expedition," in vol. 1 of* Harriman Alaska Expedition

As our zodiak purred across the sea toward Hall Island, the *Clipper Odyssey*
dissolved into the fog behind us. I was suddenly aware that we were far from
civilization. Aside from my ten companions and those in a few nearby Zodiacs, the
only humans in contact with us for more than two hundred miles were on that now
invisible ship. We were connected to the ship via radio and radar reflector, but they
seemed an alarmingly frail lifeline. I reassured myself that the unperturbed crewman
who was steering our Zodiac seemed experienced and probably would know how to
get us back.

   Well, I was on Harriman Retraced to experience wilderness isolation—and to see
birds. Saint Matthew and Hall islands sit alone, almost in the middle of the Bering
Sea. They have always held allure for me because they are among the world's most
remote spots; no one has ever lived here except for a few military personnel during
World War II. I have studied seabirds throughout Alaska, but I had never made it to
these islands. I was eager to see their huge seabird colonies: a million birds on Saint

Matthew and 1.2 million on Hall Island. In the context of Bering Sea history, and with our current concerns about the ecological health of the region, I wondered whether these special islands could provide us with any insights into the changes that have occurred since the 1899 expedition. Today we are faced everywhere with concerns about pollution, overfishing, and other human pressures on seabirds. Could we learn anything here about pristine populations?

My apprehensions faded away as the cliffs of Hall Island materialized out of the fog. The Zodiac settled to a stop. A dark rock wall stretched as far as we could see: great iron-gray buttresses, black alcoves like ruined chimneys, green scraps of ledges from which new towers soared higher. We strained to see the top of the precipice, but it disappeared into the mist hundreds of feet above us.

As we moved along the shoreline, we were surrounded by seabirds, on the cliffs, on the water, in the air. It was exactly as John Burroughs described it in 1899. Black-legged kittiwakes, their plumage white as snow, huddled on rows of nests that seemed plastered to sheer rock, with a few half-grown chicks among them. Black-and-white common and thick-billed murres stood shoulder to shoulder on ledges no wider than a windowsill. Black, long-necked pelagic cormorants were visible in shadowed hollows. Pairs of white glaucous gulls and their downy gray youngsters stood on the broadest ledges. On rocks at the bottom of the cliff were lines of more birds—horned puffins with oversized orange bills, black pigeon guillemots with red feet and white shoulders. Flying birds filled the air. Many birds on the water preened, scratched, and rested, while others dived below the surface, then popped into view again a moment later.

We moved slowly along the coast, keeping far enough from the cliff not to alarm the birds on the ledges or the Steller sea lions that were relaxing at the edge of the water. Easing close to a pinnacle, we gazed at murres that covered its slope like tiles on a roof. All around us were the cries of birds. "The cackling of innumerable voices made an incessant murmur above the sound of the sea," wrote Charles Keeler a hundred years ago on this same island. Another seabird for which Hall Island is famous is the fulmar. At 420,000 birds, Hall Island's population of this species is one of the four largest in Alaska. Ironically, we could not see the fulmars because their cliff-top nest sites were hidden in the fog.

Because we were now only midway through our Alaska coastline reconnaissance, it was difficult to know whether this was the most spectacular seabird colony we would see. In the Gulf of Alaska, we had seen mountainous East Amatuli Island, home to two hundred sixty thousand birds; the little rocky triplets near Kodiak; Aghiyuk Island, which has five hundred thousand birds; and a dark cove near Unga Village with more than fifty thousand black-legged kittiwakes. Over forty thousand seabirds nest on little Bogoslof Island, whose jagged volcanic rocks are among the youngest on earth.

Just yesterday we had landed on Saint George Island and hiked for an hour up fog-soaked tundra slopes. We had peered over the edge of a thousand-foot cliff to see legions of seabirds clinging to the ledges, yet these were only a fraction of the island's

2.5 million nesting birds. The star of Saint George's seabirds is the red-legged kitti-wake, with its striking ruby legs—80 percent of the species' entire world population nests on this single island. On neighboring Saint Paul Island we had looked down another cliff at murres and puffins. Red-legged kittiwakes find their most northerly nesting spot among that island's two hundred thousand seabirds.

Soon after our stops at Saint Matthew and Hall islands, we would land on Saint Lawrence and Little Diomede islands. I had spent time at both these northern seabird colonies in other years, and I had marveled at the vast numbers of sparrow-sized least and crested auklets nesting in slopes of tumbled rock. Little Diomede Island has over eight hundred thousand seabirds; Saint Lawrence Island may be the largest colony in North America, with at least 3.5 million birds. But compared with all of Alaska's other remote seabird colonies, Saint Matthew and Hall islands are unique in their isolation.

As we floated next to Hall Island, seabirds were hunting for food all around us. Gulls were perched on the rocks, some intently watching murre nests in hopes of stealing an egg or chick. As we drew closer, a twinkling in the mist took shape as a flock of kittiwakes and gulls, hovering lightly and splashing to the water to seize fish. Gulls and kittiwakes cannot dive and therefore must fish near the surface. Gulls are the most versatile of the seabirds; although they can catch fish for food, they will hap-pily eat the eggs or chicks of other birds, dead animals, garbage—or your sandwich. In contrast, the murres and guillemots around us bobbed on the waves, dipped their heads below the surface to watch for prey, and dived with a gentle plop. Occasionally a murre surfaced with a fish in its bill, rose slowly into the air on whirring wings, and ascended to its chick on a ledge.

The graceful birds that were floating peacefully near us could be misunderstood: as predators, they are savagely efficient. A seabird is a superb feeding machine, with thick waterproof feathers, webbed feet for speed, a deadly fish-catching bill, and extra eyelids for seeing underwater. Surface-feeding birds have long, narrow wings for hours of travel across the ocean, while divers have short, stubby wings for swimming underwater, sometimes to depths greater than four hundred feet. All these attributes allow seabirds to chase and capture prey fish.

With the ocean surrounding us containing countless fish, many in our party assumed that Alaskan waters are a virtual smorgasbord of feeding opportunities for seabirds. Despite this bounty, only a few prey are suitable for birds. Most eat small fish or squid up to six inches long, and smaller seabirds, such as auklets, depend on animal plankton that float and drift in the ocean. Seabirds tend to select the most nutritious and oily fish, such as capelin, sand lance, and small herring, especially while feeding their young. For efficiency, they seek out compact schools of prey where hunting success is high, rather than spending a lot of energy looking for the odd fish here and there.

However, the adaptations that serve the seabirds so well in the water also carry a serious disadvantage. For seabirds, life would be impossible away from the sea. They know how to find food only in the ocean (although a few also visit lakes), and many are

FIGURE 39. *Seabird rookery, Saint Matthew Island.*
Credit: Edward S. Curtis. Source: Harriman family collection.

clumsy on land. Therefore seabirds spend most of the year at sea. Only in summer do they come to land, to nest and raise their young, and even at this time they stay as close to the sea as possible.

Seabirds must nest close to their food, but why do they crowd onto the cliffs of these small, desolate islands? As we looked up from the Zodiac, we could hardly comprehend how many birds covered the immense walls. In 1899, the same frenetic scene amazed Keeler as he maneuvered along Hall Island's ledges and gazed over the edge of the cliffs: "A wonderful scene lay below us. Some great splinters of rock . . . stood out in the water[,] . . . the waves dashing about their bases, while all over their sides, upon every ledge, crowded the seabirds. Below and opposite on the precipitous volcanic face of the island was an almost solid front of birds—bustling, bobbing, and bowing, some sitting passively on their single eggs, and many standing, with their faces turned toward the rock wall which rose above them."

Examining the cliffs with binoculars, I could see the ledges where murres were clinging precariously and other ledges where kittiwakes were perched securely in their nests. The rows of birds crowded onto ledges repeated themselves thousands of times across the sheer cliff face. To depart from its ledge, a bird would simply drop into space. The kittiwakes glided gracefully on the air currents, but the heavy, short-winged murres plunged toward the ocean with whirring wings until they gained enough speed to fly. It seemed certain that an incoming murre would crash-land on its nesting ledge, yet it always settled on the spot with the precision of a ballet dancer.

The birds have learned to cope with these cliffs, and so their nests are inaccessible to many potential predators. Seabirds that do not nest on cliffs seek other refuges from predation: guillemots and some auklets nest in crevices and slopes of jumbled rock; tufted puffins and the tiny storm petrels create their own hiding places by digging burrows; gulls nest on flat islands. Most seabirds avoid open tundra, where they could easily be hunted by foxes, falcons, ravens, and large gulls.

The vast crowds of birds on Hall Island illustrate another key strategy that helps tip the balance in favor of survival: nesting in colonies. It was the colonial behavior of seabirds that most awed the scientists on both the 1899 and 2001 expeditions— thousands upon thousands of birds all nesting in one small area. Colonial nesting provides several advantages. Many birds can share the limited space on a few small islands. The uproar and agitation that meet a predator when it approaches a colony often distract and deter it and quickly alert the rest of the colony to trouble in its midst. Finally, a seabird whose livelihood depends on finding schools of fish may increase its chances by watching its successful neighbors return and then following them on the next feeding trip.

All animals do their best to avoid becoming someone else's meal. However, avoiding predators is especially important for seabirds; they reproduce so slowly that it is hard to make up for lost offspring. Additionally, many seabirds do not start nesting until they are four or five years old, a late start in comparison with many other bird species. Individuals of some species, like the kittiwakes, lay two or three eggs each spring, but several species, including fulmars, murres, puffins, and auklets, lay just a single egg. It takes the entire summer for most seabirds to raise just one family: most incubate their eggs for about a month, and, after hatching, the chicks stay in the nest for three to eight weeks. While the chicks are growing, the parents protect and feed them. In an instant, months of effort can be lost to a single hungry gull, bad weather, or starvation.

When so many factors interact to influence births and deaths—bad weather, predators, changing food supplies—how do we know the number of seabirds that survive? The answer is that we count them. This is a sizeable job because there are nearly two thousand colonies in Alaska and the Russian Far East combined. To monitor these seabirds, counts are conducted every one to three years at a few selected colonies. I have spent many long hours on the brink of a cliff, sitting on tundra sprinkled with yellow and purple flowers, counting and re-counting seabirds on ledges below me, or waiting until a bird moved a fraction of an inch and revealed the egg beneath its breast.

From the relative comfort of the *Clipper Odyssey*, I thought back to a day in July 1996, when three other biologists and I floated for hours in a Zodiac near the north shore of Saint Lawrence Island, counting seabirds. We became cold despite our rain gear and thick clothing, and stiff and sore from hours of holding up our binoculars. To count the thousands of birds, we divided the cliff mentally into small sections—

100 murres and 56 kittiwakes on that ledge, 250 and 85 between the ledge and the patch of lichen, and so on. If we lost count, we had to start over. The work is exacting, but also rewarding and necessary. It is vital to keep track of the health of each species—whether its population is going up or down—so we can try to protect those that need our help.

Once we have learned how many birds are nesting on Hall Island (or Saint Lawrence), what do our counts tell us about changes during the past century? In comparing our counts with the observations of 1899, the greatest challenge we face is that science has changed dramatically in the past one hundred years. The Harriman scientists did not count the seabirds. This is not surprising because most early natural scientists were collectors. They shot birds, measured them, made paintings of them, and filed them away in museum drawers. Throughout the 1899 expedition, artist Louis Agassiz Fuertes and ornithologist Albert Fisher shot many dozens of birds for this purpose, and two taxidermists prepared "study skins" for examination and shipment to museums. Oddly, Fisher did not publish a scientific report about birds for the Harriman volumes. As was the norm in 1899, Keeler and Burroughs wrote lyrical descriptions of the birds' beauty and abundance, listing the names of the species they noticed. If it had occurred to them to count vast seabird colonies, the prospect would have been overwhelming. It would have also seemed unnecessary, for ecological concepts were in their infancy, including those concerning animal populations and the ecosystems that support them. Although several people on the *George W. Elder* were concerned with human threats to wild populations, such as Merriam and Henry Gannett, no one was worried yet about seabirds.

Looking back over the century, we can say that the list of Bering Sea seabird species found in 2001 is quite similar to the 1899 list. In the course of our Harriman Retraced voyage, we saw all the species identified in 1899 and some that the Harriman reports did not mention: pelagic and red-faced cormorants, glaucous-winged gull, common murre, crested auklet, and red-legged kittiwake. Have those birds taken up residence in the Bering Sea during the past hundred years? More likely the Harriman observers overlooked some species during their brief visits or else did not think them worth mentioning. Several other expeditions did record the presence of these species in the Bering Sea colonies between 1841 and 1914. Fisher himself saw the common murre, according to his unpublished notes, but it never appeared in the final reports. We are left to wonder how the actual sizes of seabird populations have changed over the past century. Scientific monitoring of Alaska's seabird populations began only in the 1970s, when we realized that human activities such as oil exploration could affect the Bering Sea environment on a large scale.

One fact is certain, and it is encouraging: our scientific capabilities and knowledge have improved radically since 1899. Modern technology, such as miniature radios for tracking birds across the oceans via satellite, would have been science fiction to the 1899 scholars. Our most crucial advantage today may be the modern sta-

tistical methods we have for designing research to help us understand seabird populations better.

From 1976 through the early 1980s, we saw major declines in seabird populations,
a phenomenon that worried scientists and conservationists. Seabird colonies normally
fluctuate somewhat in size, but this problem occurred throughout the Bering Sea and
Gulf of Alaska and suggested that a widespread cause was responsible. Since the mid-
1980s, many Alaskan seabird populations have been stable or increasing. Declining
populations continue to concern us in the Pribilof Islands and Prince William Sound.
Both the black-legged and red-legged kittiwake populations have declined steadily in
the Pribilofs for the past twenty-five years. Our greatest concern is for the red-legged
kittiwake on Saint George Island. This single colony contains the majority of the
species' population on earth. We are also seeing declines in the northern fulmar on
Saint George and in the thick-billed and common murre on both Saint Paul and Saint
George. In Prince William Sound, several seabird species were severely affected by the
Exxon Valdez oil spill, and some have not yet returned to their pre-spill numbers. The
reasons for these trends are being studied—and hotly debated.

Heated debates have become a routine part of our attempts to address seabird-
population declines, in part because our scientific understanding of the natural world
has improved so much. With more accurate monitoring of seabird populations, we
often can discover which species are in trouble and where. However, it is more diffi-

FIGURE *40. A. K. Fisher and Louis Agassiz Fuertes specimen collecting earlier in the voyage
on Kodiak Island. Credit: Edward S. Curtis. Source: Harriman family collection.*

cult to learn why they are declining or what to do about the problems. Our better understanding of ecosystems reveals that many different factors, singly or in combination, might be responsible.

Many scientists are concluding that the major factors underlying seabird declines are climate change, fisheries, and pollution. For instance, climate and commercial fisheries may have changed the food supply of seabirds in the Pribilof Islands; the failure of marine birds to regain their former numbers in Prince William Sound seems to be due to lingering oil pollution and a climate-caused lack of prey fish. To complicate matters, the predominance of these factors differs with the bird species and with location. The food requirements and adaptations of seabirds dictate where they can nest. Some seabirds are widespread, but others are confined to small areas. Each species hunts within the habitat to which it has become adapted over thousands of years. Auklets form large colonies only where ocean currents bring zooplankton from the deep ocean onto the continental shelf. Red-legged kittiwakes hunt for deep-ocean fish just beyond the shelf edge, so they must nest near this habitat: in the Pribilofs and Aleutians. Common murres and shearwaters specialize in water about 150 feet deep. Because they need to live in specific habitats, seabirds cannot just pick up and leave an area, even if prey becomes scarce or a catastrophe occurs.

Oil is the threat that many people think of first in the marine environment. The massive 1989 *Exxon Valdez* spill in Prince William Sound killed 250,000 seabirds. Some died because their oil-soaked feathers could not insulate them from the cold; others were poisoned while trying to preen themselves. This oil continues to foul some shorelines of Prince William Sound even in 2001. Several populations of seabirds, such as marbled and Kittlitz's murrelets, pigeon guillemots, and common murres, have not yet recovered from the spill. Although the *Exxon Valdez* spill is the best known, oil pollution is a serious threat everywhere on Alaska's coast. The fishing vessel *Windy Bay* hit a rock and leaked thirty-five thousand gallons of fuel into Prince William Sound on August 4, 2001, two days after we passed that spot. At least a hundred seabirds were killed. And, as we explored Saint Matthew Island, we saw a rusted hull on the rocks—the *Milos Reefer*, a freighter that ran aground in 1989 and spilled more than 237,000 gallons of fuel. Although these incidents do not make the national news, they are having an impact on Alaska's environment.

As we delighted in Alaska's magnificent coast and admired its birds, we learned that even we ourselves must take care not to harm them. While floating in our Zodiac below the vast crowds of birds on Hall Island, we assumed that we could not affect them. But once, as our boat slipped closer, the birds began to glance around urgently and then burst into the air. We hastily backed away. Disturbance, even if unintentional, can cause birds to lose their eggs or desert a colony. The loudest intruders, such as sightseeing planes, can disturb them from as far as half a mile away. A hiker's misplaced foot can collapse the soft soil above seabird burrows. As more people come to enjoy Alaska's magnificent landscape and wildlife, these seemingly isolated events can have an increasing impact on seabirds. Environmental educators and the eco-tourism industry are already collaborating so that people can appreciate the sensitivity of seabirds as well as their beauty.

History tells us humans have inadvertently caused other problems for seabirds. In spite of the Aleutian Islands' remoteness, their seabird colonies have suffered severely from introduced mammals. Seabirds coexisted with Natives in the Aleutian Islands for thousands of years, but after newly arrived Russian and U.S. fur farmers introduced foxes there, these predators devastated many seabird populations. Foxes have died off or have been removed on some islands, and seabirds are recovering. Nowadays the introduced Norway rat is perhaps the greatest threat to Alaska's seabirds. Rats are voracious predators; they can swim ashore from shipwrecks or boats in harbors, can climb any cliff, and are almost impossible to eradicate. Communities such as Saint George and Saint Paul have highly organized programs to keep rats away. This threat is so important that biologists have formed emergency teams to surround new shipwrecks and intercept rats before they can invade seabird colonies.

Explaining changes in seabird populations becomes more complex when we turn to the influence of climate change. In the mid-1970s, when we began to study the diets of seabirds, Pribilof birds were feeding their chicks plenty of energy-rich capelin. By 1980, however, they were eating more low-calorie species such as pollock. Ocean conditions had shifted, making it difficult for the birds to obtain their preferred fish, with the result that many chicks were not getting enough to eat. The entire North Pacific Ocean warmed in the late 1970s, providing one explanation for the food problems. Widespread climate shifts and changes in marine ecosystems have been occurring every few decades for centuries. Many believe that cooler conditions will return to the Bering Sea, but we cannot say with certainty that the original conditions will reestablish themselves. If this cyclical warming were to become predominant, as might occur with global climate change, Alaska's ecosystems could be affected profoundly.

Intensive commercial fishing may also be contributing to declines of seabirds in two possible ways: birds get caught directly in fishing gear, and fisheries may catch enough fish to compete directly with birds or to change the marine ecosystem. During the 1990s, more than 18,000 seabirds were accidentally caught each year in Alaska's offshore long-line and trawl fisheries. Most of this by-catch does not appear to be affecting bird populations, but there is concern about several species, particularly fulmars and albatrosses. Fishermen are now required to use devices that keep most birds away from long-line gear. The long-term effect of fisheries could be more serious: the dramatic reduction of seabird prey near breeding colonies or threats to the larger marine ecosystem from huge harvests of fish year after year.

Although I care deeply about the birds themselves, I know that they are also telling us a larger story. Ecologically, bird populations are the canary in the coal mine. The health of seabird populations is an indicator of the health of the ecosystem. If seabirds are experiencing problems, other parts of the system may be in trouble as well.

Many people have a stake in the continued health of Alaska's seabirds: bird-watchers, scientists, coastal residents, and the tourism industry. But no one has a greater interest in seabirds than coastal Native communities. Seabirds have been part of their cultures for as long as they have lived in the Bering Sea and Gulf of Alaska. These creatures inhabit their legends and art. Gulls and other seabirds, for example, were considered to be helping spirits for Yup'ik Eskimo hunters. Many Native communities continue to include subsistence harvests of seabirds as part of their way of life. On both sides of the Bering Sea, villagers collect eggs, and hunters harvest adult seabirds, particularly in spring when other food is scarce. Birds and eggs are shared throughout a village.

When problems of the Bering Sea are debated today, the dialogue sometimes becomes quite intense. Many groups—local residents and visitors, commercial fishers and subsistence hunters, scientists and managers—have deep concerns. We need to protect fish stocks, marine mammals, seabirds, and people's ways of life. The issues are complex; the solutions are sometimes uncertain or even (as with global warming) far away. Debate is a useful way to air all the issues. It is also the way in which various groups can express their points of view as the government considers and decides on management strategies, such as limiting catches for fisheries or controlling oil leaks from vessels.

The good news for Native communities, birdwatchers, and marine ornithologists is that seabird populations in most parts of Alaska are healthy. We are fortunate that most Alaskan colonies are now protected in federal wildlife refuges, national parks, and a few privately managed areas. Because most of Alaska's fifty million seabirds breed in only fifteen hundred colonies, the protection of these areas is an important part of our efforts to maintain healthy seabird populations. We remain concerned about seabirds in a few areas, however, and we must be vigilant in protecting them. We also must not forget that seabirds need protection of their feeding areas at sea.

As our exploration of Hall and Saint Matthew islands drew to a close, I felt both uplifted and sobered. Like Fuertes, Keeler, and Fisher a hundred years before, we were entranced by the seabirds at these remote wilderness islands. We were awed by the vitality of the innumerable thousands of birds and by their deep isolation. But our visit to this special place also showed us that not even the most remote speck of land in the Bering Sea can escape the pressures and problems of the modern world. The shipwreck teetering on the rocks beside Saint Matthew Island reminds us that the rest of the world is not far off. In a way, this is good. We need to remember that the seas and oceans of the world and their islands are all connected with each other— and powerfully influenced by our own species.

Finally, although no one was ready to leave Hall Island, it was time to go back to the *Clipper Odyssey*. The Zodiac headed out toward the empty sea. Then, to my relief, our ship materialized out of the mist.

PART FIVE

INTO RUSSIA, HOMEWARD TO NOME

❦

{Cape Dezhnev, Russia}

CLIMBING TO THE DESERTED VILLAGE

Lean into the hill, our guide says.
Grab hold of grasses, wormwood.
The balance of younger years is gone;
feet stray. Lean, our guide says. Lean.
This is where you learn to trust the land.

Climbing the trail of rock and bone,
you reach the bowhead jaws
that once held up an umiak; stop.
Resting on walrus skulls you look
up to the broken houses of hunters
gone north: moved to Uelen by the Soviets,
who themselves went away.

Earth will protect you.
See how this season of beach rye
holds soil, rib, cliff—even your hand
that reaches out, five-fingered
like the whale's hand. There is room.
Earth will compensate for what is lost.

— SHEILA NICKERSON

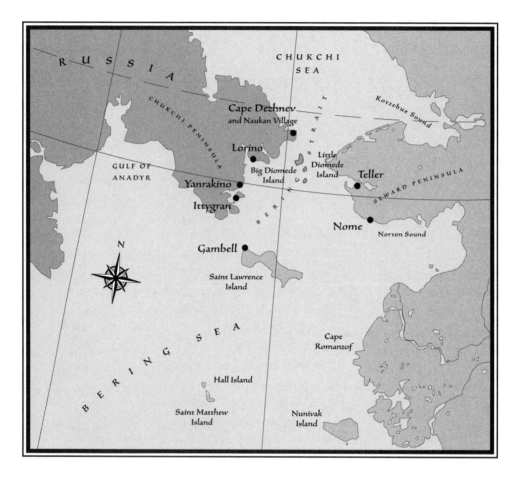

Across the Bering Sea, Yanrakino to Nome

Beringia

14–16 August 2001

The horn calling the Zodiacs back to the ship pierced the fog and reached us with a jolt. Exploring the towgambellering, seabird- and guano-covered cliffs of Hall Island had taken on a dreamlike quality. Visibility was limited, so cliffs packed with birds and haulouts covered with loafing sea lions slipped in and out of the gauze that surrounded our slow-moving boat. The sounds of water working the rocks, bird calls, and sea lion growls were amplified and hung in the heavy air. The raw beauty of these fog-framed scenes drew us in and, for the time, took us far away from the everyday world. No one was ready to break away at this point, and our enchanted time with a pod of sea lions delayed us further.

From below the surface, at the edge of visibility, appeared the head of a Steller sea lion, then a small group of heads, followed by dozens of heads—a pod of fifty or sixty sea lions materialized before our eyes. With the Bogoslof story still fresh in our minds, we reacted instantly to put distance between our boats and the pod. As we pulled away, they followed; we backed up farther, and they moved with us. After a few minutes we realized we were the center of the pod's interest and possibly their entertainment for the day. Their behavior was so carefree that this group must have never encountered human hunters in boats.

Unlike Bogoslof, which is a restricted breeding colony, Hall Island is a haulout site for nonbreeders. The sea lions following us were most likely nonbreeding juveniles that had dispersed from their birth colonies or males that had been run off by dominant breeding bulls and were now biding their time on a "bachelor island." A portion of the pod engulfed our Zodiac, and curious, bobbing faces surrounded us. We turned off the engine and immediately heard the snorts they made as they blew clouds of seawater into the air. I made eye contact with an individual just a few feet away who was staring at me. It was not a casual crossing of sightlines;

FIGURE 41. *A Siberian Yup'ik camp at Plover Bay, Russia.*
Credit: Edward S. Curtis. Source: Harriman family collection.

we studied each other, gathering information for our separate needs and purposes. Being wary of anthropomorphizing, I remain confident in reporting that these sea lions were having fun among themselves and with the delighted but hesitant humans. For as long as they chose, we could not lose them. They breached into the air and splash-landed, circled our boats, blew water in all directions, and bobbed around us like giant corks. As we made our way back toward the ship, I was sad when they had had enough of us and broke away, disappearing as quietly into the fog as they had arrived. I cherished the innocence of our encounter but worried that they were not warier.

On August 14 we left Hall Island late in the afternoon, and, for the first time, our course significantly departed from the 1899 route. In

1899, having missed Hall and Saint Matthew islands in the fog after leaving Saint Paul, the Harriman Expedition sailed directly to Plover Bay, a small Yup'ik settlement near what is now the deep-water port of Provideniya, the region's government center, located on the Chukchi Peninsula's southern point. Remarkably, as the sea-weary John Burroughs points out, after all their effort getting there, they spent little time on their Siberian adventure: "We traveled two hours in Asia." They sailed north along the coast into the twilight, but sea conditions deterred them from making other Russian landings. They could not pass through the Bering Strait, Burroughs reported, as "a little farther north the ice pack closed the gateway to the Arctic Ocean." The *Elder* turned instead east and south toward North America, passing within sight of the Diomede Islands and King Island. The immediate goal was to reprovision in Port Clarence, an anchorage for the Bering Sea and Arctic whaling fleet, located on Alaska's Seward Peninsula.

As expected near the end of long journey, the mood on the *Elder* shifted from outward-bound exploration to thoughts of home. From this northernmost point of the 1899 voyage, Captain Peter Doran now steered his ship southward, stopping briefly at Saint Lawrence Island, then making short landings at the previously elusive Hall and Saint Matthew islands. Harriman's expedition from this point forward focused on Seattle. During this leg of the journey the *Elder* made the ill-fated stop at the Saanya Kwaan's Cape Fox Village and collected totems. Also during this passage, Harriman himself confirmed that the voyage was drawing to an end. When asked to share in an exceptional view of the Fairweather Range, he made his often-quoted declaration: "I don't give a damn if I never see any more scenery!" The very challenges that prompted this ambitious but exhausted man's journey to Alaska were now calling him back.

Our 2001 journey would end on the Seward Peninsula, but not before we pushed farther than the *Elder* had sailed. Expense and the time constraints of our contemporary, busy lives made sailing back to Seattle impractical. The convenience of air travel made the decision for us—Nome would mark the end of the 2001 voyage. But from the outset of our planning we had wanted to look beyond the 1899 expedition's accomplishments, and as we left Hall Island, we began this new chapter. The technically advanced *Clipper Odyssey* would take us farther north than our 1899 colleagues had been and

FIGURE *42. A group picture taken on Cape Fox Village beach toward the voyage's end.*
Credit: Edward S. Curtis. Source: Harriman family collection.

would allow us to spend more time along the thinly charted Chukchi Peninsula's coastline. We knew this reconnaissance could only start an exploration that would have to be completed sometime in the future.

We were aware that in the last leg of our voyage we were sailing into the heart of a geographic region, Beringia—a place that marks the beginning of an epic time in the earth's history. Although the dates of human migration across the Bering Land Bridge are debated, there is little disagreement that at the peak of its emergence a thousand-mile-wide piece of land connecting Asia and North America was the route used by plants, animals, and humans migrating in both directions between Siberia and Alaska. Like the mountains of the Southeast's Alexander Archipelago, the Bering Land Bridge emerged again during the last ice age, about thirteen thousand years ago. A vast swath of relatively shallow continental shelf appeared as the earth's temperatures dropped; free water was transformed into glacial ice, and the sea level fell three hundred feet. With time, grasses invaded the raw earth and a semiarid steppe came to cover the land that would only temporarily connect two continents. Shortly, we would be sailing over the top of it.

Fittingly, our first landing on this leg was Saint Lawrence Island, a mountainous island seventy by twenty-five miles, at the gates of the Bering Strait—and a visible remnant of the land bridge now reclaimed by the sea. Saint Lawrence Island also began a new, surreal chapter of our voyage, in which the ancient cultures of Beringia were connected with the most dangerous of twentieth-century geopolitics. In the same conversation we could speak of walrus-skin boats and nuclear warheads.

Our destination was Gambell, or Sivuqaq, a village of 650 people on Saint Lawrence's Northwest Cape. As we approached from Niyrakpak Lagoon, fresh winds from the north piled up the lagoon's shallow waters into breaking waves and made a landing too dangerous. The *Odyssey* rounded the cape to the west looking for protection in the headland's lee and lowered a single Zodiac to scout a landing site. After traveling in our small boat just outside the shore break for some distance, we found a reasonable landing place. Suffice it to say that this was one of the more exhilarating arrivals of the voyage, as we timed our landings on the beach in and among three-to-four-foot waves. To the credit of our expert crew, there is no tale of swamped Zodiacs to tell. Nonetheless, our arrival must have been entertaining for community leaders Wilbur Booshu, Melvin Apassingok, and Gerold Soonagrook, who watched from the shore.

A small fleet of all-terrain vehicles awaited us on the beach. Following greetings, they transported us over a remarkable landscape composed almost entirely of golf-ball–sized gravel. The village itself sits on this "plain of gravel," which shifts and adjusts under each step. Once we were in the community center, we heard for the first time a version of a story that would be repeated throughout our travels in the north Bering Sea. Our new friends told us they are the Yup'ik. The community today is most closely related to the Siberian Yup'ik living on parts of the Chukchi coast, but their common ancestry extends to Central Yup'ik and Inupiaq living on the Bering Sea and Arctic coasts of Alaska. They are all hunters, sometimes called Eskimos, who share an ancient heritage bound and shaped by the sea. Regional differences certainly exist, but at their cultural core they are a maritime people whose social organization and subsistence culture are based on hunting whale, walrus, seal, fish, seabirds, waterfowl, and polar bear. Even with the pervasive influences of Western society, signs of subsistence living are everywhere in Gambell: fish drying on racks, the remains of a butchered whale, bone piles, walrus skulls defining dumps and work yards, and walrus skins stretched on drying racks. Umiaks, traditional walrus skin–covered hunting boats are under construction, and others stand ready along the beach.

The Saint Lawrence Yup'iks, like other Native people of Beringia, have a culture that has evolved in response to an extreme environment. Summers are short, with an average temperature of around forty-one degrees. Precipitation occurs three hundred days a year. Fog and gale winds are common. Pack ice engulfs the island in mid-November and breaks up at the end of May. During this time the days grow darker until the sun does not rise at all; then the days lengthen slowly as the summer solstice and midnight sun approach. Average winter temperatures range between minus-two and ten degrees Fahrenheit, with extreme cold sometimes reaching minus-thirty degrees.

I waited at the shoreline for the last Zodiac back to the ship and looked higher up the beach at the group of people waving good-bye, kind people who had hosted our visit and shared their day and good company with us. It was chilling to consider how a people so well prepared to deal with one set of harsh conditions had once suddenly found themselves so utterly vulnerable in the face of others.

Burroughs described the situation on Saint Lawrence one hundred years ago: "Not many years ago there were on St. Lawrence many encampments of Eskimo embracing sev-eral hundred people. Late one autumn some whalers turned up there with the worst kind of whiskey, with which they wrought ruin of the natives, persuading them to exchange most of their furs and other valuables for it, and leaving them so debauched and demoralized that nearly all perished of cold and hunger the following winter. Village after village was found depopulated, the people lying dead in their houses." He was describing the famine of 1879, during which survivors near Gambell and Saint Lawrence's other village, Savoonga, were too weak to bury their dead. Instead, they used their homes as crypts that, with time, became sacred burial sites. When in 1899 he observed the impact of Western culture on the Native people of the Bering Sea, George Bird Grinnell came to this plain-spoken conclusion: "The outlook for the immediate future for these Eskimos is gloomy. . . . [Westerners] have taken away their women, and debauched their men with liquor; they have brought them strange new diseases . . . and in a very short time they will ruin and disperse the wholesome, hearty, merry people whom we saw."

We knew this story all too well. It had been repeated in one form or another since we left Prince Rupert's temperate rainforests. Now, just short of the Arctic Circle, we were hearing it again. But, more important, in revisiting this nightmarish period in the Yup'ik and Inupiaq past, we needed to be clear about who stood before us on the beach: a resilient people whose culture and religion were so strong that they had overcome the unspeakable. As their longer history has shown, they have again and again found ways to confront harsh conditions and move beyond them into the future.

Not to be forgotten, the future into which the Yup'iks are moving lies on an island under

U.S. jurisdiction, in a region where Native communities have been entangled in the relationship between the United States and the former Soviet Union. Provideniya, Russia, is less than 50 miles away from Saint Lawrence Island in the United States. From Gamble, the Russian border is just 18 miles to the west; Nome is 185 miles to the east. For millennia, these distances had more to do with properly provisioning an umiak for a whale hunt or visiting relatives who could be found on either coast than with international tensions. For many of us from "away," Americans who grew up during the cold war, our understanding has been more abstract; Russia was first an idea, then a place. With little direct experience, much of what most Americans know about this region is embedded in U.S-Soviet relations as portrayed on the nightly news. For decades, the broader, more dangerous relations between ideological rivals displaced an understanding of the people and cultures that rim the north Bering Sea. The matter was much simpler for us in a sense; one was either Russian or American, and we knew the difference.

Our visit to Gambell, then the Inupiaq subsistence communities of Teller, north of Nome, and Little Diomede in the Bering Strait quickly blurred the lines between nations. Political realities and ancient traditions are woven together as a matter of routine in these communities. In Teller, signs of subsistence hunting and fishing were mixed with the early-morning image of the postmaster raising the U.S. flag over the post office. As we walked toward the community center, sled dogs tethered in neighborhood yards vigilantly studied our intentions, and their barking telegraphed the news of our approach up the road. Moments later we watched traditional dances and saw clothing reflecting both Siberian and Inupiaq styles. The drums, covered with walrus stomach and beaten with walrus tusk, were of a kind used on both the Chukchi and Seward peninsulas. On the way back to the ship, members of our Young Explorers Team joined a pickup basketball game on a schoolyard court.

Later that day we found that the relationship between Little Diomede Island and Russia is more dramatic. Little Diomede is just two-and-a-half miles from Big Diomede Island, in Russia. Between the two islands runs the international date line, which is also the boundary between Russia and the United States. From Little Diomede you look into both Russia and "tomorrow." For members of this community, the international date line and the iron curtain were one and the same, as family groups were kept apart by the politics of others. After meeting with Mayor Dora Ahkinga and Elders Orville Ahkinga Sr. and Pat Omiak Sr., we walked through the village center up the mountainside on a narrow footpath into an area of homes. There we met a fellow who identified himself as a hunter; he was working on two walrus skins stretched on drying racks. He explained that the villagers use only female walrus skins for their boats because the females have much less scar tissue and damage from fighting, which regularly occurs among males. We asked where he hunted; he pointed to different locations not far offshore, sites determined by season and weather, by where there was ice or open water. He was quick to remind us that he and his fellow hunters are forbidden to cross the international date line into Russia to hunt. He gazed out toward Big Diomede for a moment, then smiled and said, "But I don't see no date line."

A World Turned Upside Down, Twice: Chukchi Peninsula

18–19 August 2001

Those among us who had been day-dreaming about exploring the globe's faraway places since middle-school geography class were about to experience one of the most interesting intersections the world map has to offer. At 7:15 P.M. we had left Little Diomede, heading due west for Big Diomede, the international date line, and Russian waters. As we crossed the date line, which corresponds to the one-hundred-eightieth meridian, the *Odyssey*'s stern was in the United States on Thursday, August 16, and its bow in Russia on Friday, August 17. We were also in the middle of the Bering Strait, where the waters of the Bering and Chukchi seas meet. Cape Dezhnev, the easternmost point on the continent of Asia, was twenty-five miles ahead, and Cape Prince of Wales, the westernmost point in North America, was thirty miles off the stern. At this point you can see two continents, separated by only fifty-five miles that just an ice age ago was a land bridge.

At the southern end of Big Diomede, or Ostrov (island) Ratmanova as the Russians call it, a Russian ship met us. It transported three customs officials who cleared us into Russia and stayed on board the *Odyssey* for the duration of the Chukchi exploration. Sailing north along the Big Diomede coast, some of us tended to the official business of passports and visas, while others watched the seemingly slow-motion life of more than 150 walrus lying about a haulout. A fog bank rolled in behind us, swallowing all we had just seen; the silver-gray cloud of fog seemed to push us gently north into the Chukchi Sea.

The geographers on board had one more goal to accomplish in the remaining hours of this day. With Big Diomede off our stern, we set a course of six degrees, just a little east of north. At 11:36 P.M. we gathered on the bridge in the twilight to watch the Global Positioning System (GPS) unit, which uses a network of satellite signals to determine precise latitude and longitude locations on the

FIGURE *43. A quiet moment for Edward H. and Mary W. Harriman on the deck of the* George W. Elder *during the return voyage. Credit: William A. Averell. Source: Manuscripts Special Collections, University Archives, University of Washington Libraries, Harriman 195.*

earth's surface. The ship's GPS receiver ticked off our position in minutes and seconds as we moved north until we arrived at latitude 66°33": the Arctic Circle. With a cheer, we celebrated this imaginary line, which separates the Arctic from the Subarctic and demarcates the southern limit of the area where the sun neither sets on the summer solstice (June 21) nor rises on the winter solstice (December 22). In a world with many disputes, we had the satisfaction of a day that confirmed many irrefutable facts of nature and some very old agreements between navigators and mapmakers.

We would go no farther north on this voyage. Shortly after midnight, the *Clipper Odyssey* set on a course of 199 degrees southsouthwest for Cape Dezhnev. In just hours, we would make landfall on the Chukchi Peninsula and observe the Far Eastern remains of the Soviet experiment. For weeks we had been seeing examples of entrepre-

neurial drive spurred on by the promise of free-market rewards; now we would experience the other side of the ideological rivalry that gripped the twentieth century. When we entered the north Bering Sea the day before, cultural anthropologist David Koester, a member of our "floating university" and a Russian Far East specialist, gave a lecture to help prepare us for what lay just ahead:

For the people of Plover Bay who encountered the 1899 expedition, the Soviet government was still more than a quarter century away. When Soviet power did arrive, it came with an ideology dramatically different from that of the individuals and corporations seeking gold-rush wealth in Alaska. The destructive forces affecting the lives of the Native populations of Alaska were haphazard and not centrally planned. Soviet interventions, however, were carried out with the grand humanitarian ideology of socialist reform, which was transformed in stages by the turning screw of Soviet domination.

In the 1940s the Soviet government organized collective farms, known as *kolkhozy*. In Chukchi these were, of course, not actually farms but increasingly segmented and specialized versions of traditional harvesting activities: reindeer herding, sea mammal hunting, and fishing. Eventually, the government industrialized processing of the animals as well. Some of the young people present in Plover Bay when the Harriman expedition visited could have witnessed the construction of the Plover Bay sea mammal processing plant in 1948. It processed sea mammal meat, hides, tusks, fat, and fish products from the catch provided by the local *kolkhoz*. Reindeer herding was simi-

larly collectivized, with the more profound effect of settling the formerly nomadic herding populations. Perhaps the greatest disruption to the lives of the indigenous peoples of the Russian North Pacific Region came not with collectivization but with resettlement of populations. The new villages were not sited for their capacity to sustain traditional subsistence practices, and *kolkhozy* that had been profitable when they were located near procurement territories soon showed losses as transportation costs increased.

The Cold War had a direct impact on the lives of Yup'ik Eskimos near the coast. The government closed villages and created multiethnic towns with the intention of interrupting historical ties with related villages across the Bering Sea in Alaska. The government sought to introduce new,

FIGURE *44. A Siberian Yup'ik family at Plover Bay, Russia, studying the visitors. Credit: Edward S. Curtis. Source: Harriman family collection.*

223

bureaucratized production activities and curtail "risky" subsistence practices. Reindeer herding was considered more profitable and closer to the agricultural model on which the *kolkhozy* were built nationwide. With this, support for sea mammal subsistence decreased. According to Ol'ga Murashko, in the early 1960s there were nearly 700 hunters in ninety-six brigades involved in sea mammal hunting; by the end of the 1960s there were only 357 sea mammal hunters in sixty-three brigades.

The *sovkhoz* era, a new phase in both political and economic development, brought more changes, as the government introduced livestock, fur, and chicken farming. With this new economic infrastructure came a huge influx of settlers, with the goal of creating a total industrial-agricultural economy combining local and imported activities. The positive side, temporarily at least, was that central government then provided medical and consumer services and supported communications and transportation. The down side for these once independent and self-sustaining cultures was a high dependence on a distant government—Moscow was four thousand miles away—for supplies of fuel, animal feed, food, and communications.

When the Soviet government collapsed in the early nineties, many communities were left with homes dependent on now-scarce resources: electricity for cooking and oil, gas, or firewood for heating. The state stores that had provided staple foods collapsed along with the government. The flow of medical supplies nearly stopped, and alcoholism, a problem over much of Russia, increased, as high-profit activities associated with the sale and production of alcohol thrived.

The result of the collapse has been a difficult wave of efforts to revive traditional subsistence practices. The problem of distance from subsistence harvest areas, brought about by resettlement, has become even more acute. Fuel for transportation, heating, and cooking quickly became difficult to obtain. The only communities that are doing relatively well are those with sufficiently diversified economies and access to local resources that provide self-sustaining sources of food.

Captain Michael Taylor's order to drop anchor off Cape Dezhnev at Naukan Village came at 6:37 A.M. on August 18. From the deck, a collage of grays and whites blurred the boundaries between the choppy sea, unsettled sky, and mountainous rock outcrops that blended into patches of green, wind-worked shrubs. We wore the heavy coats, hats, and gloves of winter while waiting for the Zodiacs to be lowered. Fog and broken pieces of low clouds raced by the ship and down the strait, driven by a constant, cold wind.

Once in the boats, we headed for the shoreline and a narrow gravel beach pinched off by the abrupt rise of the mountain face. Large snowfields along the beach were tucked against the mountain's toe. Farther up the face more snow filled the deeper, shaded ravines. Our landing parties collected on the beach, then followed our Russian guide, Sergey Frolov, single file up a steep, narrow switchback trail. The simple rock and dirt path formed the route into a village that once was home to more than three hundred Siberian Yup'iks. Centuries of foot traffic had worn the stones smooth.

The village site is no more than a leveling-off of the mountainside before it again rises steeply to the peak. This one small, remote place, looking out over the Bering Strait and eons-old marine mammal–migration routes, embodied the sweeping history shared by Koester. A wider path about a half mile long led along the cliff edge north, separating the village remains from the precipice. Two parallel rows of weathered whale ribs were all that remained of drying racks for meat and fish and for storing the village's umiaks. Scattered along the upper side of the cliff path were carefully constructed circular rock meat caches, pits fifteen feet across and eight feet deep, which reminded me of a New England root-cellar hole. Lichen-covered whale and walrus bones scattered along the path identified the work that had taken place in this part of the village.

The path forked gently uphill into a cluster of stone house foundations, the village proper. These foundations were also circular or oblong, some being thirty feet or more across. Whale-rib and driftwood rafters that had supported animal-skin roofs still spanned the foundations of a few homes. Further upslope, higher than any other construction, was the burial ground. Easily seeing the deliberate organization of the vanished community, I could image the village at work, going about its social life and carrying out the chores necessary to prepare for the winter just ahead.

Little remained of this community, which had been inhabited for more than two thousand years, once the second largest Native community on the Chukchi Peninsula. In 1958, the Soviet government declared Naukan an "unpromising" village and relocated the residents to Nunyamo, a collective farm that failed in the 1970s. A culturally rich people intimately tied to the Bering Sea ecosystem became drifters. In 1899 George Bird Grinnell expressed dismay about the seemingly "inevitable conflict" between Western and Native cultures, saying, "Wherever the two touch each other, the weaker people must be destroyed." Grinnell's opinion was informed; in the U.S. West he had seen the results of Native resettlement following the Indian wars of the 1870s. The powerful irony that met us just a little farther down the ancient path brought Grinnell's dire words into the present.

The cliff path continued northward, ending at a ravine that drew a sharp line between the Yup'ik community and a Soviet military outpost. The outpost, a projection of power at the door of its ideological adversary just fifty-five miles away, also lay in ruin. The materials for the half-dozen rectangular buildings in various states of collapse were obviously manufactured elsewhere and brought to the site: milled beams numbered for assembly; plaster and lath; decorative millwork around the windows and doors; pitched roofs with eaves and soffits. A building that appeared to be the headquarters, with the date 1963 above its door, was falling into its own cellar. Surveying from the slope above the compound and the Bering Strait beyond it, I searched for words to explain what had gone on here. Many came to mind, but the Soviets' own lingered: *unpromising.* The time span between the establishment of the Soviet Union in 1917 and its disintegration in 1991 was seventy-four years. Not nearly enough time to smooth stones on a path.

At midday, the *Odyssey* weighed anchor and headed south-southwest along the magnificently raw and beautiful Chukchi coast. Unsettled weather gave way to clearing skies and diminishing winds. With just seventy thousand people throughout the expansive Chukchi Region, there is little sign of human activity. At

2:00 P.M. we rounded Mys (cape) Kriguygun on a westward course for Lorino, the largest rural community on the peninsula. In 1953, Lorino was a small Native village that, with a declaration of the Soviet government, became the site of the new Lenin Collective Farm. The nomadic Chukchi reindeer herders of the interior, the sedentary maritime Chukchi of the coast, and the Yup'iks were gathered together and resettled in Lorino. The surviving residents of Naukan were eventually settled there also. For a time the heavily subsidized socialist economy of Lorino thrived from the development of commercial reindeer and fox farming and marine mammal hunting.

The Lorino that Harriman Retraced visited in 2001 was a community living in a twilight zone between remnant traditional cultures and a collapsed Soviet system. Little in their ancient subsistence or contemporary socialist histories had prepared the Native people or local administrators for an abrupt transition toward a market economy. Imagine a small, remote, rural city of fifteen hundred people, with a municipal infrastructure—schools, water system, waste treatment, communications, transportation, healthcare, fuel supplies, food distribution—where almost overnight state and federal support disappears, along with the most prominent financial players. This is Lorino today, with its decaying, stark, Stalinist-looking buildings, rusting infrastructure, and machines and vehicles that have been repaired so often that they can be best described as "contraptions."

The Soviet bureaucrats responsible for assembling this state farm moved on, leaving the local government to struggle. Those left were a generation divorced from their traditional subsistence cultures, and, as a result of

central planning and policymaking, they had little governmental experience. Attempts at reviving their subsistence culture have been slowed by depleted marine mammal stocks. Local stocks had been reduced in the process of providing feed to the fox farms. That issue aside, even a healthy, local marine mammal population could not support an artificial concentration of fifteen hundred people. Hunters now travel considerable distances to find fewer animals. The anchoring of the *Odyssey* off Lorino created a contrast so sharp that many of us were uneasy. In a few moments we would leave a ship projecting wealth and luxury to enter a community where poverty shortened peoples' lives.

As we had found in many instances on our journey, the spirit of the people we met was often distinct from the circumstances in which they found themselves. And they were not looking for our sympathy. As we approached the Lorino beach in our Zodiacs, a large dance troupe in traditional dress was waiting for us, loudly beating walrus-skin drums amid a cacophony of greeting calls. The commotion on the beach signaled our arrival at the village. Residents streamed down from the sandy bluff on which the town sat to the wide, sandy beach below. By now the sky was clear and crystal blue, the sun August-bright, and the Bering Sea a reflecting pond. With this warm, uproarious welcome, the ship's party and the community—elders, mothers, fathers, children, teenagers—melded into a single group communicating through interpreters or a mix of words and often comical sign language. Quizzical looks, hesitant nods, and bursts of laughter alternated with those wonderful moments where broad smiles signaled a breakthrough and understanding. Some of us rediscovered that speaking English louder does not necessarily improve communication.

The community's craftspeople were ready for business. Their stands and display blankets stretched end to end along the foot of the sandy bluff. It was like the scene John Burroughs had described in Port Clarence: "They had all manner of furs, garments, baskets, ornaments, and curios for sale. . . . An animated and picturesque scene they presented, and dozens of cameras were leveled at them."

In the midst of the festivities, a small number of non-Native Russians, some in military uniforms, others in Western clothes, watched the goings-on, aloof observers. Oblivious to the sentinels, the crowd formed a broad circle around the dancers and drummers, who began their performance. Elder dance leaders stood behind the younger dancers, stoically evaluating their students. Following the dancing, young men performed comedy skits full of stylized buffoonery. The end of the skits marked the start of the umiak races along the shore. The bright sun backlit the sails and the walrus-skinned hulls that glowed yellow-brown. Just off shore, behind the umiaks, the *Odyssey* lay at anchor.

Before the end of the festivities, I left the gathering for a meeting with Roman Abramovich, the new governor of the Chukchi Region. He is the individual charged with leading the mineral-rich but poverty-stricken post-Soviet region into the future. To look at him, you would not know that the unassuming, boyish thirty-four-year-old, dressed in jeans, was a highly successful entrepreneur and skilled politician—who personally wanted to assess the opportunities that shipborne visitors wishing to spend hard cash might present. Although Lorino's modern history could not have been more different from that of the Alaska coast towns we had been visiting, the conversation we had with him about the economic potential of tourism was remarkably similar. Lorino villagers, who expressed approval of Governor Abramovich to us, seem to appreciate his efforts and to feel that he understands their problems and tries to solve them. They credit him with finding the resources to keep the electric power plant and schools operating.

The governor, and his entourage of assistants and bodyguards, met us at the edge of the crowd; discussions were held with his staff as to how the visit would take place. An invitation to the governor to attend a dinner in his honor aboard the *Odyssey* was respectfully declined. He was uncomfortable dining at a banquet while just a short distance away Lorino struggled. When a fact-finding tour was accepted as a substitute for the dinner, we all set off for the ship. The tour, led by Captain Taylor and his officers, ended in the ship's lounge. There we talked about the hundred-year-old connection between Russia and the Soviet Union and Harriman Retraced. The governor was well aware of the geopolitics that had shaped the modern relationship between the United States and Russia and the role that W. Averell Harriman had played in fostering relations between the two countries. Averell was eight years old when he first visited Russia as part of his father's expedition. In adulthood, he pursued a career that resulted in a lifetime of return visits and involved him deeply in relations between the United States and Russia: as Franklin Roosevelt's ambassador to the Soviet Union from 1943 to 1946, secretary of commerce under Harry Truman, and manager of the Lend-Lease program. Years later, under President John Kennedy, Averell served as assistant secretary for Far Eastern Affairs and participated in the Nuclear Test-Ban Treaty negotiations. Capping a career of relations-building with the Soviet Union, he founded the Harriman Institute for Advanced Study of the Soviet Union at Columbia University.

During our shipboard conversation, we discussed the end of the cold war, the future that our children would inherit, and how cooperation could improve that future. The only stumble came when the governor proposed that a renewed military-industrial complex was an economic engine that made sense for his country, "that good leaders know not to take it too far." The governor seemed to enjoy the pregnant pause as the ecologist processed his proposal. The first thing that came to my mind was an August 14 story in the *Odyssey*'s satellite newspaper—headlined "Rumsfeld: Negotiating with Russia Is 'Cold War Thinking'"—about the proposed withdrawal of the United States from the Antiballistic Missile Treaty. Hoping to avoid a slippery diplomatic slope as we floated in Russian waters, I stuck to what I knew and suggested that although the military-industrial complex was certainly an option, so too were projects like the joint International Space Station and the economic opportunities its emerging science and technology represented. He smiled and nodded at my satisfactory response, and we moved on to the status of sealing in the Pribilofs. With a signal from an aide, the conversation drew to a close, and the group made its way to the stern. After handshakes and farewells, the powerful visitors loaded back into Zodiacs and headed for shore. Leaning on the stern rail watching the governor's boat approach shore, with Yup'iks, Chukchis, Americans, and Russians gathered on the beach just beyond, I wished for "good leaders" in our future.

{Little Diomede}

THE VIEW FROM THE SHIP

See how the houses run up the hill,
away from the waves, on stilts.
See how they fall, or fly off
the side, leaving their legs
behind. See, high above,
those crosses huddled on talus—
how the race ends there,
in a silent crowd of rock.

— SHEILA NICKERSON

Chukchi Drummer

© PATRICIA SAVAGE

CHAPTER FOURTEEN

DISCOVERING ALASKA

∾

R I C H A R D   N E L S O N

After a time the Eskimo left the ship to return to the beach. . . . There was a continuous
camp of natives stretching all along the curving beach for a mile or more.

> – *George Bird Grinnell, "Natives of the Alaska Coast Region,"*
> *in vol. 1 of* Harriman Alaska Expedition

A GUSTY NORTH WIND poured through the gateway of the Bering Strait, tearing holes in the fog, scattering swarms of whitecaps across brilliant blue water. From high lookouts on the *Clipper Odyssey*'s decks, everyone peered excitedly ahead. Finally, a shoulder of pale brown stone glimmered a few degrees off the bow, broadened and rose higher, then resolved itself into the impassive self-containment of an island. A second island came into view, separated from the first by two miles of fretting sea. The channel, which looked broad and ample at first, seemed to shrink as we came near, until it felt like a narrow defile between impinging rock walls.

All of us had dreamed of laying eyes on this pair of islands, and we couldn't suppress the urge to recite their names, as if the words created them out of myth, as if they shaped what had seemed almost imaginary into something real, as if our utterances made comprehensible the vastly different worlds lying to port and starboard:

Big Diomede—Little Diomede
Russia—Alaska
Old World—New World
Eastern Hemisphere—Western Hemisphere

Our ship eased between the islands, nosing into the gale and tide. We angled closer to the flank of Little Diomede, which now cut a high arc across the sky. At the base of a precipitous talus slope, stuck there like a tick on a cow's haunch, was a cluster of weathered houses perched atop wooden stilts, with a network of trails running between. Thousands of seabirds—auklets, murres, gulls—whirled about the island and above the village, making the rounds between their nests and the neighboring sea. Adding another element to this remarkable scene, a herd of walrus lolled among the waves just ahead, then surged away, regarding us disdainfully, snorting spray into the wind. Their enormous brown bodies, plainly visible in the clear water, looked like drifting chunks of earth. I was reminded of an Inupiaq Eskimo word for walruses on a floating ice pan: *nunavak,* "piece of land."

The ship came ponderously to a halt and dropped anchor, filling our ears with the resonant clatter of chain links running through cold steel—a noise that had signaled the start of many mornings and made me feel as though I was awakening inside a massive alarm clock. Everyone lined up along the rails, peering toward the village, where a growing cluster of residents looked back with seemingly equal interest.

I had never seen a more improbable place for a human settlement, nor could I have conceived of a community that so visibly demonstrated the tenacity, irrepressibility, and ingenuity of the Eskimo people. What other group of humans, anywhere on earth or at any time in history, would be capable of inhabiting such a feral and daunting place? But the birds in the air and the walruses in the sea gave an immediate, eloquent explanation, for this narrow channel teems with exuberant, edible life, nourished by powerful currents rushing between the Bering and Chukchi seas.

Inflatable Zodiacs dropped like spiders from the davits and began ferrying brightly bundled passengers to shore. I stood with binoculars on the ship's uppermost deck, savoring the sight of villagers greeting newcomers. Here we were, in the year 2001, renewing an ancient tradition as wandering humans converged in the midst of the Bering Strait, their senses focused wholly on the pleasures and rewards of discovery.

For countless millennia, people have been discovering Alaska. In every tribe and culture, throughout all eras and generations, among the myriad camps and communities, men and women and children have undertaken to explore the immeasurable complexity of their northern world. By studying the landscapes, waterways, skies, weather, plants, and animals around them, people have accumulated the knowledge required for subsistence, survival, and success. Their discoveries have shaped a diverse array of cultures and lifeways, creating uniquely Alaskan legacies of science and technology, religion and art, society and community.

Waiting my turn for a shuttle to the island, I reflected on my own experiences in Alaska and how most of those experiences grew out of the discoveries made over thousands of years by people from diverse cultural traditions. I realized it was impossible to comprehend my own relationship to Alaska without understanding how all of us have discovered this place and how these discoveries have shaped our comprehension of Alaska itself.

FIGURE 46. *Inupiaq women and children at Port Clarence, Seward Peninsula.*
Credit: Edward S. Curtis. Source: Harriman family collection.

Almost forty years ago, I had arrived in another Inupiaq Eskimo village called Wainwright, situated on the arctic coast some four hundred miles north of Little Diomede. To carry out my work as an anthropologist, I acquired a team of dogs, sewed harnesses and built a sled, made a kayak, purchased caribou-hide clothing, learned to shoot a rifle, and started my apprenticeship as a hunter. Soon I was traveling widely on the tundra and sea ice, spending long nights in remote camps, listening to the elders, and making discoveries that would profoundly affect the course of my life.

Now, fragments of the Inupiaq language began drifting through my mind—words for the different kinds of sea ice, words for the wind and weather, words for the animals, and words for places on the land. Thinking about those places and longing to hear the sounds, I whispered their names to myself:

> *Qilamittagvik:* "place to hunt ducks with ivory bolas"
>
> *Pingusugruk:* "big hill thrust up by the permafrost"
>
> *Qayiaqsigvik:* "place where a kayak was lost"
>
> *Nannugvik:* "place of the polar bear"
>
> *Anaktuuq:* "place where there are caribou droppings"
>
> *Mitqutailat:* "place of the arctic terns"
>
> *Ulguniq:* "where a standing thing fell and left its traces"
> (the Inupiaq name for Wainwright Village)

The two-thousand-mile coastline traversed by our voyage was stitched together by a chain of names like these—in the Tlingit, Haida, Chugach, Danaina, Alutiiq, Aleut, Yup'ik, and Inupiaq languages—adding to the uniqueness and meaning of every cape and headland, bay and cove, islet and pinnacle, river and estuary.

Once, as I traveled by dog team with an Inupiaq man, he had pointed out a single stone no taller than my knee on the featureless tundra plain. Then he had told me a name for the place, which as far as I knew was distinguished mainly by the presence of that stone. I had imagined then how the land around us was embellished with thousands of names, shimmering like diamonds in the minds of those who listened and remembered. Some of these names are so ancient that no one recalls what they mean or how they came to be. Others are recent enough that villagers can translate and explain them. And still others have been given by newcomers from Russia, France, Britain, and the United States. Earlier in our voyage, much notice had been given to names assigned by the Harriman Expedition in 1899, especially in Prince William Sound—names like Smith Glacier, College Fjord, Harvard Glacier, Harriman Fjord. Regardless of their origin, place names reflect the process of discovery—people exploring, studying, utilizing, inhabiting, celebrating, and embedding themselves into the landscape. These names remind us that people have lived in Alaska for a prodigious length of time, and they reveal that a deeply abiding human history is written everywhere, whether the names are inscribed on maps or in memory.

Only one Alaskan place has a completely different story—a place that is remarkable not for the richness of its human history but for the nearly complete absence of such a history. It is called Saint Matthew Island, a place we visited just a few days ago. This island is one of most isolated tracts of land in the Northern Hemisphere and one of the few bits of terrain outside the Antarctic that has never been permanently settled by people.

The different histories of Saint Matthew and Little Diomede bring sharply into focus the nexus between humans and land in Alaska. Several times over the past thirty thousand years, the Diomedes have switched their identity from islands in the strait to mountains overlooking a broad isthmus of land. Before the final inundation of this isthmus by rising sea levels, ancestral Native Americans gradually moved across and entered the New World for the first time. This migration was one of the greatest events in the history of human discovery.

We often forget that Alaska's landscapes and waterways have been intimately known for many thousands of years. We overlook this essential fact because most of Alaska looks as pristine as Saint Matthew Island, and so we consider it a wilderness, as if it had never been settled at all. And, in fact, except for areas now experiencing the impact of modern industry, land clearing, or other developments, the long-inhabited Alaskan terrain is still fundamentally unaltered, the plant communities remain intact, the fauna is undiminished and diverse.

AS WE POUNDED shoreward in a Zodiac, chill wind and stinging spray on our faces, I abandoned these ruminations and focused on the near-at-hand. We scrambled up a tide-slick concrete ramp into the mingle of villagers and visitors, each of us joining a small group headed by a local guide. Our leader, a soft-spoken man with a shy smile, took us up a steep, rock-lined path with clapboard dwellings pinched close on either side. At one of the houses, he pointed out a long-handled dip-net. It was not used in the water, he explained, but on the mountainside above us, where hunters concealed themselves among the boulders and adroitly snagged seabirds winging past. Farther on, he showed us a box containing some of the freshly killed birds.

Around many homes, we saw the stout, dense, bleached bones of walrus, and at the village edge canted wooden drying frames with walrus hides lashed onto them looked like enormous, translucent, rawhide-covered drums. Our guide spoke of hunting in winter for seals and polar bears on the perpetually grinding, cracking, heaving ice between Little Diomede and Big Diomede islands. He told of men drifting away on the pack ice: some were never seen again, and some, by nothing more than chance, landed on Saint Lawrence Island 150 miles to the south, then returned to their homes like apparitions of the dead.

After touring the village, many of the *Clipper Odyssey*'s party jammed into a small general store and bought ivory carvings, then walked to the nearby school gym to watch traditional Inupiaq dancing. During those hours, I realized that as we followed the route of the 1899 Harriman Alaska Expedition, we were also retracing the course of my life in Alaska. Earlier in the voyage, we had visited Kodiak Island, where I first came to Alaska in 1961 to help a team of archaeologists and zoologists studying prehistoric human ecology. Researchers dug into middens filled with clam shells, fish bones, sea mammal bones, and artifacts, which revealed how people had used their coastal environment since ancient times. I thought of the hands that shaped each tool, of the eyes that for centuries looked over the sprawl of sea and islands, of the songs and stories that celebrated their lives. The soil of that place seemed to come alive.

After Kodiak, the *Clipper Odyssey* had sailed out along the Aleutian Islands. Passing the emerald mountainsides and indigo volcanic cliffs took me back to my second Alaska trip in 1963, when I had worked as a trowel hand for an archaeological dig on tiny Ananuliak Island, halfway out the chain. As we sailed farther north, I had reflected on my experiences living with Inupiaq Eskimos and with their inland neighbors, the Koyukon Indians. Both of these peoples have flourished in difficult and challenging environments by making the fullest use of their intellectual powers, by studying every detail of their world, by developing a potent self-assurance, and by integrating themselves fully into the encompassing natural community.

Traveling with Inupiaq and Koyukon people, I had begun to recognize my own physical connections to the environment—an awareness so deeply engrained in my companions' minds that they might never put it into words. On the first hunt of my life, I had joined a group of Inupiaq men and their dog teams, searching far inland for herds of migratory caribou. Afterward, exhausted from a long trip back to the village, I had unloaded the caribou meat from my sled, cut off a piece, and cooked it in a frying pan. Sitting down to eat, I had suddenly comprehended that we humans, in common with every other creature, must sustain ourselves by taking other life, whether we do it ourselves or have someone else do it for us. This may be the single most important lesson I have ever learned.

The connection between Alaskan Native people and their surroundings is manifested not only in physical and ecological ways but also in religious traditions centered around a spiritual relationship between humans and nature. In many communities, these older religious ways have been displaced or diminished by Christianity, but they remain strong among the Koyukon Indians, who live by hunting, trapping, and gathering in an immense, forested wildland along the Yukon and Koyukuk rivers. Koyukon elders recount sacred stories of a dreamlike primal world created by the Great Raven, a world in which animals and people lived together, spoke a common language, and possessed abilities we might call supernatural. Since that distant time, spiritual power has permeated all of nature: animals and plants, wind and rain, sun and stars, mountains and rivers, and the earth itself.

To honor these spirits, hundreds of rules govern the ways that people behave toward everything in nature. For example, it is important never to insult any animal or brag about hunting exploits, lest the offender suffer loss of hunting or fishing luck or in serious cases become sick, even die. The grizzly bear is so sensitive and volatile that Koyukon people are reluctant even to say its proper name. Moose have a more benign character, but the hunter who kills a moose should butcher it carefully, waste nothing, and honor the sacredness of its meat. Trappers are instructed to put unusable parts of beavers or muskrats back into the water, so the animals will be reincarnated. Even trees and other plants have consciousness. If someone strips the bark from a freshly cut birch log in winter, the bare log should be covered with snow or brought inside the house, not left "naked" out in the cold.

Almost every animal is imbued with its own special genius. For instance, porcupines have a gift for knowing the land in all its details, as revealed by their habit of roaming widely and circuitously, as if they are immersed in the pleasures of geography. The loon's power is that of beauty, manifested in its striking plumage and ululating voice. "When a loon calls on a lake," an old Koyukon saying goes, "it is the greatest sound a person can hear." Huge spruce trees give protection to travelers who sleep under their sheltering boughs. A red squirrel chattering at night warns that someone is going to die. A wolverine's carcass is so radiant with spiritual power that children should be kept away from it.

Another way of showing respect toward the environment is by using it responsibly, and long before Europeans came into their homeland Koyukon people had developed a sophisticated ecological sensibility and clearly understood the importance of conservation. For example, hunters avoid taking too many moose or bears or wolves; trappers focus on catching only adult beavers; large-meshed fishnets are used so that small fish will not be caught. Although these practices are exactly what Western wildlife science would advise, in Koyukon communities the consequences for violations are not just practical or ecological but also spiritual because excessive use offends or alienates the natural world.

Prior to European times, other Alaskan Native cultures likely followed moral and ethical codes similar to those that still govern the Koyukon people's behavior toward the natural community to which they belong. These codes, founded on principles of respect, humility, and gratitude toward the environment, may help to explain the pristine land and undiminished wildlife that constitute Alaska's enduring legacy of wildness—a gift from countless generations who have lived here before us.

NEAR THE END OF our visit to Little Diomede village, I stood beside several large, skin-covered umiaks perched upside-down on a wooden rack. Looking over toward Big Diomede, I imagined riding in such a boat across the water to explore the hidden niches and coves along that far shore. Then I remembered the early days of our Harriman voyage, gliding in the *Clipper Odyssey* on the silky, sunlit fjords of south-eastern Alaska and easing against the dock in Sitka, my home community for the past two decades.

My life in this outer-coast town has been strongly influenced by what I learned during my years with Alaskan Native people. I've sought closeness to the land and water, not just as a source of recreation in beautiful surroundings but also for the bounty of venison, salmon, halibut, lingcod, clams, huckleberries, salmonberries, and edible greens. Eating these wild foods each day gives nourishment to my spirit as well to as my body, reminds me that I am not only living in this place but also living from it, that I am literally a part of it, because the earth and waters of southeast Alaska flow inside my veins.

Harvesting directly from what Alaska provides also brings constantly to mind the importance of using it responsibly, carefully, respectfully. In a book called *The Island Within*, I wrote a small credo about my relationship to the forests around my home, drawing from the teachings of Koyukon people:

> I've often thought of the forest as a living cathedral, but this might diminish what it truly is. If I have understood Koyukon teachings, the forest is not merely an expression or representation of sacredness, nor a place to invoke the sacred; the forest is sacredness itself. Nature is not merely created by God; nature is God. Whoever moves within the forest can partake directly of sacredness, experience sacredness with his entire body, breathe sacredness and contain it within himself, drink the sacred water as a living communion, bury his feet in sacredness, touch the living branch and feel the sacredness, open his eyes and witness the burning beauty of sacredness. And when he cuts a tree from the forest, he participates in a sacred interchange that brings separate lives together. . . .
>
> I am cautious and self-protective here, as anywhere, but I believe that a covenant of mutual regard and responsibility binds me together with the forest. We share in a common nurturing. Each of us serves as an amulet to protect the other from inordinate harm. I am never alone in this wild forest, this forest of elders, this forest of eyes.

Like the Koyukon people and others of similar beliefs, I feel an obligation to give something back in return for the sustenance of food, the grace of water, the shelter of forests, the beauty of mountains, the peace of wildness. And I believe we should not use the forests and wildlife beyond their ability to replenish themselves, following the example set by many Alaskan Native people for millennia. We must work to protect the gifts so abundantly given by the Alaskan environment.

About 40 percent of Alaska is public wildland managed by the U.S. government on behalf of all its citizens. These Alaskan national wildlands belong equally to everyone. Unlike private lands, they are not locked up but locked open, accessible to people from anywhere in the country or the world.

When we participants in the 2001 voyage trekked ashore outside cities or villages, we were nearly always in a national forest, national park, or national wildlife refuge. These Alaskan lands are among the most spectacular, pristine, and biologically rich places remaining on the earth. Their designation as public land is among the highest achievements of U.S. democracy. Perhaps greater than anything that we as a people have created are these places where we have chosen to leave the original creation intact.

Every citizen of the United States and the world today is given the gift of freedom to wander at will on the magnificent public lands of Alaska. Even their names have a kind of magic:

Tongass National Forest
Misty Fjords National Monument
Glacier Bay National Park
Admiralty Island National Monument
Chugach National Forest
Katmai National Park
Alaska Maritime National Wildlife Refuge
Denali National Park
Yukon Delta National Wildlife Refuge
Bering Land Bridge National Reserve

Through conservation activism, I have come to a deeper appreciation not only of America's public wildlands but also of the privileges afforded by living in a democracy, where we are free to speak and act on behalf of our environment. Advocating for responsible, ethical, sustainable use of our environment is the ultimate and most vital form of patriotism, and conservationists can take pride in being patriots for the land, helping to protect the source of our lives and livelihoods.

It is also worth remembering that conservation is fundamentally conservative—it emphasizes the importance of moving slowly and cautiously, showing respect for values that are old, venerable, and bequeathed to us by ancestors far wiser than ourselves. Working on behalf of the environment is a way to honor those elders, who include not only people like the Inupiaq and Koyukon but also people of European ancestry. In fact, the roots of the modern U.S. conservation movement can be traced directly to several members of the Harriman Expedition, notably John Muir, George Bird Grinnell, and John Burroughs.

WHAT COULD BE more gratifying than to know that much of the land and water-ways traversed by the *Clipper Odyssey* in 2001 remains as beautiful, as wild, as biologi-cally rich today as it was during the voyage of the *George W. Elder* a century ago? We can celebrate the fact that grizzly bears still roam the forests of Baranof Island, that kittiwakes and puffins still throng the waters of Glacier Bay, that humpback whales still roll in the fjords of Prince William Sound, that wolves still howl on the Katmai Peninsula, that polar bears still prowl the pack ice around Saint Lawrence Island, that walruses still swim in the frigid waters of the Bering Strait. In an era of environmen-tal loss and ecological disarray, we are privileged to discover—as so many generations have before us—the abounding beauty and unfathomable wildness of Alaska. In this discovery we find not only comfort, pleasure, and fascination but also hope.

Perhaps, ultimately, the most important lesson of Alaska's enduring land is that humans can inhabit a fragile terrain over vast spans of time without depleting its bounty. Therefore, we should not regard ourselves as unalterably a blight on the earth. We have a rightful place, not just as pilgrims admiring the scenery from afar but as members of our sustaining natural community. We are citizens of a world that gives us life and elevates our spirits. But true citizenship is something we must earn. It requires a will to approach the land with humility, respect, and restraint—lessons we can learn from the people who lived here for thousands of years before us.

ALTHOUGH OUR VISIT to Little Diomede lasted only a few hours, it was an extraor-dinarily powerful experience. As we pulled away from the shore, I watched the village dwindle astern, until it abruptly vanished behind the shoulder of Big Diomede, and we sailed on into a gray mist, leaving one world and entering another.

When our anchor clattered down the next morning, I looked out at the moun-tainous foreland of Cape Dezhnev. To understand the geography, hold both hands in front of you, palms and fingers pointing toward each other, about an inch apart. The middle finger on your left hand is Cape Dezhnev, Siberia, the easternmost point in Asia; the middle finger on your right hand is Cape Prince of Wales, the westernmost point in Alaska; and the intervening space is the fifty-mile breach of the Bering Strait. For years, I had read about this place, and now I was insuppressibly excited to see it for the first time. After catching an early Zodiac to the beach, I hiked up the steep, grassy, windblown slope to a broad terrace punctuated everywhere with abandoned houses that once constituted Naukan Village. Wandering among the remains, I thought of the crowded gymnasium on Little Diomede, throbbing with songs and drumbeats and dancers' footsteps. And I imagined those sounds drifting on winter gales through the emptied houses of Naukan.

Beyond the farthest of these dwellings were several larger, deteriorating Soviet stucco buildings, strewn with wires and disintegrating remnants of what must have been electronic surveillance equipment. At the northernmost end, an ivory-colored lighthouse stood on the shoulder of Cape Dezhnev, elegantly and compellingly dominating the scene. From the base of the lighthouse, I looked out over the whitecapped waters, and there beneath a bright, broken overcast trailing veils of rain I saw both of the Diomede Islands. Farther on, barely visible along the remote eastern horizon, was the low, dark silhouette of Alaska's mainland.

Then I looked out over the vast, submerged Bering Land Bridge, remembering the ancient people who had moved their villages and hunting camps eastward across the steppes into a new world. For thousands of years since that first arrival, humans have been discovering Alaska—naming the animals and plants and places, learning the intricacies of the terrain, creating ways to make livelihoods on their homelands, enshrining their discoveries in stories and songs.

We are still discovering Alaska. Natives and non-Natives, scientists and naturalists, philosophers and theologians, homesteaders and fishermen, villagers and urbanites, children and elders are probing the mysteries, braiding humankind more deeply into the northern world. And, of all that remains for us to learn, the most important, by far, is how to live here in ways that preserve Alaska's natural heritage for those discoverers yet to come.

> *We shall not cease from exploration*
> *And the end of all our exploring*
> *Will be to arrive where we started*
> *And know the place for the first time.*
> – T. S. Eliot, "Four Quartets"

Steller Sea Lions

© PATRICIA SAVAGE

And Then It Was Gone,
East across the Bering Sea

19–20 August 2001

The modern-day "bug hunters, mole catchers and trappers of mice, diggers of worms and experts on ice" are scheduled to arrive in Nome August 19. Nome is the terminus of the *Clipper Odyssey*'s trip. From here the participants will fly away.

– *The Nome Nugget*, 16 August 2001

Overnight the *Clipper Odyssey* made an easy sail seventy miles south-southwest from Lorino to the southern end of the Chukchi Peninsula and into the last day of the 2001 expedition. Before sunrise we entered a huge embayment that enveloped the peninsula's most southeastern coast. Four mountaintop islands, Ostrov Arakamchechen the largest, stretched along the shore as reminders of the land bridge and its ice-age explorers. Today, Arakamchechen is the site of the largest walrus haulout in the Bering Sea, with the total number of walruses estimated at forty thousand. The wildlife- and nutrient-rich Straits of Seniavin, "Whale Alley," separate the mainland from the islands. Named for the once abundant bowhead and gray whales that worked the strait's waters during migration, Whale Alley was the homeland of the Old Bering Sea people, a maritime culture dating to the first century. At first light, we lowered a Zodiac and headed for the north shore of the archipelago's second-largest island, Ostrov Yttygran, to scout an ancient ceremonial gathering place that Russian anthropologists first documented in 1976. The people who worshiped here abandoned Whale Alley sometime in the seventeenth century, and we have no clear explanation of why, or where, they went.

Withdrawn into early-morning thoughts as the Zodiac bounced toward shore, the engine making too much noise for conversation, I became conscious of a habit of mine that had developed early in the voyage. When exploring in unfamiliar waters, I would unconsciously mark the location of the base ship in relation to the Zodiac. These were quick

FIGURE 47. *Sky and water. Credit: Edward S. Curtis. Source: Harriman family collection.*

glances mixed with hundreds of others, but they sorted themselves as being a little more important. I discovered the search image fixed in my mind's eye, ready to be recalled. On occasion, the realization that we were in a very remote place, far from home, would penetrate the excitement of exploring, and instinctively I would search out the large white vessel waiting at anchor for our return. The mood of the sky and horizon might change, or the size of the seas, but the waiting ship was a constant that emboldened our wanderings. At this moment, we were as far from home on this voyage as we would go. The fast-approaching beach and need for reaction interrupted my musings, and I scanned for the ship to mark its location.

Yttygran's ancient ceremonial site was as interesting and mysterious as anything we had so far encountered. To accompany our visit,

the rising sun broke through an overcast horizon, providing dramatic light that sparkled off the frost-covered tundra and its profusion of wildflowers in bloom—bog saxifrage, larkspur, Alaska poppy, Kamchatka rhododendron. Our attention was quickly drawn to the whalebones stretching over a quarter mile along the rise just above the gravel beach. Pairs of bowhead whale skulls were buried at regular intervals along the route, nasals down, occipital bones exposed. A double row of bowhead jaw and rib bones, buried like poles, paralleled the shoreline. Interspersed with these structures were massive whale skulls and what appeared to be dug pits.

Following the promenade, we came upon a carefully constructed stone amphitheater looking out toward the sea. Standing whale ribs were deliberately placed around its perimeter. In later times, two small Yup'ik villages also existed on Yttygran, but their people were resettled in the 1950s to the newly established New Chaplino on the mainland to the south. The former residents of these villages claim no relation the Old Bering Sea people, and their village histories provide no reference to the more ancient culture that left these whalebone relics behind.

Leaving with many more questions than we had arrived with, we departed Yttygran by midmorning for Yanrakynnot, a Chukchi village. Located on the mainland, at the north entrance to Seniavin Straits, the village is another variation of Soviet-era resettlement. Unlike the Yup'iks, or maritime Chukchis, who lived in small population centers along the coast, the interior Chukchis are the majority Native culture on the Chukchi Peninsula. Most of Yanrakynnot's four hundred residents descend from the nomadic reindeer herders who moved about the interior Yanrakynnot tundra until they were forced into the new village's sedentary lifestyle. Fox farming, intended to be the core of their economy, soon proved unprofitable, and government support shrank to almost nothing by the time of the Soviet collapse. Reminiscent of Lorino, but significantly smaller and more isolated, the community struggles into an uncertain future.

Like those of Lorino, the people of Yanrakynnot also greeted us warmly under another afternoon of clear skies and sunshine. They had prepared for us a field day of activities that included wrestling matches among bare-chested young men, dog-sleds-on-wheels races, dancing and drumming, and a reindeer-antler lasso contest. Many things—shoes and boots, pants and shirts, hats, lassoes, and the crafts for sale—were made from some part of a reindeer. The offering of fish

soup and whale meat was accepted with appreciation—and just a little hesitation. The villagers were clearly excited about our visit, explaining that we were the second set of visitors to the village in three years. They welcomed us up the bluff covered with blooming forget-me-nots and into the village. As in a village anywhere, cats and dogs were wandering about, a radio was playing through an open window, boys were playing on a basketball court, and people were sitting on their stoops enjoying the commotion our visit created. The warmth and goodwill that the community offered us without hesitation were in stark contrast to the predicament that a failed government had bequeathed them. With so many complaints available to them, the only concern we heard was from a group of whale hunters who complained that in the fall and winter wolves tried to feed on the catch that was brought to the beach for butchering.

It had been a long, busy day and, without warning, a melancholy thought that I had been avoiding abruptly appeared: this was the last time we would be returning "home" from an exploratory landing during Harriman Retraced. For over thirty days our voyage followed an intense, relentless schedule, filled with countless images, ideas, and emotions. To manage the pace, we were constantly living in the moment. Suddenly, with Yanrakynnot fading off our stern, this amazing voyage was coming to an end; the moment had arrived.

The tone back on board the ship clearly had changed. When we left the ship at first light that morning for the Russian shore, we had again been heading out to explore and to absorb all we could from the environment that surrounded us—what a special opportunity and privilege. When we set foot back on the ship, it was as if a switch had been thrown. At 5:00 P.M. we weighed anchor, and Captain Michael Taylor set a course directly for Nome. With this signal the crew and expedition members turned their attention to what would greet them in the morning: the dock at Nome, hotels, and plane connections. The everyday world that we had chosen to suspend for a month was back. All the boxes of equipment and supplies had to be packed, the computers cased, the artwork crated. In the few hours that remained we had no time for lectures, discussions of one hundred years of change, or presentations of project results. Our grander goals gave way to the immediate; packing up our cabins was all-consuming. Clean clothes, dirty clothes, wet boots, books, cameras, paperwork all needed to find there way back into the duffels in which they had arrived. I sat on the edge of my bunk, surveying what seemed an impossible task and grew edgier by the moment.

The exchanges in the passageways shifted from "What did you see today, and where will we be tomorrow?" to good-byes, the trading of addresses, handshakes, and hugs. Important things that hadn't been said made their way into the conversations. A transformation had occurred. A group of individuals had agreed to join an adventure and found themselves living together on a small ship. The group had become a community of its own, bound together by adventure and exploration, the daunting scope of its mission, daily struggles with ideas and values, camaraderie and friendship, and "the ship." As in any small community, there were laughs, individual and group epiphanies, gossip, and goodwill. We shared in all the good days and found our ways through the rocky ones. We came to know each other's temperaments and how to build relationships and avoid confrontations. Our immersion into an instant community, coupled with the intensity of our mission, was emotionally and intellectually powerful, draining. We were tired; it was time to go to the home.

The transition dominated every corner of the ship except for the bridge. While the rest of the ship was going about housekeeping tasks in anticipation of arrival at Nome, the bridge was focused on the immediate task of crossing the Bering Sea. Unlike much of the coastal navigating we had done, this run was a straight shot for 190 miles across open water. It was a beautiful evening as the sun skimmed the western horizon and Chukchi Peninsula dropped off the stern. The bridge was quiet, as open seas and an expansive horizon extended before us. Our major goals had been accomplished; the outward voyage was literally behind us. For the first time we were not extending our route, but heading back—with one possible complication.

The weather reports had been tracking a tropical low that had crossed the Aleutians near Dutch Harbor. Gale winds of forty to fifty miles per hour were reported and seas of fifteen to twenty feet. The storm front was headed north into the Bering Sea. To this point our voyage in the Bering Sea had been charmed; we had enjoyed mostly clear skies, sunshine, and comfortable seas that reflected the clouds and sky. Since we had rounded Scotch Cap Pinnacle in Unimak Pass and entered the Bering Sea nine days earlier, the weather had been with us, with no hint of the conditions that can combine to make the Bering Sea one of the most tumultuous and dangerous in the world. If the low caught up with us during the night, we would be experiencing a Bering Sea we had not yet seen.

It would also make our arrival in Nome considerably more complicated. The open coast of Nome takes a pounding in a strong south wind, and docking becomes impossible. If this became the case, the *Odyssey* would have to anchor offshore, and all of us, and our gear, would have to be shuttled by Zodiac into a sheltered area of the port. This was a soggy prospect at best and a tough way to end the voyage. In addition, if the seas were too rough for Plan B, we would have to head for the sheltered port of Teller to the north and bus back down to Nome. As a hedge, the captain increased our speed, which would burn more fuel and get us to Nome earlier than necessary but, we hoped, ahead of the storm. We collapsed into bed that night not knowing what the Bering Sea was about to serve up or what shape our departure might take. Harriman Retraced was not over just yet.

At first light, the view from our window was a dock. Teller, where we had been just days before, did not have a dock large enough for our ship, so this must be Nome. Fumbling about the cabin, I remembered our visit to Yakutat. During our welcoming, healing ceremony there, a Tlingit elder presented us with an eagle feather and the tribe's prayer. They asked that we be allowed to travel safely under the eagle's wing and that fair weather be with us for the remainder of our voyage. To the very last day, the blessing held. The sun was rising over Nome, the storm would not arrive until later in the day, and I was deeply grateful to the Yakutat Tribe and the spirit of the eagle feather that traveled with us. I wondered what

the *Clipper Odyssey* would encounter when she headed back out to sea that afternoon. How would she handle the swells and wind that challenged her hull? Now that was someone else's concern. Soon the ship broke into barely organized mayhem as people, luggage, equipment, and farewells all merged toward the gangway and waiting buses.

One by one the buses left the dock for Nome and the charter flight to Anchorage. A group of us stood around the gangway talking with the captain and crew, stalling until the last bus. Inevitably, we had to say our good-byes and board the remaining orange school bus. I ungracefully worked my way down the narrow aisle to the back seats, wrestling with laptops and daypacks. Completing the mental checklist of the possessions that should be sitting next to me on the seat, I settled in for the ride. The bus rolled down the pier as I drifted out of the chatter going on around me. Unconsciously, but deliberately, my eyes swept the scene surrounding us until I was twisted, looking over my shoulder out the back window. My line of sight intersected with the ship, white against the dock and the Alaskan horizon. Over the years of planning, all my efforts had been focused on beginnings: getting Retraced launched, making it to the ship, staying on task, making the observations that needed to be made. In the small space of this newest moment, the Harriman Alaska Expedition Retraced and Mr. Harriman's 1899 expedition were joined in the past. As the bus made its way down the long pier, the *Clipper Odyssey*, framed by the bus window, grew smaller, more distant. With the turn of a corner, what remained was a vivid image in my mind's eye.

Long-tailed Jaeger, Saint Matthew Island

CHAPTER FIFTEEN

IN SEARCH OF THE FUTURE:

Sustainability, Ecosystems, and Economics

♪℃

THOMAS S. LITWIN

T HERE IT WAS: the same enticing tourism poster that we had seen at the beginning of our expedition. It greeted us now as we passed back through Seattle at
the end of our voyage: "Join the Adventure, Visit Alaska." In tow we had volumes of
journal entries and observations, thousand of photographs, hours of film, countless
conversations—many pieces of a story. My journal entry for the day says, "amazing
trip, a flood of unorganized images, memories, and emotions; . . . for the time being,
I will set analysis aside."

Like all field researchers on a reconnaissance, we echoed the worry of our colleagues in 1899: "What do we do with all this information?" A fast-paced voyage,
brief visits to many places, and countless issues seemed to defy organization. The
words of C. Hart Merriam, John Burroughs, George Bird Grinnell, and John Muir
as they led us along our route were reassuring. Exploration and discovery—the heart
of learning and new ideas—will forever change the world we once knew. These are
the powers that pull us into the future. But first, as their writings of volcanoes, people,
glaciers, and fish tell us, you must make the journey. Our journey through time and
over water had been completed; the poster image triggered a cascade of thoughts
that could not have existed when we first gazed on it en route to Prince Rupert.

As we stood bedazzled in a long airport ticket line, memories of Tlingit dancers,
breaching humpbacks, calving glaciers, and growling sea lions were dreamlike, as they
mixed with the immediate commotion of the airport around us. Charles Keeler's poem
"Alaska," written abroad the *George W. Elder* in June of 1899, also had new meaning. To
hold the world at bay for just another moment, I pulled the poem from my carry-on:

Fiords of the far west shore, where peaks sublime
Are cloudward thrust 'neath folds of glistening snow,
With hoar and frigid streams that tideward flow,
Sculpturing their cliff and crags which mount and climb
Full in the sight of heaven—grim heirs of time,
Stern children of eternity, that grow
Austere and terrible 'mid storms that blow
Their lusty trumpets in the tempest's prime.
What joy is this to float upon the tide,
So blue, so beautiful, to gently glide
'Mid islets forested, past shores that stand
Dark portals opening to enchantment's land,
Where all is but a dream, soon to be
Lost in the purple mist of memory.

I had read Keeler's poem many times, but for the first time we shared a common experience with the travelers of 1899. They were partners who only now could help us look back over time and see the changes that had unfolded across a century. With that gift of understanding they had brought us to the present. Now, it was for the travelers of 2001 alone to grapple with how the momentum of one hundred years would burst into the twenty-first century and, moment by moment, flow toward the next.

THE 1899 PARTICIPANTS spent considerable time describing the magnificence they observed, as well as their concerns. The treatment of Native Alaskans, the depletion of otter and fur-seal populations, overfishing, and the raucous influence of the gold rush were just a few of the issues that expanded their understanding of how profoundly human activities can alter our world. As Bob Peck explained during our voyage, the conservationists aboard the *Elder*—Muir, Burroughs, Grinnell, Merriam—inspired by what they had discovered in Alaska, went on in their careers to continue the cause for conservation, environmental protection, and Native rights. They were part of an era in conservation that coincided with the birth of ecology as a discipline and were the first to benefit from a growing understanding of ecological relationships. The boom-and-bust economics of natural resource consumption they observed in Alaska reinforced observations made throughout the country: natural systems have limits, and when those limits are exceeded, a bust follows, the resource is depleted, and the ecosystem becomes less stable and is possibly headed for collapse. The fundamental economic and ecological understanding that a depleted natural resource or destroyed ecosystem is not available to meet a societal need would eventually lead to the concept of sustainability. Onboard the *Clipper Odyssey* the idea came up often during the intense discussions involving logging, tourism, oil, and the Bering Sea fisheries.

During the twentieth century, these understandings began to slowly bring conservation thinking into a world that had previously seen the land and seas as boundless, the resources within them never-ending. When a resource became depleted in an area and went bust, the industry simply moved on to the next area within a seemingly infinite wilderness. The twentieth century's technological revolution progressed, and the world grew smaller as advances in transportation, communications, and commodities-distribution systems kept pace with society's increasing consumer demands. As David Policansky explained in Orca, salmon began to be packed in a new technology called a "can" and shipped from Alaska, eventually making its way across the United States on an expanding network of railroads. The growing urban centers of the East Coast demanded more, and they got it; but the salmon population collapsed. With technology and the incentive of market demand, it became increasingly easy to open wilderness, and, with growing efficiency, the speed with which a boom could be started and finished accelerated. People who found themselves in the aftermath of a bust, such as Native Alaskans, immigrants, and homesteaders, were left to their own devices.

Make no mistake, countless positive contributions also were made during this era, and a globally unrivaled standard of living emerged in the United States. Compared with many people in the world, most Americans go comfortably through their day unconscious of the wealth created throughout the twentieth century and the societal benefits that resulted. This was a century whose accomplishments often simultaneously produced spectacular benefits and dire consequences.

Those who studied the consequences were forced to question the sustainability of such benefits. Generations of conservation activists emerged, seeking to balance natural resource consumption and environmental protection. They began to shape an idea that today has the attention of ecologists and economists alike: overshoot. Given that the human population has grown from 1.6 billion in 1899 to 6.1 billion in 2001, the question is deceptively simple: Can the world's societies continue to consume natural resources at the current rate without overshooting the earth's ability to provide the resources necessary for their own survival? This question, which is being asked on a global scale, is the same question that Grinnell asked about salmon and Merriam about fur seals on the Alaska coast.

Debates centering on various forms of this question have spanned a century, and in the United States a commitment to environmental protection expanded throughout the governmental and private sectors. Since 1899, in Alaska and in the lower states, the conservation of natural resources has greatly improved, and the previously unbridled pace of unsustainable economics and environmental destruction has slowed.

During this same transitional period, with the commercial goals of oppression and exploitation achieved, devastated Native communities in Alaska and the lower states found themselves in governmentally managed programs that were often characterized by neglect. As a result of what can only be one of the twentieth century's greatest stories of perseverance and cultural tenacity, this situation is changing. Throughout the 2001 voyage we met Native leaders, elders, and their communities determined to regain self-determination and on a path of cultural reconstruction and economic independence. At least in Alaska, it seems, a nation is being reborn within a nation. The imperialistic relationships of Western and Native cultures in the eighteenth, nineteenth, and twentieth centuries are, sadly, not unique to Alaska. Importantly, the struggles and strategies used by Native Alaskan communities as they move into the twenty-first century may hold promise for indigenous people around the world. That is their story to tell.

THROUGHOUT OUR VOYAGE aboard the *Clipper Odyssey*, we saw many successful examples of conservation and environmental protection—large protected areas of maritime refuges and national parks, regulatory harvest limits. In the course of our coastal voyage, we could not avoid the observation that terrestrial conservation practices during the past one hundred years have evolved at a much faster pace than those for the open marine environment. Brad Barr, a 2001 expedition scholar and senior policy advisor for the National Oceanic and Atmospheric Administration's National Marine Sanctuary System, confirmed our observation as we approached the Arctic Circle:

> On land, there is a long and rich history of place-based management by federal agencies. At the time of the Harriman Expedition, this concept was just being put into practice, and institutions were forming to guide its development. Just twenty-seven years before the 1899 expedition, Yellowstone became the first national park, but the National Park Service was not created until 1916. Now there are 384 areas of national park land encompassing 83.3 million acres that have been visited by more than 270 million people. Similarly, the U.S. Forest Service was established in 1905, with the first national forest reserves designated in 1891. Currently, there are 177 national forests and grasslands protecting 192 million acres of land. The first National Wildlife Refuge, Pelican Bay in Florida, was created in 1903, but it was not until 1939 that the Fish and Wildlife Service was established. One of the first federal actions to manage wildlife occurred in 1868, when President Ulysses S. Grant declared the Pribilof Islands a northern fur-seal reserve. Today, there are more than 520 refuges nationwide covering 93 million acres. The Bureau of Land Management was late on the scene, being created in 1946, but it now manages about 264 million acres nationwide. Of all the lands managed by these agencies, 37 percent are located in Alaska.
>
> In the oceans, there are far fewer protected areas compared to the amount of area set aside for conservation on land. While terrestrial national parks, national

forests, and national wildlife refuges constituted approximately 18 percent of the U.S. land mass, national marine sanctuaries accounted for only 0.4 percent of the area of the U.S. Exclusive Economic Zone, which is roughly equivalent to the land area of the United States. By comparison, there are thirteen national marine sanctuaries, but more than nine hundred protected terrestrial areas. But this is changing, and increasingly the concept of "place" is being applied to marine ecosystem conservation efforts.

Historically, management of both terrestrial and marine resources has been focused largely on individual species, or in some cases groups of species with similar life histories. An example of this is fisheries management, where actions center on limiting the harvest of a species' population, based on surveys and mathematical estimates. In its simplest form, if the stock is declining, harvests are decreased, and, conversely, if stocks are increasing, fishing effort can be increased. This form of management gives little, if any, attention to the ecosystem in which those fish live, or to the dynamic interactions between species and their environment.

Recognizing the importance of ecosystem dynamics to management decision making, fisheries managers are looking more closely at the whole system within which a fish lives. This has been done largely through the establishment of closures. These are biologically important areas for species, such as spawning areas, that are closed to fishing or restricted for periods of time when the fish in that area are most susceptible to adverse impacts from fishing. The 2001 expedition had firsthand experience with the closure of the Bogoslof Steller sea lion rookery. A three-mile zone around Bogoslof Island prohibited vessels from approaching the island and potentially disturbing the endangered sea lions and their pups. Another Alaskan example is the restriction of cruise-ship entry into Glacier Bay National Park and Preserve to help protect important humpback-whale feeding grounds.

Single-species management like that used with the sea lion or humpback whale remains in use today, but the concept of ecosystem management is increasingly being seen as a more effective management strategy. Understanding the interactions of species with their habitats and the dynamic, sometimes chaotic, nature of their ecosystems holds promise for helping managers achieve a sustainable use of marine resources.

Marine Protected Areas (MPAs), such as national marine sanctuaries, are being used to speed the important ideas of ecosystem management into marine conservation strategies. MPAs are widely regarded as an important tool in the efforts to conserve marine ecosystems worldwide. MPAs have the potential to preserve marine biodiversity, help reverse devastating declines in fish stocks, protect unique areas and biotic communities, support efforts to recover endangered species, and conserve representative habitats of the world's oceans. As in the early days of terrestrial ecosystem protection, MPAs holds great promise, but there are many issues to be considered, and more research and analysis to be conducted. Still, it is clear that

MPAs will have a role in the future of Alaskan marine-ecosystem conservation, and it is for Alaskans to decide if national marine sanctuaries will be a future part of Alaskan marine conservation.

New approaches to conservation, such as the marine sanctuaries, carry on the legacy of the previous century, enhanced by advances in scientific understanding. Kathy Frost's research on marine mammals, Paul Alaback's investigations of old-growth forests, the seabird studies of Vivian Mendenhall, and the work of thousands of other scientists have provided the basic knowledge necessary for improving existing conservation strategies and creating new approaches. In the aftermath of the *Exxon Valdez* oil spill, one of the most comprehensive ecosystem-scale research programs was born, the Gulf of Alaska Ecosystem Monitoring and Research Program (GEM). GEM is a state-of-the-art interagency scientific effort, and it serves as a model for cooperative marine-ecosystem research around the world. Computer-based technologies are being used to integrate ecological principles, economic data, and social issues into the design of marine preserves in such diverse areas of the globe as the Gulf of California, Australia's Great Barrier Reef, and the Bahamas. These advances were unimaginable in 1899.

At no time in history has our ability to conserve resources through scientifically and technologically based methods been so promising. Creating more ecosystem-scale preserves and implementing scientifically derived environmental regulations will continue to be critical parts of an environmental protection strategy well into the future. But as demand for resources increases in step with a growing world population, and emerging nations emulate the consumerism of wealthy nations, science alone cannot be expected to address the serious social challenges inherent in overshoot. If ecosystem preserves are to be more than natural museums whose resources have to be constantly defended and ecosystem research more than forensic science, an environmental ethic for the twenty-first century must be constructed on a broad social base.

When the *Clipper Odyssey* sailed into Prince William Sound, we also sailed into a debate about drilling for oil in the Arctic National Wildlife Refuge that echoed debates around the world. A protected portion of an ecosystem spanning the top of the globe, with ecological communities and species that exist nowhere else in the Milky Way galaxy, also has another resource below it: oil. How do we ascribe the values of scarcity in this situation to make a decision about drilling for oil? Science and engineering can inform this debate, but they cannot relieve society of making a value judgment. Engineers can propose technology for greatly reducing the probability of an oil spill and state-of-the-art methods for cleaning one up. Wildlife scientists can tell in "parts per million" how much oil it takes to kill a seabird. But neither discipline is intended to help society at large understand the value judgments that are involved or the investment momentum that has to be considered when it weighs wilderness protection against the benefits of an industry that will not exist at the end of the twenty-first century.

Instead, we are often left to make complex decisions on the basis of imperfect simplifications. In political debates, we are often presented with oversimplifications like "having jobs or protecting the environment." In such cases, we, as citizens, are really being asked to stop thinking. Anyone who faces the monthly bills or understands self-esteem knows that we need jobs. We also know that over 60 percent of the human body is composed of water: our brain is 70 percent water, our blood is 82 percent water, and our lungs are 90 percent water. Much of the grown food we eat ranges between 85 and 95 percent water. To the best of our knowledge, the earth, our environment, is the only place in the solar system where a life-sustaining amount of water exists. The same life-sustaining importance applies to the air we breathe, which fires the respiration in our cells and brings the bodies of all living things, including our own, to life. When presented with a choice between jobs or the environment, are we being asked to choose between a job and the clean water and air we need to have a healthy life? With such simplifications we continue to perpetuate the dangerous myth that somehow contemporary human societies and their economies stand separate from the earth processes and ecosystems that support their very existence. Instead of socially or environmentally unsustainable either/or choices, we need an evolving twenty-first-century environmental ethic that begins to dissolve artificial distinctions between societal needs and environmental protection. As many of our hosts in the Native Alaskan and Chukchi communities we visited would tell us, they are, in the final analysis, one and the same.

The ability of the United States to move toward and provide leadership for a sustainable future may not be as fanciful as it first might seem. At the start of the twenty-first century, the United States is the sole superpower and one of the wealthiest nations. Our educational and healthcare systems provide services only dreamed about in many parts of the world. The United States can afford to use its power and wealth to provide leadership into a socially and environmentally stable and sustainable future. It is a choice a democracy has. Many of the pieces required to begin framing a twenty-first-century ethic, and its translation into working business and social models, are already well into development. Significant work is underway around the world in the formative disciplines of ecological economics, sustainability science, ecological sociology, and ecological psychology, as well as within the environmental sciences and engineering. The integration of information across these disciplinary boundaries is essential for creating the broad-based social-policy recommendations needed to support sustainability goals. Equally important is the wide dissemination of policy recommendations and educational materials in a form usable by governments, policymakers, advocates, and kindergarten through high school educators. With so much of the framework already in place, there is no need to stand befuddled at the start of the twenty-first century. What is needed is an understanding of the choices and of the values that drive the decision making that surrounds them.

No matter what, the momentum of the twentieth century will surely result in significant environmental pressures well into the new century, pressures that will have to be faced by a growing human world population. Although an abundance of natural resources drove the economics and social institutions of the United States in the decades after 1899, the economics of scarcity may well shape the social institutions of the twenty-second century. How the earth's ecosystems and societies fare at the end of this century depends on choices and how quickly they are made. A society committed to sustainability and careful use of natural resources through an understanding of scarcity will be different from one in which scarcity is suddenly a desperate realization. For now, we are left to explore a future that is still unknown, provisioned with a knowledge of the past, ideals for a twenty-first-century ethic, and a wish: that the group of explorers who retrace the routes of the 1899 and 2001 expeditions in the year 2100 can look back and repeat the words of our gentle friend John Burroughs: "We have gone far and fared well."

Appendix:
MEMBERS OF THE 2001
AND 1899 EXPEDITIONS

Members of the 2001
Harriman Expedition Retraced

THE SCIENTIFIC PARTY

Thomas S. Litwin, Ph.D., expedition leader and director, Clark Science Center, Smith College, Northampton, Massachusetts

Paul B. Alaback, Ph.D., associate professor of ecology, School of Forestry and Conservation, University of Montana, Missoula

Vera Alexander, Ph.D., dean, School of Fisheries and Ocean Studies, University of Alaska Fairbanks

Brad Barr, senior policy advisor, Conservation Policy and Planning Branch, National Marine Sanctuary System, National Oceanic and Atmospheric Administration, Woods Hole, Massachusetts

Lawrence Charters, National Ocean Service, National Oceanic and Atmospheric Administration, Silver Spring, Maryland

William Cronon, Ph.D., professor of history, geography, and environmental studies, Department of History, University of Wisconsin at Madison

Kristine J. Crossen, Ph.D., professor of geology and chair, Department of Geology, University of Alaska Anchorage

Aron L. Crowell, Ph.D., Alaska director, Arctic Studies Center, National Museum of History, Smithsonian Institution, Anchorage

Kathryn J. Frost, Alaska Department of Fish and Game, retired; affiliate associate professor of marine science, University of Alaska Fairbanks

Alison Hammer, National Ocean Service, National Oceanic and Atmospheric Administration, Silver Spring, Maryland

Kim Heacox, author and photographer, Glacier Bay Institute, Gustavus, Alaska

David Koester, Ph.D., associate professor, Department of Anthropology, University of Alaska Fairbanks

Maureen Litwin, community events coordinator, Smith College, Northampton,
Massachusetts

Vivian M. Mendenhall, Ph.D., marine bird coordinator, retired, Division of Migratory
Bird Management, U.S. Fish and Wildlife Service, Anchorage

Richard Nelson, Ph.D., cultural anthropologist, writer, and conservationist, Sitka, Alaska

Brenda L. Norcross, Ph.D., professor of fisheries oceanography, University of Alaska
Fairbanks

Robert McCracken Peck, curator of art and artifacts and fellow of the Academy of
Natural Sciences of Philadelphia

David Policansky, Ph.D., scholar in the Board on Environmental Studies and Toxicology,
National Research Council, Washington, D.C.

Kay Sloan, Ph.D., coauthor of *Looking Far North: The Harriman Expedition to Alaska, 1899*,
and professor of English, Miami University, Oxford, Ohio

Pamela A. Wight, president, Pam Wight & Associates, Edmonton, Alberta, Canada

Rosita Worl, Ph.D., president, Sealaska Heritage Institute; professor of anthropology,
University of Alaska Southeast, Juneau

VISITING SCHOLARS

Elaine Abraham, M.A.T., Tlingit elder and secretary of the Board of Commissioners,
Alaska Native Science Commission

Anne Castellina, superintendent, Kenai Fjords National Park, Seward, Alaska

Molly McCammon, executive director, Exxon Valdez Oil Spill Trustee Council, Anchorage

FILMMAKERS AND PHOTOGRAPHERS

Kim Heacox, photographer, Glacier Bay Institute, Gustavus, Alaska

Lawrence R. Hott, director and filmmaker, Haydenville, Massachusetts

Allen Moore, filmmaker

Stephen McCarthy, filmmaker

ARTISTS AND POET

Sheila Nickerson, Ph.D., poet laureate of Alaska, emeritus, Bellingham, Washington

Patricia Savage, wildlife artist, Raleigh, North Carolina

Kesler Woodward, MFA, professor of art emeritus, Art Department,
University of Alaska Fairbanks

SHIP'S OFFICERS AND EXPEDITION LEADERS

Michael Taylor, master and captain (Clipper Cruise Lines)

Mike Messick, expedition leader (Zegrahm Expeditions), Castle Valley, Utah

Allen White, assistant expedition leader (Zegrahm Expeditions), Falkland Islands

Lynne Greig, cruise director (Zegrahm Expeditions), Seattle

Michael Breen, chief officer

Peter Millington, chief engineer
Juliana Jenny, purser
Craig Murray, hotel manager

PHYSICAN

Marjory Vanderly

NATURALISTS

Dale Chorman, Homer, Alaska
Carmen Field, Homer, Alaska
Conrad Field, Homer, Alaska
Sergey Frolov, Petropavlovsk-Kamchatskiy, Russia

YOUNG EXPLORERS TEAM

Salah Aboulhouda, student, Nelson Lagoon, Alaska
Claire Baldwin, student, Wasilla, Alaska
Debbie Chalmers, teacher, Juneau, Alaska
Natasha Dallin, student, McGrath, Alaska
Devon Ducharme, student, Northampton, Massachusetts
Elizabeth Litwin, student, Whately, Massachusetts
Megan Litwin, student, Whately, Massachusetts
Jonas Parker, student, Sitka, Alaska
Douglas Penn, teacher, Girdwood, Alaska

SMITH COLLEGE STUDENT SCHOLARS

Allison Eberhard, Rolling Hills, California
Julia O'Malley, Juneau, Alaska
Allison Sayer, New York, New York

Members of the 1899 Harriman Alaska Expedition

(As reported in C. Hart Merriam, ed., *Harriman Alaska Expedition*, vol. 1)

THE HARRIMAN FAMILY

Edward H. Harriman, patron of the expedition, Arden, New York
Mrs. E. H. Harriman
Miss Mary W. Harriman
Miss Cornelia Harriman
Carol Harriman
Averell Harriman

Roland Harriman

W. H. Averell, Rochester, New York

Mrs. W. H. Averell

Miss Elizabeth Averell

Miss Dorothea Draper, New York City

THE SCIENTIFIC PARTY

William H. Brewer, professor, Sheffield Scientific School, Yale University,
New Haven, Connecticut

John Burroughs, ornithologist and author, West Park, New York

Wesley R. Coe, Ph.D., assistant professor of comparative anatomy, Yale University,
New Haven, Connecticut

Frederick V. Coville, curator, National Herbarium, and botanist,
U.S. Department of Agriculture, Washington, D.C.

Dr. William Healey Dall, paleontologist, U.S. Geological Survey, and honorary curator of
mollusks, U.S. National Museum, Washington, D.C.

Walter B. Devereux, mining engineer, Glenwood Springs, Colorado

Daniel G. Elliot, curator of zoology, Field Museum, Chicago

Benjamin K. Emerson, professor of geology, Amherst College, Amherst, Massachusetts

Bernhard E. Fernow, professor and dean of the School of Forestry, Cornell University,
Ithaca, New York

Dr. Albert K. Fisher, ornithologist, Biological Survey, U.S. Department of Agriculture,
Washington, D.C.

Henry Gannett, chief geographer, U.S. Geological Survey, Washington, D.C.

Grove Karl Gilbert, geologist, U.S. Geological Survey, Washington, D.C.

Dr. George Bird Grinnell, editor, *Forest and Stream*, New York City

Thomas H. Kearney Jr., assistant botanist, U.S. Department of Agriculture,
Washington, D.C.

Charles A. Keeler, director, Museum of the California Academy of Sciences,
San Francisco

Trevor Kincaid, professor of zoology, University of Washington, Seattle

Dr. C. Hart Merriam, chief, Biological Survey, U.S. Department of Agriculture,
Washington, D.C.

John Muir, author and student of glaciers, Martinez, California

Dr. Charles Palache, mineralogist, Harvard University, Cambridge, Massachusetts

Robert Ridgway, curator of birds, U.S. National Museum, Washington, D.C.

William E. Ritter, president, California Academy of Sciences, and professor of zoology,
University of California, Berkeley

De Alton Saunders, botanist, South Dakota Experiment Station, Brookings, Seattle

Dr. William Trelease, director, Missouri Botanical Garden, St. Louis

APPENDIX

ARTISTS

Frederick S. Dellenbaugh, New York City
R. Swain Gifford, New York City

BIRD ARTIST

Louis Agassiz Fuertes, Ithaca, New York

PHYSICIANS

Dr. Lewis Rutherford Morris, New Jersey
Dr. Edward L. Trudeau Jr., Saranac Lake, New York

TAXIDERMISTS AND PREPARATORS

Leon J. Cole, Ann Arbor, Michigan
Edwin C. Starks, Biological Survey, Washington, D.C.

PHOTOGRAPHERS

Edward S. Curtis, Seattle, Washington
Dr. J. Inverarity, Seattle, Washington

CHAPLAIN

Dr. George F. Nelson, New York City

STENOGRAPHERS

Julian L. Johns, Washington, D.C.
Louis F. Timmerman, New York City

SHIP'S OFFICERS

Peter Doran, captain
Charles McCarty, first officer
J. F. Jordan, pilot
J. A. Scandrett, chief engineer
Joseph V. Knights, steward

At Orca, Prince William Sound, Captain Omar J. Humphrey of the Pacific Steam Whaling Company joined the ship and accompanied the party to the Bering Strait and back to Unalaska. His detailed knowledge of the coast proved of much value in navigating the ship. M. L. Washburn of the Alaska Commercial Company also joined the expedition at Orca and went with it to Kodiak. On the return voyage J. Stanely-Brown of the North American Commercial Company came aboard at Dutch Harbor, Unalaska, and accompanied the party on the homeward voyage and the overland journey.

SUGGESTED READINGS
AND REFERENCES

CHAPTER ONE: *View from a Seattle Hotel Window*

Burroughs, John. "Narrative of the Expedition." *Narrative, Glaciers, Natives,* vol. 1 of *Harriman Alaska Expedition.* Edited by C. Hart Merriam. New York: Doubleday, Page, 1901.

Dall, William Healey. "The Discovery and Exploration of Alaska." *History, Geography, Resources,* vol. 2 of *Harriman Alaska Expedition.* Edited by C. Hart Merriam. New York: Doubleday, Page, 1902.

Ford, Corey, with drawings by Lois Darling. *Where the Sea Breaks Its Back: The Epic Story of Early Naturalist Georg Steller and the Russian Exploration of Alaska.* Anchorage: Alaska Northwest Books, 2000.

Gannett, Henry. "General Geography." *History, Geography, Resources,* vol. 2 of *Harriman Alaska Expedition.* Edited by C. Hart Merriam. New York: Doubleday, Page, 1902.

Goetzmann, William H., and Kay Sloan. *Looking Far North: The Harriman Expedition to Alaska, 1899.* New York: Viking Press, 1982.

Grinnell, George Bird. "The Natives of the Alaska Coast Region." *Narrative, Glaciers, Natives,* vol. 1 of *Harriman Alaska Expedition.* Edited by C. Hart Merriam. New York: Doubleday, Page, 1901.

Klein, Maury. *The Life and Legend of E. H. Harriman.* Chapel Hill: University of North Carolina Press, 2000.

Merriam, C. Hart, ed. *Harriman Alaska Expedition.* 13 vols. New York: Doubleday, Page, and Washington, D.C.: Smithsonian Institution, 1901–1914.

Muir, John. *Biography of Edward Henry Harriman.* New York: Doubleday, Page, 1912.

Rennick, Penny, editor. *The Best of Alaska Geographic: Our First 100 Issues. Alaska Geographic* 27 (1) (2000).

CHAPTER TWO: *For the Benefit of Others*

Brewer, William H. Pocket field journal. Sterling Memorial Library, Yale University, New Haven, Connecticut.

Burroughs, John. Expedition journal. Huntington Library, Los Angeles.

Dellenbaugh, Frederick. Expedition diary. Beinecke Rare Book and Manuscript Library, Yale University, New Haven, Connecticut.

Gilbert, Grove Karl. *Glaciers and Glaciation,* vol. 3 of *Harriman Alaska Expedition.* Edited by C. Hart Merriam. Washington, D.C.: Smithsonian Institution, 1910.

Goetzmann, William H., and Kay Sloan. *Looking Far North: The Harriman Expedition to Alaska, 1899.* New York: Viking Press, 1982.

Grinnell, George Bird. Expedition diary. The Southwest Museum, Los Angeles.

Harriman, Averell. Souvenir album. Averell Harriman Collection, New York.

Harriman, Edward H. Preface. *Narrative, Glaciers, Natives,* vol. 1 of *Harriman Alaska Expedition.* Edited by C. Hart Merriam. New York: Doubleday, Page, 1901.

Keeler, Charles. Keeler family papers. Bancroft Library, University of California, Berkeley.

Merriam, C. Hart, editor. *Harriman Alaska Expedition.* 13 vols. New York: Doubleday, Page, and Washington, D.C.: Smithsonian Institution, 1901–1914.

Muir, John. *Biography of Edward Henry Harriman.* New York: Doubleday, Page, 1912.

———. *John of the Mountains: Unpublished Journals of John Muir.* Edited by Linnie Marsh Wolfe. Boston: Houghton Mifflin, 1938.

———. *Travels in Alaska.* Boston: Houghton Mifflin, 1915.

EXPEDITION LOG ONE: *Seattle to Prince Rupert*

Burroughs, John. "Narrative of the Expedition." *Narrative, Glaciers, Natives,* vol. 1 of *Harriman Alaska Expedition.* Edited by C. Hart Merriam. New York: Doubleday, Page, 1901.

Clark, J. P. (Rear Admiral, Hydrographer of the Navy). *The Coast of British Columbia from Cape Caution to Portland Inlet with Queen Charlotte Islands and from Sitklan Island to Cape Fox, Alaska.* Admiralty Charts and Publications NP 26, 7th ed. British Columbia Pilot, vol. 2. Published by the Hydrographer of the Navy, 1999.

EXPEDITION LOG TWO: *The First Morning, Sunrise at Cape Fox Village*

Essenhigh, N. R. (Rear Admiral, Hydrographer of the Navy). *South-East Alaska Pilot, from Dixon Entrance to Cook Inlet.* Admiralty Charts and Publications NP 4, 6th ed. Published by the Hydrographer of the Navy, 1993.

Goldschmidt, Walter R., and Theodore H. Haas. *Haa Aaní, Our Land: Tlingit and Haida Land Rights and Use.* Seattle: University of Washington Press, and Juneau: Sealaska Heritage Foundation, 1998.

Sealaska Corporation. *Celebration 2002: Restoring Balance through Culture.* Juneau: Sealaska Corporation, 2000.

CHAPTER THREE: *Standing with Spirits, Waiting*

Cole, Douglas. *Captured Heritage: The Scramble for Northwest Coast Artifacts.* 1985. Reprint. Norman: University of Oklahoma Press, 1995.

Tsosie, Rebecca. "The Native American Graves Protection and Repatriation Act: A Discussion Paper on the Issue of 'Culturally Unidentifiable' Native American Human Remains." Presented at a symposium on the Native American Graves Protection and Repatriation Act, Arizona State University, Tempe, 2000.

Worl, Rosita. "Tlingit *At.óow*: Tangible and Intangible Property." Ph.D. diss., Harvard University, Cambridge, Massachusetts, 1998.

EXPEDITION LOG THREE: *Repatriation Unfolds, Metlakatla to Ketchikan*

Grinnell, George Bird. "The Natives of the Alaska Coast Region." *Narrative, Glaciers, Natives,* vol. 1 of *Harriman Alaska Expedition.* Edited by C. Hart Merriam. New York: Doubleday, Page, 1901.

EXPEDITION LOG FOUR: *Into the Rain Forest, Wrangell-Wragell Narrows*

Burroughs, John. "Narrative of the Expedition." *Narrative, Glaciers, Natives,* vol. 1 of *Harriman Alaska Expedition.* Edited by C. Hart Merriam. New York: Doubleday, Page, 1901.

Connor, Cathy, and Daniel O'Haire. *Roadside Geology of Alaska.* Missoula, Mont.: Mountain Press, 2003.

Gilbert, Grove Karl. *Glaciers and Glaciation,* vol. 3 of *Harriman Alaska Expedition.* Edited by C. Hart Merriam. Washington, D.C.: Smithsonian Institution, 1910.

CHAPTER FOUR: *Fernow's Prediction*

Alaback, Paul B. "Biodiversity Patterns in Relation to Climate in the Temperate Rainforests of North America." *High Latitude Rainforests of the West Coast of the Americas: Climate, Hydrology, Ecology and Conservation.* Edited by R. Lawford, P. B. Alaback, and E. R. Fuentes. *Ecological Studies* (Springer-Verlag, Berlin) 116 (1995).

———. "A Sense of Place and Time—the Tongass Rainforest." *The Book of the Tongass.* Edited by D. Snow and C. Servid. Minneapolis: Milkweed Editions, 1999.

Burroughs, John, John Muir, et al. *Alaska, the Harriman Expedition, 1899.* 1901. Reprint. New York: Dover, 1986.

Cardot, J., Clara E. Cummings, Alexander W. Evans, C. H. Peck, P. A. Saccardo, De Alton Saunders, I. Thériot, and William Trelease. *Cryptogamic Botany,* vol. 5 of *Harriman Alaska Expedition.* Edited by C. Hart Merriam. Washington, D.C.: Smithsonian Institution, 1910.

Durbin, Kathie. *Tongass, Pulp Politics, and the Fight for the Alaska Rainforest.* Corvallis: Oregon State University Press, 1999.

Fernow, Bernhard E. "Forests of Alaska." *History, Geography, Resources,* vol. 2 of *Harriman Alaska Expedition.* Edited by C. Hart Merriam. New York: Doubleday, Page, 1902.

Harris, A. S. "Clear-Cutting, Reforestation and Stand Development on Alaska's Tongass National Forest." *Journal of Forestry* 72 (1974): 330–337.

Keeler, Charles. Keeler family papers. Bancroft Library, University of California, Berkeley.

Merriam, C. Hart, editor. *Harriman Alaska Expedition.* 13 vols. New York: Doubleday, Page, and Washington, D.C.: Smithsonian Institution, 1901–1914.

Muir, John. *John of the Mountains: Unpublished Journals of John Muir.* Edited by Linnie Marsh Wolfe. Boston: Houghton Mifflin, 1938.

Rogers, Andrew Denny, III. *Bernard Eduard Fernow: A Story of North American Forestry.* Princeton, N.J.: Princeton University Press, 1951.

U.S. Forest Service. *Multi-use Plan for Admiralty Island, North Tongass National Forest, Region 10.* Juneau, February 26, 1964.

EXPEDITION LOG FIVE: *Navigating the Islands and into the Cities*

Gannett, Henry. "General Geography." *History, Geography, Resources,* vol. 2 of *Harriman Alaska Expedition.* Edited by C. Hart Merriam. New York: Doubleday, Page, 1902.

CHAPTER FIVE: *All That Glitters*

Alaska Department of Environmental Conservation, Alaska Cruise Ship Initiative. *Report on Behalf of the Alaska Cruise Ship Initiative (ACSI). June 1, 2000 to July 1, 2001.* Part 2: *Report.* Juneau, 2001.

Burroughs, John. "Narrative of the Expedition." *Narrative, Glaciers, Natives,* vol. 1 of *Harriman Alaska Expedition.* Edited by C. Hart Merriam. New York: Doubleday, Page, 1901.

Harriman, Edward H. Preface. *Narrative, Glaciers, Natives,* vol. 1 of *Harriman Alaska Expedition.* Edited by C. Hart Merriam. New York: Doubleday, Page, 1901.

Muir, John. *Travels in Alaska.* Boston: Houghton Mifflin, 1915.

Reges, Robert. Recorded in House of the State of Alaska, House Transportation Committee. Minutes, April 19, 2000. Available at http://www.legis.state.ak.us.

Young, S. Hall. *Alaska Days with John Muir*. New York: Fleming H. Revell, 1915.

EXPEDITION LOG SIX: *A Wilderness Debate in Glacier Bay*

Burroughs, John. "Narrative of the Expedition." *Narrative, Glaciers, Natives*, vol. 1 of *Harriman Alaska Expedition*. Edited by C. Hart Merriam. New York: Doubleday, Page, 1901.

CHAPTER SIX: *The Politics of Beauty*

Abbey, Edward. *Beyond the Wall: Essays from the Outside*. New York: Henry Holt, 1984.

Bohn, Dave. *Glacier Bay, the Land and the Silence*. San Francisco: Sierra Club Books, 1967.

Lopez, Barry. *Arctic Dreams: Imagination and Desire in a Northern Landscape*. New York: Scribner, 1986.

Muir, John. *Hetch Hetchy Damming Scheme*. Memorandum, May 14, 1908. Sierra Club Collection, William E. Colby Memorial Library, San Francisco.

Tocqueville, Alexis de. *Democracy in America*. 1835. Reprint. New York: Penguin Putnam, 2001.

EXPEDITION LOG SEVEN: *Sailing into Open Waters*

Burroughs, John. "Narrative of the Expedition." *Narrative, Glaciers, Natives*, vol. 1 of *Harriman Alaska Expedition*. Edited by C. Hart Merriam. New York: Doubleday, Page, 1901.

Hill, Amy. *Marine Biology: An Introduction to Ocean Ecosystems*. 2nd ed. Portland, Me.: J. Weston Welch, 2002.

Merriam, C. Hart, editor. *Harriman Alaska Expedition*. 13 vols. New York: Doubleday, Page, and Washington, D.C.: Smithsonian Institution, 1901–1914.

CHAPTER SEVEN: *Salmon and Statehood*

Cooley, Richard. *Politics and Conservation: The Decline of the Alaska Salmon*. New York: Harper & Row, 1963.

Grinnell, George Bird. "The Salmon Industry." *History, Geography, Resources*, vol. 2 of *Harriman Alaska Expedition*. Edited by C. Hart Merriam. New York: Doubleday, Page, 1902.

Naske, C.-M., and H. Slotnick. *Alaska: A History of the Forty-ninth State*. 2d ed. Norman: University of Oklahoma Press, 1987.

National Research Council. *Upstream: Salmon and Society in the Pacific Northwest*. Washington, D.C.: National Academy Press, 1996.

Royce, W. F. "Managing Alaska's Salmon Fisheries for a Prosperous Future." *Fisheries* 14 (2) (1989): 8–13.

Sustainable Salmon Fisheries Policy for the State of Alaska. Juneau: Alaska Department of Fish and Game and Board of Fisheries, 2000.

EXPEDITION LOG EIGHT: *Risk and Reward—Prince William Sound*

Yergin, Daniel. *The Prize: The Epic Quest for Oil, Money, and Power*. New York: Free Press, 1993.

CHAPTER EIGHT: *Beyond Serenity*

Arata, C. M., J. S. Picou, G. D. Johnson, and T. S. McNally. "Coping with Technological Disaster: An Application of Conservation of Resources Model to the *Exxon Valdez* Oil Spill." *Journal of Traumatic Stress* 13 (2000): 23–29.

Berger, M. "Lingering Effects? Sound Still Not Recovered from Spill." *Cordova Times*, September 6, 2001.

Brown, E. D., J. Seitz, B. L. Norcross, and H. P. Huntington. "Ecology of Herring and Other Forage Fish as Recorded by Resource Users of Prince William Sound and the Outer Kenai, Alaska." *Alaska Fishery Resource Bulletin* 9 (2) (2002): 75–101.

Burroughs, John, John Muir, et al. *Alaska, the Harriman Expedition, 1899.* 1901. Reprint. New York: Dover, 1986.

Carls, M. G., G. D. Marty, T. R. Meyers, R. E. Thomas, and S. D. Rice. "Expression of Viral Hemorrhagic Septicemia Virus in Prespawning Pacific Herring (*Clupea pallasi*) Exposed to Weathered Crude Oil." *Canadian Journal of Fisheries and Aquatic Science* 55 (1998): 1–10.

"Fishermen Express Dismay over *Exxon Valdez* Ruling." *New York Times*, November 9, 2001.

Lethcoe, J., and N. Lethcoe. *A History of Prince William Sound, Alaska.* Valdez, Alaska: Prince William Sound Books, 1994.

Nelson, Richard. *The Island Within.* New York: Vintage Books, 1989.

Muir, John. "Notes on the Pacific Coast Glaciers." *Narrative, Glaciers, Natives*, vol. 1 of *Harriman Alaska Expedition*. Edited by C. Hart Merriam. New York: Doubleday, Page, 1901.

Norcross, Brenda L., and E. D. Brown. "Estimation of First-Year Survival of Pacific Herring from a Review of Recent Stage-Specific Studies." *Herring: Expectations for a New Millennium*. Edited by F. Funk, J. Blackburn, D. Hay, A. J. Paul, R. Stephenson, R. Toresen, and D. Witherell. Sea Grant publication AK-SG-01-04. Fairbanks: Alaska Sea Grant, University of Alaska Fairbanks, 2002.

O'Driscoll, P. "Ten Years Later, Case Is Hardly Closed—for Many, Optimism Drowned in Oil." *USA Today*, March 22, 1999.

Picou, J. S., and D. A. Gill. "The *Exxon Valdez* Disaster as Localized Environmental Catastrophe: Dissimilarities to Risk Society Theory." *Risk in the Modern Age*. Edited by M. J. Cohen. London: Macmillan, 2000.

———. "The *Exxon Valdez* Oil Spill and Chronic Psychological Stress." *Exxon Valdez Oil Spill Symposium Proceedings*. Edited by S. D. Rice, R. B. Spies, D. A. Wolfe, and B. A. Wright. *American Fisheries Society Symposium* 18 (1996): 879–893.

Rice, S. D., R. B. Spies, D. A. Wolfe, and B. A. Wright, editors. *Exxon Valdez Oil Spill Symposium Proceedings. American Fisheries Society Symposium* 18 (1996).

EXPEDITION LOG NINE: *From the Chugaches to the Chiswells*

Ashmead, William H., Nathan Banks, A. N. Caudell, O. F. Cook, Rolla P. Currie, Harrison G. Dyar, Justus Watson Folsom, O. Heidemann, Trevor Kincaid, Theo. Pergande, and E. A. Schwarz. *Insects Part I*, vol. 8 of *Harriman Alaska Expedition*. Edited by C. Hart Merriam. Washington, D.C.: Smithsonian Institution, 1910.

Ashmead, William H., D. W. Coquillett, Trevor Kincaid, and Theo. Pergande. *Insects Part II*, vol. 9 of *Harriman Alaska Expedition*. Edited by C. Hart Merriam. Washington, D.C.: Smithsonian Institution, 1910.

Coe, Wesley R., and Alice Robertson. *Nemerteans, Bryozoans*, vol. 11 of *Harriman Alaska Expedition*. Edited by C. Hart Merriam. New York: Doubleday, Page, 1904.

Dall, William H., and C. C. Nutting. *Land and Fresh Water Mollusks, Hydroids*, vol. 13 of *Harriman Alaska Expedition*. Edited by C. Hart Merriam. Washington, D.C.: Smithsonian Institution, 1910.

Eisen, Gustav, and Katherine J. Bush. *Enchytraeids, Tubicolous Annelids*, vol. 12 of *Harriman Alaska Expedition*. Edited by C. Hart Merriam. Washington, D.C.: Smithsonian Institution, 1910.

Rathbun, Mary J., Harriet Richardson, S. J. Holmes, and Leon J. Cole. *Crustaceans*, vol. 10 of *Harriman Alaska Expedition*. Edited by C. Hart Merriam. Washington, D.C.: Smithsonian Institution, 1910.

Verrill, Addison Emery. *Monograph of the Shallow-Water Starfishes of the North Pacific Coast from the Arctic Ocean to California (with 110 Plates)*, Part 1: *Text*, vol. 14 of *Harriman Alaska Expedition*. Edited by C. Hart Merriam. Washington, D.C.: Smithsonian Institution, 1914.

CHAPTER NINE: *One Century at a Time*

Black, Lydia T. "The Story of Russian America." *Crossroads of Continents: Cultures of Siberia and Alaska.* Edited by William W. Fitzhugh and Aron L. Crowell. Washington, D.C.: Smithsonian Institution Press, 1988.

Burroughs, John. "Narrative of the Expedition." *Narrative, Glaciers, Natives*, vol. 1 of *Harriman Alaska Expedition*. Edited by C. Hart Merriam. New York: Doubleday, Page, 1901.

Crowell, Aron L. *Archaeology and the Capitalist World System: A Study from Russian America.* New York: Plenum, 1997.

————. "Prehistory of Alaska's Pacific Coast." *Crossroads of Continents: Cultures of Siberia and Alaska.* Edited by William W. Fitzhugh and Aron L. Crowell. Washington, D.C.: Smithsonian Institution Press, 1988.

Crowell, Aron L., Amy F. Steffian, and Gordon L. Pullar, eds. *Looking Both Ways: Heritage and Identity of the Alutiiq People.* Fairbanks: University of Alaska Press, 2001.

de Laguna, Frederica. *The Archaeology of Cook Inlet, Alaska.* 2d ed. Anchorage: Alaska Historical Society, 1975.

Demientieff, Martha. "Alutiiq Paths." *Looking Both Ways: Heritage and Identity of the Alutiiq People.* Edited by Aron L. Crowell, Amy F. Steffian, and Gordon L. Pullar. Fairbanks: University of Alaska Press, 2001.

Fienup-Riordan, Ann. *The Living Tradition of Yup'ik Masks: Agayuliyararput, Our Way of Making Prayer.* Seattle: University of Washington Press, 1996.

Fitzhugh, William W., and Aron L. Crowell, eds. *Crossroads of Continents: Cultures of Siberia and Alaska.* Washington, D.C.: Smithsonian Institution Press, 1988.

Grinnell, George Bird. "The Natives of the Alaska Coast Region." *Narrative, Glaciers, Natives*, vol. 1 of *Harriman Alaska Expedition*. Edited by C. Hart Merriam. New York: Doubleday, Page, 1901.

Holmberg, Heinrich. *J. Holmberg's Ethnographic Sketches.* Edited by Marvin W. Falk; translated by Fritz Jaensch. Fairbanks: University of Alaska Press, 1985.

Liapunova, R. G. "Relations with the Natives of Russian America." *Russia's American Colony.* Edited by S. F. Starr. Durham, N.C.: Duke University Press, 1987.

Lukin, Shauna. "Subsistence Fishing." *Looking Both Ways: Heritage and Identity of the Alutiiq People.* Edited by Aron L. Crowell, Amy F. Steffian, and Gordon L. Pullar. Fairbanks: University of Alaska Press, 2001.

Madsen, Roy. "Tides and Ties of Our Culture." *Looking Both Ways: Heritage and Identity of the Alutiiq People.* Edited by Aron L. Crowell, Amy F. Steffian, and Gordon L. Pullar. Fairbanks: University of Alaska Press, 2001.

Muir, John. *John of the Mountains: Unpublished Journals of John Muir.* Edited by Linnie March Wolfe. Madison: University of Wisconsin Press, 1979.

Pullar, Gordon L. "Contemporary Alutiiq Identity." *Looking Both Ways: Heritage and Identity of the Alutiiq People.* Edited by Aron L. Crowell, Amy F. Steffian, and Gordon L. Pullar. Fairbanks: University of Alaska Press, 2001.

————. "The Qikertarmiut and the Scientist: Fifty Years of Clashing World Views." *Reckoning with the Dead: The Larsen Bay Repatriation and the Smithsonian Institution.* Edited by Tamara L. Bray and Thomas W. Killion. Washington, D.C.: Smithsonian Institution Press, 1994.

Steffian, Amy F. "Cúmilalhet—Our Ancestors." *Looking Both Ways: Heritage and Identity of the Alutiiq People.* Edited by Aron L. Crowell, Amy F. Steffian, and Gordon L. Pullar. Fairbanks: University of Alaska Press, 2001.

EXPEDITION LOG TEN: *Sad to Go, Crossing the Shelikof Strait*

Burroughs, John. "Narrative of the Expedition." *Narrative, Glaciers, Natives,* vol. 1 of *Harriman Alaska Expedition.* Edited by C. Hart Merriam. New York: Doubleday, Page, 1901.

Merriam, C. Hart. Alaska Journal, entry for July 3, 1899. Library of Congress, Washington, D.C.

Personal Account of the 1964 Tsunami. Collection of the Kodiak Historical Society, Kodiak, Alaska.

U.S. Geological Survey. *Can Another Great Volcanic Eruption Happen in Alaska?* USGS Fact Sheet 075–98. Anchorage: Alaska Volcano Observatory, 1998.

EXPEDITION LOG ELEVEN: *Westward, the Alaska Peninsula off Starboard*

Emerson, B. K., Charles Palache, William H. Dall, E. O. Ulrich, and F. H. Knowlton. *Geology and Paleontology,* vol. 4 of *Harriman Alaska Expedition.* Edited by C. Hart Merriam. Washington, D.C.: Smithsonian Institution, 1910.

Gannett, Henry. "General Geography." *History, Geography, Resources,* vol. 2 of *Harriman Alaska Expedition.* Edited by C. Hart Merriam. New York: Doubleday, Page, 1902.

Gedney, Larry. *Shumagin Islands Likely Site for Next Major Earthquake.* Article 628. Fairbanks: Geophysical Institute, University of Alaska, 1983.

CHAPTER TEN: *Ghosts of Unga*

Black, Lydia T., Sarah McGowan, Jerry Jacka, Natalia Taksami, and Miranda Wright. *The History and Ethnohistory of the Aleutians East Borough.* Alaska History Series 49. Fairbanks: Limestone Press, 1999.

Pels, Jacquelin Ruth Benson. *Unga Island Girl [Ruth's Book].* Walnut Creek, Calif.: Hardscratch Press, 1995.

EXPEDITION LOG TWELVE: *Starting North*

Admiralty Sailing Directions, Bering Sea and Strait Pilot, NP 23. 5th ed. Taunton, Somerset, England: Hydrographic Department, British Ministry of Defence, 1980.

Burroughs, John. "Narrative of the Expedition." *Narrative, Glaciers, Natives,* vol. 1 of *Harriman Alaska Expedition.* Edited by C. Hart Merriam. New York: Doubleday, Page, 1901.

Gannett, Henry. "General Geography." *History, Geography, Resources,* vol. 2 of *Harriman Alaska Expedition.* Edited by C. Hart Merriam. New York: Doubleday, Page, 1902.

Haslam, D. W. (Rear Admiral, Hydrographer of the Navy). *Bearing Sea and Strait Pilot. North-west and North Coasts of Alaska from Cape Douglas to the Alaska-Canada Boundary, the Aleutian Islands, and the North-east Coast of Siberia from Mys Lopatka Peninsula to Vicinity of Mys Yakan with Off-Lying Islands.* Admiralty Charts and Publications NP 23, 5th ed. Published by the Hydrographer of the Navy, 1980.

Muir, John. *John of the Mountains: Unpublished Journals of John Muir.* Edited by Linnie Marsh Wolfe. Boston: Houghton Mifflin, 1938.

CHAPTER ELEVEN: *Crosscurrents and Deep Water*

Burroughs, John. "Narrative of the Expedition. *Narrative, Glaciers, Natives,* vol. 1 of *Harriman Alaska Expedition.* Edited by C. Hart Merriam. New York: Doubleday, Page, 1901.

Dall, William Healey. "The Discovery and Exploration of Alaska." *History, Geography, Resources,* vol. 2 of *Harriman Alaska Expedition.* Edited by C. Hart Merriam. New York: Doubleday, Page, 1902.

Gannett, Henry. "General Geography." *History, Geography, Resources,* vol. 2 of *Harriman Alaska Expedition.* Edited by C. Hart Merriam. New York: Doubleday, Page, 1902.

Merriam, C. Hart. "Bogoslof, Our Newest Volcano." *History, Geography, Resources,* vol. 2 of *Harriman Alaska Expedition.* Edited by C. Hart Merriam. New York: Doubleday, Page, 1902.

National Marine Mammal Laboratory. *Steller Sea Lion Research.* 2004. Available at http://nmml.afsc.noaa .gov/AlaskaEcosystems/sslhome/stellerhome.html.

National Research Council. *The Bering Sea Ecosystem.* Washington, D.C.: National Academy Press, 1996.

————. *Decline of the Steller Sea Lion in Alaskan Waters: Untangling Food Webs and Fishing Nets.* Washington, D.C.: National Academy Press, 2003.

Reidman, M. *The Pinnipeds: Seals, Sea Lions and Walruses.* Berkeley: University of California Press, 1990.

Restoring Alaska: Legacy of an Oil Spill. Alaska Geographic 26 (1) (1999).

Seals, Sea Lions and Sea Otters. Alaska Geographic 27 (2) (2000).

Washburn, M. L. "Fox Farming." *History, Geography, Resources,* vol. 2 of *Harriman Alaska Expedition.* Edited by C. Hart Merriam. New York: Doubleday, Page, 1902.

EXPEDITION LOG THIRTEEN: *Only on Earth!*

Gannett, Henry. "General Geography." *History, Geography, Resources,* vol. 2 of *Harriman Alaska Expedition.* Edited by C. Hart Merriam. New York: Doubleday, Page, 1902.

Merriam, C. Hart. "Bogoslof, Our Newest Volcano." *History, Geography, Resources,* vol. 2 of *Harriman Alaska Expedition.* Edited by C. Hart Merriam. New York: Doubleday, Page, 1902.

————. Alaska Journal, entry for July 8, 1899. Library of Congress, Washington, D.C.

Partnow, Patricia H. "Teaching with Historic Places." *The Seal Islands: Fur Seal Rookeries National Historic Landmark, the Pribilof Islands.* Anchorage: National Park Service, National Trust for Historic Preservation, and St. George Tanaq Corporation, n.d.

Pribilof School District. *Pribilof Islands Stewardship Program.* St. Paul Island, Alaska, n.d. Available at www.Pribilofs.k12.ak.us/district/stewardship.

Wingspread Statement on the Precautionary Principle. Racine, Wis.: Wingspread Conference Center, January 23–24, 1998.

CHAPTER TWELVE: *Conservation Comes to Alaska*

Bade, William Frederic. *The Life and Letters of John Muir.* 2 vols. Boston: Houghton Mifflin, 1924.

Elliott, Henry Wood. *The Condition of Affairs in the Territory of Alaska.* Washington, D.C.: U.S. Treasury Department/Government Printing Office, 1875.

Goetzmann, William, and Kay Sloan. *Looking Far North: The Harriman Expedition to Alaska, 1899.* Princeton, N.J.: Princeton University Press, 1982.

Grinnell, George Bird. "Destruction of the Fur Seals." *Forest and Stream,* May 19, 1900.

Muir, John. "Pacific Coast Glaciers." *Narrative, Glaciers, Natives,* vol. 1 of *Harriman Alaska Expedition.* Edited by C. Hart Merriam. New York: Doubleday, Page, 1901.

Peck, Robert McCracken. *A Celebration of Birds: The Life and Art of Louis Agassiz Fuertes.* New York: Walker, 1982.

————. "A Cruise for Rest and Recreation." *Audubon* 84 (1982): 95.

Sterling, Keir B. *Last of the Naturalists: The Career of C. Hart Merriam*. New York: Arno Press, 1977.

Stolozenburg, William. "Danger in Numbers." *Nature Conservancy Magazine* 54, no. 2 (summer 2004).

EXPEDITION LOG FOURTEEN: *Wilderness Islands—Hall and Saint Matthew*

Merriam, C. Hart. Alaska Journal, entry for July 9, 1899. Library of Congress, Washington, D.C.

CHAPTER THIRTEEN: *Seabirds at the Edge of the World*

Burroughs, John. "Narrative of the Expedition." *Narrative, Glaciers, Natives*, vol. 1 of *Harriman Alaska Expedition*. Edited by C. Hart Merriam. New York: Doubleday, Page, 1901.

Hunt, G. L., Jr., and G. V. Byrd. "Marine Bird Populations and Carrying Capacity of the Eastern Bering Sea." *Dynamics of the Bering Sea*. Edited by T. R. Loughlin and K. Ohtani. Sea Grant. Publication AK-SG-99-03. Fairbanks: Alaska Sea Grant, University of Alaska Fairbanks, 1999.

Hunt, G. L., Jr., M. B. Decker, and A. Kitaysky. "Fluctuations in the Bering Sea Ecosystem as Reflected in the Reproductive Ecology and Diets of Kittiwakes on the Pribilof Islands, 1975 to 1991." *Aquatic Predators and Their Prey*. Edited by S.P.R. Greenstreet and M. L. Tasker. Cambridge, Mass.: Blackwell, 1996.

Hunt, G. L., Jr., F. Mehlum, R. W. Russell, D. B. Irons, M. B. Decker, and P. H. Becker. "Physical Processes, Prey Abundance, and the Foraging Ecology of Seabirds." *Proceedings of the Twenty-second International Ornithological Congress* (1999): 2040–2056.

Irons, D. B., S. J. Kendall, W. P. Erickson, L. L. McDonald, and B. K. Lance. "Nine Years after the *Exxon Valdez* Oil Spill: Effects on Marine Bird Populations in Prince William Sound, Alaska." *Condor* 102 (2000): 734–737.

Keeler, Charles. "Days among Alaska Birds." *History, Geography, Resources*, vol. 2 of *Harriman Alaska Expedition*. Edited by C. Hart Merriam. New York: Doubleday, Page, 1902.

National Research Council. *The Bering Sea Ecosystem*. Washington, D.C.: National Academy Press, 1996.

Rhode, E. "St. Matthew and Hall Islands: Oasis of Wildness." *Alaska's Seward Peninsula. Alaska Geographic* 14 (3) (1987).

U.S. Fish and Wildlife Service. *Beringian Seabird Colony Catalog: An Automated Database*. Anchorage: U.S. Fish and Wildlife Service, Migratory Bird Management Division, 2001.

EXPEDITION LOG FIFTEEN: *Beringia*

Burroughs, John. "Narrative of the Expedition." *Narrative, Glaciers, Natives*, vol. 1 of *Harriman Alaska Expedition*. Edited by C. Hart Merriam. New York: Doubleday, Page, 1901.

Grinnell, George Bird. "The Natives of the Alaska Coast Region." *Narrative, Glaciers, Natives*, vol. 1 of *Harriman Alaska Expedition*. Edited by C. Hart Merriam. New York: Doubleday, Page, 1901.

EXPEDITION LOG SIXTEEN: *A World Turned Upside Down, Twice*

Ainana, Ludmilla (Chair), and Nikolai Mymrin (Marine Mammal Specialist), Yup'ik Eskimo Society of Chukotka, Provideniya, Russia. *Report: Preservation and Development of the Subsistence Lifestyle and Traditional Use of Natural Resources by Native People (Eskimo and Chukchi) in Several Coastal Communities (Inchoiun, Lorino, New Chaplino, Sireniki, Enmelen) of Chukotaka in the Russian Far East during 1997*. Submitted to Shared Beringian Heritage Program, U.S. National Park Service, Anchorage, March 1999.

Burroughs, John. "Narrative of the Expedition." *Narrative, Glaciers, Natives*, vol. 1 of *Harriman Alaska Expedition*. Edited by C. Hart Merriam. New York: Doubleday, Page, 1901.

Grinnell, George Bird. "The Natives of the Alaska Coast Region." *Narrative, Glaciers, Natives,* vol. 1 of *Harriman Alaska Expedition.* Edited by C. Hart Merriam. New York: Doubleday, Page, 1901.

Murashko, Ol'ga. "Chukotka: Proshloe, nastoiashchee i budushchee okhotnikov na morskogo zveria." *Zhivaia Arktika* 2 (2000): 55–57.

CHAPTER FOURTEEN: *Discovering Alaska*

Nelson, Richard. *The Island Within.* New York: Vintage Books, 1991.

CHAPTER FIFTEEN: *In Search of the Future*

Brower, Michael, and Warren Leon. *The Consumer's Guide to Effective Environmental Choices: Practical Advice from the Union of Concerned Scientists.* Three Rivers, Mich.: Three Rivers Press, 1999.

Cronon, William. *Nature's Metropolis, Chicago and the Great West.* New York: Norton, 1991.

————, editor. *Uncommon Ground: Rethinking the Human Place in Nature.* New York: Norton, 1995.

Daily, Gretchen C., and Katherine Ellison. *The New Economy of Nature: The Quest to Make Conservation Profitable.* Washington, D.C.: Island Press/Shearwater Books, 2002.

Daly, Herman, and Joshua Farley. *Ecological Economics: Principles and Applications.* Washington, D.C.: Island Press, 2003.

Diamond, Jared. *Guns, Germs, and Steel: The Fates of Human Societies.* New York: Norton, 1997.

Exxon Valdez Oil Spill Trustee Council. *The Status of Alaska's Oceans and Watersheds: 2002.* Proceedings of a conference, Alaska's Oceans and Watersheds, Anchorage, June 18–19, 2002.

Hawken, Paul, Amory Lovins, and L. Hunter Lovins. *Natural Capitalism? Creating the Next Industrial Revolution.* New York: Back Bay Books, 2000.

Keeler, Charles. "Alaska." *Narrative, Glaciers, Natives,* vol. 1 of *Harriman Alaska Expedition.* Edited by C. Hart Merriam. New York: Doubleday, Page, 1901.

Kellert, Stephen. *The Value of Life: Biological Diversity and Human Society.* Washington, D.C.: Shearwater Books, 1997.

Meadows, Donella H., Dennis L. Meadows, and Jorgen Randers. *Beyond the Limits: Confronting Global Collapse, Envisioning a Sustainable Future.* White River Junction, Vt.: Chelsea Green, 1992.

Meadows, Donella H., Dennis L. Meadows, Jorgen Randers, and William Behrens III. *Limits to Growth: A Report to the Club of Rome.* New York: Universe Books, 1972.

Orr, David W. *Ecological Literacy: Education and the Transition to a Postmodern World.* SUNY Series in Constructive Postmodern Thought. Albany: State University of New York Press, 1992.

————. *The Nature of Design: Ecology, Culture, and Human Intention.* New York: Oxford University Press, 2002.

Pfirman, S., and the National Science Foundation Advisory Committee for Environmental Research and Education. *Complex Environmental Systems: Synthesis for Earth, Life, and Society in the 21st Century.* Washington, D.C.: National Science Foundation, 2003.

Prugh, Thomas, with Robert Costanza, John H. Cumberland, Herman Daly, Robert Goodland, and Richard B. Norgaard. *Natural Capital and Human Economic Survival.* Solomons, Md.: International Society for Ecological Economics, ISEE Press, 1995.

Roberts, Paul. *The End of Oil: On the Edge of a Perilous World.* Boston: Houghton Mifflin, 2004.

Steinberg, Ted. *Down to Earth, Nature's Role in American History.* New York: Oxford University Press, 2002.

Wilson, Edward O. *Consilience: The Unity of Knowledge.* New York: Knopf, 1998.

NOTES ON CONTRIBUTORS

Paul B. Alaback is a professor of ecology in the School of Forestry and Conservation, University of Montana, where he teaches ecology, conservation biology, and wilderness studies. He conducts research on the ecology and conservation of temperate rainforests and associated ecosystems along the Northwest coast to Alaska and in the Patagonia region of Chile and Argentina.

Vera Alexander is a professor of marine science and dean of the School of Fisheries and Ocean Sciences at the University of Alaska Fairbanks. She has conducted research on marine ecosystems in high-latitude waters, including the nearshore Ellesmere Island, the Beaufort Sea, the Chukchi Sea, the Bering Sea, and the Southern Ocean (Antarctic). Her work has focused on the role of sea ice in these systems.

Brad Barr is a senior policy advisor to the director of the National Oceanic and Atmospheric Administration's National Marine Sanctuary System. His work focuses on integrated ocean management, ocean and coastal policy development, and marine protected areas, particularly ocean wilderness issues.

William Cronon is the Frederick Jackson Turner and Vilas Research Professor of History, Geography, and Environmental Studies at the University of Wisconsin–Madison. He is an environmental historian who has studied the interactions between human beings and the landscapes in which they dwell.

Kristine Crossen is a professor of geology and the chair of the Geology Department at the University of Alaska Anchorage. She specializes in glacial marine sedimentation of the ice age, glacial and Pleistocene geology, geomorphology, the geology of Alaska, and Alaska glaciers. Her writing focuses on such topics as the Pleistocene/Holocene transition and human occupation of the central Tanana Valley of interior Alaska.

Aron L. Crowell, Alaska director of the Smithsonian Institution's Arctic Studies Center, is an arctic anthropologist and archaeologist. He is the coeditor of *Crossroads of Continents: Cultures of Siberia and Alaska* and *Looking Both Ways: Heritage and Identity of the Alutiiq People,* and he is the author of *Archaeology and the Capitalist World System: A Study from Russian America.*

Kathryn J. Frost is a marine mammal biologist who studies the natural history and ecology of seals and whales and the involvement of indigenous people in research and resource management in Alaska. She worked for the Alaska Department of Fish and Game for twenty-five years and is now an affiliate faculty member at the School of Fisheries and Ocean Sciences, University of Alaska Fairbanks.

Kim Heacox is an environmental writer, wilderness photographer, and conservationist based in Gustavus, Alaska. His books include *Alaska Light, Visions of a Wild America* and his forthcoming memoir, *The Only Kayak: Finding Friendship, Risk, and Hope among the Glaciers of Alaska.*

Thomas S. Litwin, Harriman Retraced Expedition leader, is also director of the Clark Science Center at Smith College. He is an avian ecologist who studies the relationship of human activity to ecosystem health. He is the founding director of Smith College's Environmental Science and Policy Program and an Aldo Leopold Fellow.

David Koester is an associate professor of anthropology in the Department of Anthropology at the University of Alaska Fairbanks. He studies culture history and historical consciousness in the circumpolar North, with specialization in the Russian Far East and Iceland.

Vivian M. Mendenhall is retired from the U.S. Fish and Wildlife Service. She continues to work on the biology and conservation of seabirds from her home in Anchorage.

Richard Nelson is a cultural anthropologist, writer, and conservationist. His books include *The Island Within, Make Prayers to the Raven,* and *Heart and Blood: Living with Deer in America.* He received the John Burroughs Award for nature writing and was the 1999–2001 Writer Laureate of Alaska.

Sheila Nickerson, former poet laureate of Alaska, served as editor of *Alaska's Wildlife,* the conservation magazine published by the Alaska Department of Fish and Game. Her nonfiction books include *Disappearance: A Map* and *Midnight to the North: The Untold Story of the Inuit Woman Who Saved the* Polaris *Expedition.*

Brenda L. Norcross is a professor of fisheries oceanography at the University of Alaska Fairbanks. She and her students have been actively investigating fishes and their habitats in Prince William Sound and the Gulf of Alaska since the *Exxon Valdez* oil spill in 1989.

Robert McCracken Peck, Senior Fellow and librarian of the Academy of Natural Sciences of Philadelphia, is a naturalist, writer, and historian who has traveled widely in Africa, Asia, and South America. He is the author of *A Celebration of Birds: The Life and Art of Louis Agassiz Fuertes,* a biography of one of the original Harriman Alaska Expedition participants; *Headhunters and Hummingbirds: An Expedition into Ecuador;* and *Land of the Eagle: A Natural History of North America.*

David Policansky is a scholar in the Board on Environmental Studies and Toxicology of the National Research Council. He has directed studies on a variety of natural resource matters, including studies of Atlantic and Pacific salmon. His recent publications have been on fisheries, recreational fishing, and on the use of science in decision making.

Patricia Savage grew up in North Carolina and currently resides in Raleigh, where she has been a professional artist since 1987. Her work has appeared in a limited-edition art book, *North American Endangered and Protected Species,* and in publications such as *US Art, Wildlife Art,* and *Wildlife in North Carolina.* Her paintings have been shown at a number of museums and annual shows around the world, including the Leigh Yawkey Woodson Art Museum, the Bell Museum of Natural History, the National Geographic Society, the U.S. Botanic Gardens, Walt Disney World Animal Kingdom, and Christie's of London.

Kay Sloan is a professor of English at Miami University, Oxford, Ohio. She coauthored *Looking Far North: The Harriman Expedition to Alaska, 1899* with William H. Goetzmann, and she is also the author of two novels and a book on the history of silent film.

Pamela A. Wight is the president of Pam Wight & Associates (Edmonton, Alberta, Canada), an international tourism consultancy specializing in community development, ecotourism, and resource planning and management, with considerable experience working throughout the arctic. She works for the private sector, nongovernmental organizations, and all levels of government, including the United Nations Environment Programme and the World Tourism Organisation. She is author of more than seventy tourism publications.

Kesler Woodward is professor of art emeritus at the University of Alaska Fairbanks, where he taught for two decades before retiring to paint and write full time in 2000. Woodward's paintings are included in all major public art collections in Alaska and in museum, corporate, and private collections on both coasts of the United States. *A Northern Adventure: The Art of Fred Machetanz,* published in May 2004, is his seventh book on the art and artists of Alaska and the circumpolar North.

Rosita Worl is the president of the Sealaska Heritage Institute and a professor of anthropology at the University of Alaska Southeast in Juneau.

Index

A NOTE ON THE TYPE

This book is set in Monotype Baskerville, a digital interpretation of
the metal types designed by John Baskerville (and cut for him by his punchcutter,
John Handy) in Birmingham in the 1750s. Baskerville's type is arguably the most
significant of the rationalist-spirited, Neoclassical typefaces that appeared in England
during this period, influencing as it did the later work of his compatriots Richard
Austin, who cut the original Bell type in the 1780s for the London publisher John
Bell, and William Martin (brother of Richard Martin, Baskerville's chief
assistant), whose types, promoted by the printer William Bulmer in the 1790s,
would herald the birth of English Romantic typography.

Designed and composed by Kevin Hanek

Printed and bound by Maple-Vail Book Manufacturing Group,
York, Pennsylvania